T.J. COLES is a postdoctoral resear<
Cognition Institute, working on issu
visual impairment. His thesis *The K*
online. A columnist with Axis of Logi   _ about
politics and human rights for *Counter*,   ., *Newsweek*, the *New
Statesman* and *Truthout*. His books include *Britain's Secret Wars*,
President Trump, Inc. and *Fire and Fury*.

MANUFACTURING TERRORISM

WHEN GOVERNMENTS USE FEAR TO JUSTIFY
FOREIGN WARS AND CONTROL SOCIETY

T.J. COLES

CLAIRVIEW

Clairview Books Ltd.,
Russet, Sandy Lane,
West Hoathly,
W. Sussex RH19 4QQ

www.clairviewbooks.com

Published in Great Britain in 2018 by Clairview Books

A CIP catalogue record for this book is available from the British Library

Print book ISBN 978 1 905570 97 3
Ebook ISBN 978 1 905570 98 0

Cover by Morgan Creative incorporating photo © Wavebreak Media Micro
Typeset by DP Photosetting, Neath, West Glamorgan
Printed and bound by 4Edge Ltd, Essex

Contents

Acronyms and Glossary

Al-Muhajiroun   The Emigrants. Also known as Islam4UK,
   al-Ghurabaa (the Strangers)
ARC   Advice and Reformation Committee
BCCI   Bank of Credit and Commerce International
BHJ   Bund Heimattreuer Jugend
CDC   Centers for Disease Control
CIA   Central Intelligence Agency
COG   Continuity of Government
CPC   Clandestine Planning Committee
DA   District Attorney
Daesh   The Arabic acronym for Islamic State: al-Dawlah
   al-Islamīyah fī l-ʿIrāq wa-sh-Shām – the Islamic State of Iraq and
   (Ancient) Damascus. Also known as the Islamic State of Iraq and
   Syria (ISIS) and the Islamic State of Iraq and the Levant (ISIL).
DoD   Department of Defense (US)
DRS   Département du Renseignement et de la Sécurité (Algeria)
ETA   Euskadi Ta Askatasuna (Basque Homeland and Liberty)
FBI   Federal Bureau of Investigation
FEMA   Federal Emergency Management Agency
FSA   Free Syrian Army
FSB   Federalnaya sluzhba bezopasnosti Rossiyskoy Federatsii
   (Federal Security Service of the Russian Federation)
GIA   Groupe Islamique Armé (Armed Islamic Group of Algeria)
Gladio   The generic name given to the NATO-led stay-behind
   networks after WWII.
GRAPO   Los Grupos de Resistencia Antifascista Primero de
   Octubre (First of October Anti-Fascist Resistance Groups, Spain)
HJS   Henry Jackson Society
GCHQ   Government Communications Headquarters (UK)
GWOT   Global War on Terror
ICU   Islamic Courts Union (Somalia)

INA   Iraqi National Accord

IO   Information Operation(s)

IRA   Irish Republican Army

ISI   Inter-Services Intelligence (Pakistan)

ISIL   See Daesh

ISIS   See Daesh

IW   Information Warfare

JEL   Junge Europische Legion

JSOC   Joint Special Operations Command

JTRIG   Joint Threat Research Intelligence Group

JTTF   Joint Terrorist Task Force (FBI)

KAM   Katibat al-Muhajireen (Freedom Fighters Brigade)

KBL   Katibat Al-Battar Al-Libi (Brigade of the Sword of Libya)

LeT   Lashkar-e-Taiba (Army of God, Pakistan)

LIFG   Libyan Islamic Fighting Group

MeK   Mujahideen e-Khalq

MI5   Military Intelligence Section Five

MI6   Military Intelligence Section Six

NATO   North Atlantic Treaty Organization

NIE   National Intelligence Estimate

NIFA   National Islamic Front of Afghanistan

NORAD   North American Aerospace Defense Command

NYT   *New York Times*

OAS   Organisation armée secrète (Algeria, founded in Spain)

OMY   Organisation of Muslim Youth

ÖWSGV   (Österreichischer Wander-, Sport- und Geselligkeitsverein, Austrian Association of Hiking, Sports and Society)

PLO   Palestine Liberation Organization

P20G   Proactive, Pre-emptive Operations Group

PDPA   People's Democratic Party of Afghanistan

RAF   Royal Air Force

SAS   Special Air Service

SAVAK   Sāzemān-e Ettelā'āt va Amniyat-e Keshvar (the Organization of National Intelligence and Security, Iran)

SBS   Special Boat Service

SHAPE   Supreme Headquarters Allied Command
SNC   Syrian National Council
TEDAX   Técnico Especialista en Desactivación de Artefactos
  Explosivos (Technical Specialist in Deactivation of Explosive
  Artifacts)
TFG   Transitiona Federal Government (Somalia)
UDA   Ulster Defence Association
UN   United Nations
UNGA   United Nations General Assembly
UNSC   UN Security Council
UNSCR   UN Security Council Resolution
UVF   Ulster Volunteer Force
WUCC   Western Union Clandestine Committee

Introduction

This book primarily concerns terrorism attributed to Muslim extremists ('Islamic terror'). It is also about the incomparably greater violence of the state, both the state in general and its hidden hand in terrorism. So-called 'Islamic terror' is the main focus of the book because that is the predominant form of non-state terrorism today, which is only to be expected given the increasing US-British role in the Muslim-majority Middle East and North Africa. The book also examines so-called Irish terror and the right-wing terror of Europe's Gladio networks. However, be it 'Islamic' or other forms of terrorism, the sheer power of the state and its armed forces eclipses the violence of any individual or collective terrorist organization.

From 1980 to 2003, terrorists from all over the world committed a total of 315 suicide bombings.[1] In the first few months of the Iraq War (2003) alone, the British Royal Air Force (RAF) launched 265 laser-guided Paveway II bombs 'in densely populated areas' (to quote the Ministry of Defence).[2] The Paveway II was far from being the RAF's only bomb: by the end of the year, the US-British 'coalition' had dropped or launched 29,200. From 1968 to 2009, nearly 115,000 individuals died as a result of terrorism (mostly in non-suicide bombings).[3] In collusion with the RAF, the US Air Force killed many of the 98,000 Iraqis who died in the first eighteen months of the 2003 invasion of Iraq alone.[4] The carnage was part of a deliberate strategy to target civilians, called Shock and Awe.[5]

State-terrorism is worse in scale and magnitude than non-state terrorism. But what about the state's involvement in 'smaller' acts of terror, the ones we usually think of as terrorism? The title of this book comes from Michael German, a former FBI agent. A few years ago, German told the *New York Times* that the agency was 'manufacturing terrorism cases' in order to justify its own existence. The FBI does this, says German, by taking vulnerable Arab Americans, and indeed other Americans from ethnic and religious minorities, and guiding them via agents (called handlers) to commit terrorism. Often, just before the given act of terror occurs, the FBI steps in to save the day.[6] Journalist and author Trevor Aaronson says:

> more than 150 people ... caught in sting operations never had the means and, in some cases, never had the idea for the terrorism plot ... [I]t was the FBI that provided them with everything – the bomb, the transportation, everything they needed to move forward in a terrorism plot that on their own, they never would have been able to do. And certainly, evidence suggests that in most of these cases, they never had any specific connections to terrorism.[7]

Links to the state

Not every case is 'manufactured', but many are; especially high-profile ones. In 2011, the University of California-Berkeley's Investigative Reporting Program teamed up with *Mother Jones* magazine to report on criminal prosecution statistics involving terrorism and other charges. They found that by that year, of the 508 defendants brought to court by the FBI, 48% were targeted by informants, 31% were arrested in sting operations and 10% were provoked by a handler/informant. Amazingly, 41% were not connected to a terrorist group, raising questions about how and why they came to allegedly want to commit terrorism. Only 21% were linked to 'al-Qaeda'. Twenty-nine percent were linked to other Islamic groups and 9% to non-Islamic groups.[8]

Likewise, in the UK: By 2013, 18% of British terrorism cases were connected to the group al-Muhajiroun (the Emigrants), according to the right-wing Henry Jackson Society (HJS). What the HJS doesn't bother reporting is that al-Muhajiroun's co-founder, Omar Bakri, was an MI5 informant (as we shall see).[9] Bakri's partner was Anjem Choudary. By August 2016, 850 Britons were fighting for the Islamic State in Libya, Syria and elsewhere. Commander Dean Haydon, head of the Metropolitan Police's counterterrorism unit, confirmed to the media that Choudary had recruited Britons for the Islamic

State. Choudary, recently released from prison, was connected to 500 of the 850 *jihadis.*[10]

For years, the Metropolitan Police were prevented from acting against Choudary by MI5. A source told the *Telegraph*: 'While the police might have had lots of evidence they were pulled back by the security service because he [Choudary] was one of the people they were monitoring. It was very frustrating and did cause some tension but we were told we had to consider the bigger picture'. As we shall see, the 'bigger picture' was that the secret services wanted to create a *jihadi* network in Libya and Syria to overthrow the regimes of Muammar Gaddafi and Bashar al-Assad respectively, as they had in Afghanistan and Pakistan to fight the Soviets, beginning in 1978.[11]

Back in 2002 after the 9/11 attacks, the George W. Bush administration's Defense Science Board recommended establishing a $100m per year sub-agency called the Proactive Pre-emptive Operations Group (P2OG).[12] Under the heading 'Aggressive Proactive, Preemptive Operations', the report describes influence warfare and information operations (IW/IO), 'Covert action', 'Cover & Deception', psychological operations (PSYOPS) and the use of special operations forces (SOF). The doctrine '[i]mproves information collection by stimulating reactions', i.e., provoking terrorists and setting traps, as the FBI has done for decades. It recommends: 'Vest[ing] responsibility and accountability for the P20G to a "Special Operations Executive" in the NSC [National Security Council]'.[13]

North Africa specialist and hostage negotiator Professor Jeremy Keenan writes:

> The first P2OG operation was in the Algerian Sahara in 2003, when Algeria's security and intelligence service, the Départe-ment du Renseignement et de la Sécurité (DRS) now working with the Pentagon and US intelligence services, kidnapped and took hostage 32 European tourists. Although the operation was managed by a DRS agent, the Bush administration was able to proclaim that the kidnap had been carried out by 'Bin Laden's man in the Sahara', justifying the US's launch in 2004 of a

second front or Sahara-Sahel front in the GWOT [global 'war on terror'].[14]

Social control in the form of frightening the public into supporting right-wing governments is another motive. Left-leaning governments and candidates are particularly vulnerable, as hardliners exploit terrorism and pledge to save the public from further disaster. Here's some recent, historical evidence:

From circa 1947 to 1990, MI6 and the CIA ran a secret, informal Europe-wide terror operation, loosely called Gladio. It was run from NATO offices in France and later Belgium, and touched every country in Western Europe, extending into Algeria and Turkey. Part of Gladio involved a 'strategy of tension', according to one of the terrorists (Vincenzo Vinciguerra) who was later jailed for life. Left-leaning governments were smeared as weak on terror by right-wing media and political opponents over their inability to stop the attacks. According to various parliamentary inquiries across Europe, a scholarly book by Daniele Ganser (*NATO's Secret Armies*), which draws on these and other records, and a feature-length BBC documentary, many of the 'communist' terror networks were actually far-right groups armed, trained and organized in part or in whole by the CIA and MI6. Arguably, the worst Gladio outrage was the Bologna train station bombing of 1980 in Italy, which killed 85 people and was said at the time to be the work of neo-fascists.[15]

There is also the issue of justifying foreign wars abroad. 'Al-Qaeda' (the Database), for example, was created by the CIA and MI6 as part of Operation Cyclone as a proxy force to battle the Soviets. When it became politically expedient, Britain and America blamed 'al-Qaeda' for domestic terrorism. Threats against the US were used in order to justify wars in the resource-rich Middle East, as documents (particularly *Rebuilding America's Defenses*) confirm.[16]

The deep state

This book frequently uses the term 'deep state'. The phrase deep state is widely attributed to Canadian academic, Dr Peter Dale

Scott.[17] Former Congresswoman Cynthia McKinney says of Scott's deep state theory that Scott observed four major political events in modern US history: the assassination of John F. Kennedy, the Iran-Contra Affair, 9/11 and Watergate. In each case, actors had access, at different levels, to COG: the Continuity of Government. COG is a contingency plan envisaging a surface-level government shutdown in the event of a major crisis. COG was unofficially invoked to hide the sale of weapons to Iran by the US to finance the latter's dirty war against socialists in Nicaragua (Iran-Contra) and officially implemented for the first time on 9/11.[18]

Robin Ramsay, editor of *Lobster* magazine, says of Scott and the deep state that Scott moved away from the so-called more conspiratorial and less substantive 'parapolitics' to the study of 'deep politics'; the kind of politics at the heart of so-called security establishments (originating with Turkey's intelligence infrastructure) and of the kind beyond the reach of democratic controls or oversight. It is important to note that within each state's 'deep' network lie competing factions.[19] One sticking point, for example, is the rift between intelligence analysts and operations units; the latter tend to work against the former for political reasons, which further complicates the nexus of surface- and deep-politics.[20]

In this book, 'deep state' refers to certain elements of agencies, like America's CIA, Britain's MI6 and Russia's FSB. However, in many of the cases cited here, the final decision for certain events (e.g., the decision not to kill bin Laden in 1998–99) was made by the executive, i.e., the president or the prime minister, depending on the country, not the given deep state actor.

Some criteria

The secret services (deep state) and their connections in government, corporations, the judicial system and media have several ways of 'manufacturing terrorism', as will be explored later in this book, with sources and evidence. Doubtless, some readers will be disappointed that this book does not generally go into 'disputed' areas, such as 9/11 being an 'inside-job' or the Sandy Hook massacre being a hoax. The criteria for this book are: 1) the given act must be terrorism (Sandy Hook was treated as a serious crime, not an act of terrorism) and 2) the given act of terrorism and the circumstances surrounding it must be unequivocal (i.e., most people on all sides must agree or acknowledge that it happened in a particular way), for example, via the release of declassified documents, court revelations or admissions of guilt.

September 11 as an inside-job does not fit these criteria because, although it was an act of terrorism, there is no agreement on how it was perpetrated. To give the example of the collapse of the three buildings of the WTC complex alone: Peer-reviewed journals have published the findings of physicists and chemists who discovered explosive particles in the dust of the World Trade Center.[21] However: a) there are no declassified government documents admitting this (and nor will there ever be) and b) those who support the inside-job theory are generally not in agreement about how it was done. For example: Some provide evidence that energy weapons, not chemical compounds, were used to destroy the Twin Towers and WTC7 (none peer-reviewed)[22] and others present evidence that a nuclear device was used (again, none peer-reviewed).[23] Here, there is disagreement and thus damage to the credibility of the claim (which is the role of disinformation agents). Compare this to the WTC bombing in 1993: there is unanimous agreement that an FBI-produced bomb was used in a sting operation which resulted in an act of terrorism being allowed to take place (see Chapter 8). So, to help the credibility of this book, we look only at cases that are as close to 100% provable as possible, but also where there is near-universal acceptance of what happened.

State terrorism, such as the invasion of Iraq in 2003 or the bombing of Syria by US-British-French forces, is seldom thought of as terrorism by Western media, pundits or politicians. If we focus on the kind of terrorism that we allow ourselves to think of as terrorism, namely individuals or small groups deliberately killing or harming civilians for ideological or political reasons, we see that today most terrorists claim to be Muslim. Until recently, the majority of suicide bombers were secular Tamils from Sri Lanka.[24] In the 1970-80s, terrorists included the Irish Republican Army and its affiliated groups, as well as ETA (the Basque separatists) and Italy's Years of Lead (*Anni di Piombo*). Despite Muslims now getting the blame for terrorism in general, the 1970s and '80s were deadlier in terms of terrorism than the 1990s and 2000s, according to deaths counted by the University of Maryland.[25]

Today, there are competing yet standard narratives to explain acts of 'Muslim' terrorism. On the far-right (e.g., Douglas Murray, David Horowitz), Islam is considered a violent religion and thus inherently to blame. Elements of the far- or libertarian-right (e.g., James Fetzer, Paul Craig Roberts) claim that most if not all terrorism is a hoax, that no one died in particular events and/or that actors were used to play the role of dead and injured; or that events were false-flags, i.e., committed by the West and blamed on Muslims. On the centre-right (e.g., Britain's Tory government), the narrative is that certain Muslims commit terrorism because they hate 'our way of life' (whatever that is supposed to mean). On the centre-left (e.g., Britain's Labour Party), the narrative is that Muslims are aggrieved by our foreign policy and some are inspired to commit terrorism. On the far- or progressive-left, many (e.g., Nafeez Ahmed, Mark Curtis) point out that most of the terrorists linked to plots are also linked to the deep state. On the a-political or left/progressive fringes, like the far-right, some believe that most or all acts of terrorism are false-flags or hoaxes.

The six steps

In this book, I argue a case for all of these narratives, depending on the particular event; except the one that says Islam is inherently violent and inspires terrorism: there is no evidence to support this narrative. Yet, the aggregated acts of terrorism that continue to plague Europe and America cannot be explained crudely by a single narrative, e.g., 'it was all a hoax' or 'it was all revenge for our foreign policy'. Each event must be scrutinized. In the chapters that follow, I document evidence of how the deep state manufactures terrorism using the following methods or as a result of the following actions:

1) *Promote a vicious foreign policy* (blowback). Every day, Muslims in the Middle East and North Africa are murdered, killed, blinded,

deafened, disembowelled, amputated and traumatized by British, American, French and Israeli bullets, bombs and missiles. Many of the victims are children. These routine atrocities are confined to the dusty shelves of human rights reports by the Red Cross, Doctors Without Borders, Amnesty International, Human Rights Watch and the UN and its agencies. Western media simply refuse to convey the horror of our bombings to domestic audiences, for a variety of reasons. In addition, normal people are or were forced to live under siege by *jihadi* lunatics like the Free Syrian Army, the Libyan Islamic Fighting Group and al-Nusra (Jabhat Fateh al-Sham): all of which have been trained, armed, organized and supported by America, Britain, France and/or Israel, depending on the group (as we shall see).[26] When a country is destroyed by Western military action, its food, water, medical and other supplies disrupted, jobless, angry, traumatized young men (and many women, too) are easy recruitment targets for *jihadis*. Some young terrorists think of Islam in terms of their ancestry, nationhood, community and life. Since 'Islam' (and all its associational meanings) appears to be under threat by the West, many young *jihadis* think, quite simply: you bomb us, we bomb you.

2) *Using extremists* (proxies). As noted above, terrorism is manufactured by the West for long-terms goals, including regime change in foreign countries. As soon as it became clear that neither Muammar Gaddafi of Libya nor Bashar al-Assad of Syria would open their economies to private, Euro-American financial interests (particularly oil), they changed from being close regional allies to the worst monsters on the planet. In secret – and much of it is denied to this day – MI6 and other agencies trained and organized an entire army (one plan included recruiting 100,000 *jihadis*)[27] to topple Assad's regime. This was a re-run of creating what became 'al-Qaeda' in the 1980s. These *jihadis* have now spread all over the Middle East and North Africa. The British in Northern Ireland were using the pro-British Ulster groups as proxies against the anti-British (i.e., pro-independence) Irish Republican Army.

3) *Using provocateurs* (goading). In sting operations, a terrorist or terrorist group may consist of vulnerable young men (primarily)

who are goaded into committing terrorism by agents of the deep state. Already noted above is FBI agent German's statement, the P2OG programme and the historical Gladio. In addition, there is the case of the Tsarnaev brothers, one of whom had been visited by individuals posing as FBI agents years prior to the detonation of shrapnel/pressure-cooker bombs at the Boston Marathon in 2013.[28] To give another example: British intelligence penetrated the IRA and used agents as provocateurs for the recruitment of others and the killing of informants.

4) *Green-lighting* (letting terrorists get away with crimes). As we shall see, Michael Scheuer was the head of the CIA's bin Laden unit. He told the BBC that between 1998 and 1999, the Clinton administration had nearly a dozen opportunities to kill or capture Osama bin Laden because they knew where he was. In the same documentary, it was revealed that agents had infiltrated his 'palace' and that the CIA watched his movements via a drone. It was ludicrously claimed by Scheuer that Clinton was too humanitarian to murder bin Laden with a drone (which makes no sense because Scheuer had previously said that bin Laden could have been captured) and that the 'Muslim world' would erupt if bin Laden was killed and the nearby mosque damaged; another fallacy, given bin Laden's unpopularity with the vast majority of Muslims. In Northern Ireland, the British knew about certain impending terror attacks by their Ulster allies and via their IRA informants and let them happen.

5) *Blaming enemies* (false-flag). Traditionally, false-flags were direct military attacks on targets under the guise of being committed by enemies. However, as proxy-state lines become blurred, a false-flag can include attacks carried out by proxies of the state blamed on enemies. In Northern Ireland, Britain's plainclothes Military Reaction Force murdered both Protestants and Catholics to sow confusion. Turning to Islam: In 2017, it was revealed that German soldiers known only as Maximilian T. and Lt. Franco A. (of Jägerbataillon 291) and their friend Mathias F., plotted to murder left-wing politicians by posing as Syrian refugees with forged documents. Targets included former President Joachim Gauck and Justice Minister Heiko Maas. Spokesperson Frauke Köhler

explained: 'The planned attack was intended to be interpreted by the population as a radical Islamist terrorist attack by a recognised refugee'. But this makes little sense as Franco A. used the alias David Benjamin, claiming to be a Christian fruit seller from Damascus. The media claim that a neo-Nazi group within the German military might be in operation, citing evidence of Franco A.'s alleged sympathies with Hitler.[29]

6) *Fake events* (simulations). Agencies have taken to using crisis actors pretending to be real victims. One particularly striking instance, which is easy to prove as a fake event, is a car-bombing in Iraq. Footage uploaded to LiveLeak and confirmed by Bellingcat (an online analysis group consisting largely of ex-intelligence specialists and cited in mainstream Western media) shows a car bomb exploding, people rushing to the scene, laying down and playing dead and injured, before fellow Iraqis come to 'help'. Despite proof of the car-bombing, deaths and injuries being a hoax, the news wires and thus mainstream media reported it as real.

One or more of these elements work in synch to create a 'strategy of tension' (as Vinciguerra called it), in which Islam is demonized, civil liberties eroded, hi-tech budgets (e.g., for surveillance) increased and elements of the public lending more support to foreign wars than they would have in peacetime.

Social control

So, how does the above affect society? Coupled with devastating neoliberal economic programmes which reduce wages and social safety nets, far-right politicians including Donald Trump, Nigel Farage (then-leader of the UK Independence Party) and Marine Le Pen (head of France's National Front) try to, and in the case of Trump and Le Pen succeed or almost succeed, in whipping up enough hysteria against minority targets, in this case painting all Muslims as extremists or potential extremists, for political gain. One of the consequences of scapegoating is that the entire political spectrum shifts further to the right, forcing more liberal parties to adopt stricter border controls, at least rhetorically. Another consequence is that the causes of economic hardship are obscured by this diversion strategy.

What follows is a small sample:

The USA: After 9/11, the Bush administration imposed the Patriot Act 2001. The Act criminalizes providing 'material support' to terrorists, including 'expert advice or assistance'. The court rejected this. Section 215 made it easier for agencies (notably the FBI) to gather internet users' metadata in a boon to the hi-tech industry which won more contracts. Patriot made it easier for the FBI to break into suspects' homes and copy their computer files and take DNA samples. Section 411 allows the government to expel or refuse entry to non-citizens on the grounds of their alleged use of their status 'to endorse or espouse terrorist activity', or persuade others to do so. Dr Tariq Ramadan's teaching visa was revoked under the Act, despite him being a well-known moderate. Presumably, the aim was to silence other prominent Muslims living in America from criticizing the 'war on terror'.[30] (In Chapter 7, we shall see how a false-flag anthrax attack was linked to pushing the Patriot Act.)

Great Britain: When it came to using counterterror legislation to control society, Tony Blair's Labour government (1997–2010) was one of the worst offenders.[31] The Terrorism Act 2000 made it an offense to supply material to individuals accused of property damage. When then-82-year-old German-Jewish Labour supporter and later National Executive Committee-member, Walter Wolfgang, heckled the Foreign Secretary Jack Straw at the party conference in Brighton (2005), Wolfgang was forcibly removed by security guards and prevented from re-entering under the Terrorism Act. Section 44 ballooned the number of arbitrary stops and searches by police of innocent citizens (many of them ethnic minorities, of course). Lord Carlile's annual review concluded that Section 44 actions 'could be cut by at least 50 per cent without significant risk to the public or detriment to policing'. In 2003, peace protestors were prevented from demonstrating under the Act against an arms fair in London.[32]

The post-9/11 Anti-Terrorism Crime and Security Act 2001 sought to allow for extended detention of non-citizens in the country. The Law Lords declared it unlawful, with Lord Hoffmann telling media: 'The real threat to the life of the nation ... comes not from terrorism but from laws such as these'.[33] The Terrorism Bill sought to extend detention from 14 to 90 days. It was rejected by MPs. The Serious Organised Crime and Police Act 2005 banned political protest within 1km of Parliament.[34] Max Hill QC is the Independent Reviewer of Terrorism Legislation. Following the vehicle rammings in Barcelona in 2017, Hill warned against 'thought crime' and said that many counterterrorism laws were 'unnecessary'.[35]

Spain: Under General Franco, Spain was a terror state. When the country transitioned to parliamentary representation, degrees of freedom were won. However, terrorist groups including GRAPO (First of October Anti-Fascist Resistance Groups, inactive since 2007) and ETA (Basque Homeland Liberty, now disarmed) led to antiterrorism measures being included in the Penal Code. Controversially, Article 18.1 potentially criminalizes 'apology' for terrorism, which could include anything from giving legal advice to terrorists to making satirical observations. As of 2007, 'apology' was criminalized only after a judge deemed the offence to constitute 'direct incitement'.[36]

Organic Law No. 7/2000 penalized 'glorification of terrorism', which includes actions 'to discredit, demean or humiliate the victims of terrorist offences or their families'. This is important because genuine efforts to determine if a given attack was a false-flag by the state or a simulated event which the media believe to be real could be punished as glorifying terrorism.

Even more important than persecuting the fringe who believe in false-flags and hoaxes, the Spanish government has suppressed freedom of thought and expression and ultimately criticism of government policy. Amnesty International writes of Spain: 'An exponential increase in the number of people falling foul of [the] draconian law banning the "glorification of terrorism" or "humiliating victims of terrorism" is part of a sustained attack on freedom of expression'. Under Article 578, the definitions were broadened to the point where charges jumped from three in 2011 to 38 in

2017.[37] Terror attacks in one country, like the *Hebdo* killings in Paris in 2015, have knock-on effects in that Spain, in this case, responded by further broadening the definitions of incitement. This is important because in this book we shall examine the British deep state's connection to the *Hebdo* killings. Musicians César Strawberry (of Def Con Dos) and Valtonyc (a rapper) were sentenced under Article 578: Strawberry for tweeting a joke about a cake bomb and Valtonyc for insulting the crown, threatening a politician and glorifying violence.[38]

In addition to attacking freedom, the Spanish government has bolstered its cyber security and budget and aided the hi-tech security sector with programmes like the Spider Operations, which were a series of arrests of social media users, many of whom had simply tweeted bad-taste jokes. The niece of a man who died in a terror attack defended the woman tried for making a sick joke about her late uncle, but astonishingly the court ruled that the law is effective regardless of what alleged victims think.[39]

Another effect of all of this is that activists are persecuted and right-wing elements resent it because certain Islamic extremists (whom, as we shall see, are often linked to the government) are untouched (e.g., the Muhajiroun group noted above). The right increases their pressure on 'soft governments' which allow the extremists to operate, not realizing or reporting that many are agents of the state. The right also hates being, as they see it, unable to criticize Islam for fear of being labelled 'politically incorrect'. The bad press given to Muslims in right-wing media fuels the socio-economic conditions of Muslims in Britain and France especially, which see many unemployed males drift into petty crime, making them perfect pawns to be played by the state as informants, pro-vocateurs and patsies.

Let us now turn to the deeper analysis and hard facts.

Part I

MAKING ENEMIES

Chapter 1

'Enemies are essential'

Following the collapse of the Soviet Union in the early-1990s, US and other policy planners considered which groups or nations they would consider the new enemy. As we will see, the Club of Rome thought about making humanity the enemy of itself, whilst the military lamented that the lack of real enemies hampered the development of new technologies, on which much of the US economy is based. This chapter looks at a variety of documents from the United States in order to examine the varied, sometimes conflicting, interests of different elite organizations.

Powerful organizations and affiliations, including high-ranking politicians, the so-called military-industrial-complex and the emerging hi-tech sectors, intentionally seek enemies for a variety of reasons. Here are at least eight: 1) Opening new 'defence' and surveillance markets; 2) making excuses for gathering intelligence on populations (the public being the main enemy of government); 3) winning military contracts in the pursuit of foreign enemies; 4) pursuing ulterior motives, such as securing resources in other countries; 5) scapegoating others for failed domestic policies; 6) passing laws restricting social progress under the rubric of protecting populations; 7) winning votes on a platform of counter-terrorism; and 8) making money in so-called prediction markets (i.e., taking out a hedge or an insurance policy, or short-selling stock, with foreknowledge of an impending atrocity).

After the fall

The Club of Rome was founded by wealthy elites, notably David Rockefeller, in 1968. The organization calls its founding year the 'Great Divide'. Children were losing respect for their parents. The

Civil Rights struggle of the '60s was being won. Domestic protest was forcing the Pentagon to wind down the Vietnam War, though not before it escalated. Student protests were erupting all over Europe and the USA. 'It was felt that a group of independent thinkers concerned with the long-term and deeper issues would be useful in complementing the work of the bigger organizations', like the UN, says the group.[40]

In 1991, when the Soviet Union collapsed, the Club of Rome actively looked for new ways to control the general public. Due to the ever-changing nature of politics, they decided against 'scapegoating', particularly religions and other peoples. The collapse of the Soviet Union left an ideological 'vacuum': and nature 'abhors a vacuum', the authors say, asking: 'Can we live without enemies?'. They go on to note: 'The need for enemies seems to be a common historical factor ... New enemies have to be identified, new strategies imagined, and new weapons devised'. These include the use of civil society as a soft weapon. The authors conclude that, '[i]n searching for a common enemy against whom we can unite, we came up with the idea that pollution, the threat of global warming, water shortages, famine and the like, would fit the bill ... The real enemy then is humanity itself'.[41]

Their book has circulated on the internet and has been used to promote anthropogenic climate change denial. The authors don't deny human-affected climate change, they merely cite it as a useful tool for controlling behaviour.

The Club of Rome's plan to use real-world environmental threats as a common uniting principle obviously did not work. There was far too much opposition from companies profiting from fossil fuels, as well as third world governments who charged the West with hypocrisy for telling them not to pollute (or, as they see it, 'develop'). As a direct result of those very companies wanting to control the oil and gas reserves of the Middle East and North Africa, thousands of Muslim extremists used and continue to use terrorism as a tactic to try to stop invaders from taking over their countries. Islamic terrorism became less a 'uniting' force than a dividing one.[42]

Separate to the question of their success, the above quotes exemplify the elitist mindset: that populations have to be controlled and enemies, of whatever kind, are a motivating factor.

Turning to Islamic terrorism: Samuel P. Huntington was a Professor at Harvard. A scholar for the multibusiness-funded Trilateral Commission, Huntington authored many papers and books analyzing world affairs, social movements and how elites should respond. After the collapse of the Soviet Union in the 1990s, Huntington came up with his famous 'clash of civilizations' theories, in which he argued that conflict would continue, but this time along cultural rather than ideological lines. The book quotes a *TIME* magazine article from 1992, stating: '[the] next confrontation is definitely going to come from the Muslim world. It is in the sweep of the Islamic nations from the Maghreb to Pakistan that the struggle for a new world order will begin'.[43]

Huntington's book was mostly ridiculed by people outside elite policy circles, but it deserves better treatment. The common understanding of Huntington's thesis was that monolithic civilizational blocs fight for supremacy. The most important point, however, has been overlooked: That the US needed to establish a new identity in the post-Cold War era. 'For peoples seeking identity and reinventing ethnicity, enemies are essential ... We know who we are ... when we know whom we are against', he says.[44] Huntington understood that 'sources of conflict ... are, in large measure ...: control of people, territory, wealth, and resources, and relative power, that is the ability to impose one's own values, culture, and institutions on another group'.[45] The conflict arises when victims resist. A careful reading suggests that Huntington reckoned that political elites would seek to frame conflict not as a struggle for power (which it really is), but rather, as a clash of values (or 'civilizations'), where it is easier to create enemies, identity politics and thus create a diversion from real aims.

Huntington discusses 'the ubiquity of conflict. It is human to hate', he says. Therefore, '[f]or self-definition and motivation people need enemies: competitors in business, rivals in achievement, opponents in politics'. Huntington, like the Club of Rome authors, notes that '[t]he resolution of one conflict and the disappearance of one enemy generate personal, social, and political forces that give rise to new ones'. Huntington cautions that the end of the Cold War will create a 'clash of civilizations', in which politicians will paint a world picture of civilized 'us' versus barbarous 'them'. There is a danger, says Huntington, that 'common culture ... encourages cooperation'.[46]

By implication, the US and its allies must foster identity politics. This is easy to do in a mostly white, Christianized nation like the US (though the Latino population is growing, as is secularism), which wants to secure oil in an Arab-Muslim majority region like the Middle East and North Africa. In conclusion, allies need 'common values', like defending against the barbarians: and this has helped to justify the existence of NATO in a post-Cold War world.

New enemies, new weapons

The collapse of the Soviet Union necessitated the invention and exaggeration of new threats to America's security interests in order that the US policymaking elite and war machine justifies its long-term quest for what the Pentagon calls Full Spectrum Dominance.[47]

Post-WWII advances in broadband communications, computing, digital applications, lasers, radiography, radiofrequency devices, so-called less-than-lethal weapons and sound technology created what the US military calls a Revolution in Military Affairs (RMA). Where mass bombings and force-on-force battles had been the nature of warfare during the Second World War, the Cold War changed the dynamic. Proxy wars were fought in place of direct conflict for the simple reason that both Russia and the USA possessed nuclear weapons. Even the accidental launch of a single nuclear weapon could mean the end of the world, as thousands of others could be exchanged autonomously or semi-autonomously in response.

The RMA enabled troops to target so-called non-traditional assets, such as political leaders, revolutionaries, drug lords, terrorists and community leaders with all manner of weaponry, including sonic and radiofrequency. The RMA meant that the new battleground was the entire world. It relied to an unusual extent on satellites, communication systems and tracking devices. The only trouble was that after the Soviet Union collapsed, there was an enemy vacuum, as the Club of Rome pointed out. Military planners concocted as new enemies, individuals over whom the military has no jurisdiction: drug-gangs, terrorists and political revolutionaries. These targets were hitherto the purview of law enforcement agencies.

An influential document from 1994, entitled *The Revolution in Military Affairs and Conflict Short of War*, was published by the US Army War College. The authors state: '… the successful end of the Cold War, even though it dramatically increased the need for innovation, complicates the process' of building an RMA. 'In all human endeavors, success tends to stifle innovation'. Much of the hi-tech innovation that enabled the RMA came in the post-WWII period from taxpayers who funded the military-industrial-complex in its supposed opposition to the Soviet Union. Without the Soviet menace, the excuses for new hi-tech militarism dried up. 'The natural attitude is "if it ain't broke, don't fix it"', the authors continue. In a particularly telling line about the need for enemies, the authors state: 'The fact that the United States has not faced a recent military or national security disaster has hindered the development and application of new technology to conflict short of war'. This was written seven years prior to 9/11. As we shall see, certain elements of America's policymaking elite held this attitude right up to the day of the attacks.[48]

'To many Americans, the absence of disaster shows that our national security strategy "ain't broke"', the authors continue. This implies that it had to be broken on some scale in order to justify more money for military innovation. 'Moreover, conflict short of war lacks a powerful institutional advocate able to transcend this attitude'. This was written at a time when Bill Clinton was in power. Forget Clinton's actual record, the *perception* (and perceptions are important) among the right-wing US policymaking elite, was that the Clinton administration was soft on war and shrinking the Pentagon budget.[49]

In addition to the RMA, the US Air Force still had hundreds of thousands of bombs to drop on civilian targets, as they had on Japanese and German civilians in WWII and to Vietnamese, Cambodians and Lao during the Indochina wars. The new, dispersed nature of 'conflict short of war' meant that much of the RMA prevented saturation bombing and therefore potentially meant big losses for missile, bomb and landmine companies. Certain war planners with links to the military-industrial-complex devised an air war strategy called *Shock and Awe*. They argued that a lack of genuine enemies inhibited their ability to test the strategy on a live population. Enter Iraq.

In 1996, the US National Defense University published *Shock and Awe*, a 175-page document calling for massive bombing of civilians to test the air war strategy. The principal authors were Harlan Ullman and James Wade. Ullman had business ties with the infrastructure and detection corporation, CNIguard. Wade founded Defense Group, Inc. 'which conducted' the *Shock and Awe* 'study', to quote the report. Co-authors include Keith Brendly (Defense Group, Inc.) and Charles A. Horner (a consultant). *Shock and Awe* makes for chilling reading and is worth quoting at length. Forget a single suicide bomber, as we in the West sometimes face: *Shock and Awe* calls for tens of thousands of bombs targeting civilians and civilian infrastructure; all in brazen contempt of the Geneva Conventions.[50]

> The intent here is to impose a regime of Shock and Awe through delivery of instant, nearly incomprehensible levels of massive destruction directed at influencing society writ large, meaning its leadership and public, rather than targeting directly against military or strategic objectives ... The employment of this capability ... massively destructively, strikes directly at the public will of the adversary to resist ... The major flaws and shortcomings are ... determining whether this magnitude and speed of destruction can actually be achieved using non-nuclear systems ... [T]he magnitude of Shock and Awe Rapid Dominance seeks to impose (in extreme cases) ... the non-nuclear equivalent of the impact that the

atomic weapons dropped on Hiroshima and Nagasaki had on the Japanese ... [T]he targets in each category include military, civilian, industrial, infrastructure, and societal components of a country or group.[51]

The authors write with seeming glee about the trauma that such warfare can impose on human beings:

> In Rapid Dominance, the aim of affecting the adversary's will, understanding, and perception through achieving Shock and Awe is multifaceted. To identify and present these facets, we need first to examine the different aspects of and mechanisms by which Shock and Awe affect an adversary. One recalls from old photographs and movie or television screens, the comatose and glazed expressions of survivors of the great bombardments of World War I and the attendant horrors and death of trench warfare. These images and expressions of shock transcend race, culture, and history ...
>
> [W]e seek to determine whether and how Shock and Awe can become sufficiently intimidating and compelling factors to force or otherwise convince an adversary to accept our will in the Clausewitzian sense, such that the strategic aims and military objectives of the campaign will achieve a political end.[52]

The authors conclude that there are few threats to the continental United States. Therefore, justifying the testing of this doctrine on a live population will be extremely difficult, hence the need to find or invent a new enemy.

There are two major shortcomings, say the authors. The first is the sheer number of forces needed to carry out Shock and Awe. The second 'is that with declining numbers of worthy and sufficiently equipped adversaries against whom to apply this doctrine, justifying it to a questioning Congress and public will prove more difficult'. Fortunately for them, after 9/11, the hawkish George W. Bush administration made constant inferences that Saddam Hussein, the vicious former ally of the US, had connections in his native Iraq with Osama bin Laden, the alleged suspect in the FBI's hampered 9/11 investigation. In 2003, after whipping up hysteria about weapons of mass destruction, Iraq was invaded to secure its long-term oil reserves and the US Air Force was given the chance to test Shock and Awe. The US and Britain murdered 98,000 Iraqis, according to the medical journal *The Lancet*. By 2010, one million Iraqis had died as a result of events triggered by the invasion, including US-UK divide and conquer tactics. (The US made the Shia enemies of the Sunni, and vice versa.)[53]

A catastrophic & catalyzing event

In 2000, four years after the Shock and Awe document was published, the Project for the New American Century (PNAC) published an equally chilling document. PNAC is a now-defunct organization founded by many future members of the George W. Bush administration. At one time or another, they also served as CEOs or in high positions of corporations: Bush himself, Bush senior (Carlyle Group), Dick Cheney (Halliburton), Donald Rumsfeld (General Instrument Corporation), Paul Wolfowitz (World Bank) and Richard Perle (Global Crossing Ltd.).

The PNAC document *Rebuilding America's Defenses* is also worth quoting at length. It not only reveals the plan for much of what is unfolding geopolitically today, it puts a strong emphasis on many of the technologies now being used, especially drones and the missile systems pointed at Russia. The principal author is Thomas Donnelly. Co-authors and advisors and their business ties include Barry Watts (Northrop Grumman), Dov Zakheim (System Planning Corporation) and James Lasswell (GAMA).[54]

PNAC's formal goal was 'to shape a new century favorable to American principles and interests'. The future strategic context is guaranteed by 'the preservation of a favorable balance of power in Europe, the Middle East and surrounding energy-producing region[s], and East Asia'. American business interests are assured, the document explains, by the US 'fighting and winning multiple large-scale wars, conducting constabulary missions which preserve the current peace, and transforming the U.S. armed forces to exploit the "revolution in military affairs"'.[55] The multiple, simultaneous major wars turned out to be in Afghanistan and Iraq. The use of the RMA became the massive surveillance expansion exposed by Edward Snowden. The constabulary missions included so-called counter-piracy operations in Somalia.

The document goes on to talk about using unmanned aerial vehicles (drones), which were barely in use before 9/11, to 'project military power around the globe':

> The breakpoint will come when a preponderance of new weapons systems begins to enter service, perhaps when, for example, unmanned aerial vehicles begin to be as numerous as manned aircraft ...
>
> Under the 'Land Warrior' program, some Army experts envision a 'squad' of seven soldiers able to dominate an area the size of the Gettysburg battlefield – where, in 1863, some 165,000 men fought ...
>
> [A]dvanced forms of biological warfare that can 'target' specific genotypes may transform biological warfare from the realm of terror to a politically useful tool.[56]

Perhaps most important of all, the Anti-Ballistic Missile (ABM) Treaty signed by the US and the Soviet Union restrained the development of dangerous missile systems. The PNAC document explicitly talks about backing out of the treaty: 'The Clinton Administration's adherence to the 1972 ABM Treaty has frustrated development of useful ballistic missile defenses'. Finally, the most infamous and chilling line in the document talks about needing enemies to accelerate the project. 'Further, the process of transformation, even if it brings revolutionary change, is likely to be a long one, absent some catastrophic and catalyzing event – like a new Pearl Harbor'. One year to the month of the document's publication, 3,000 people lost their lives in America's worst ever terrorist attack.[57]

'Thank you, Osama'
Many governments and corporations benefited from 9/11. Shortly after the attacks, lawyer and ex-Senator Gary Hart chaired the US

government's Commission on National Security in the 21st Century, during which he said: 'Americans are brilliant at many things, not least of which is turning lemons into lemonade. There is a chance for the President of the United States [George W. Bush] to use this disaster to carry out a phrase his father used ... and that is a "new world order"'.[58] Within a decade, the security and surveillance industry was worth $1 trillion. P.W. Singer notes that five years after 9/11, border, building and airport security was a $30bn industry, leading one private industry report to state: 'Thank you, Osama bin Laden!'.[59]

Continuing the theme of how governments benefited: One of Israel's leading newspapers, Ma'ariv, reported that several years after the attacks, Israeli Prime Minister Benjamin Netanyahu told an audience at Bar Ilan University: 'We are benefiting from one thing, and that is the attack on the Twin Towers and Pentagon, and the American struggle in Iraq'.[60] (That is actually three things.)

Four years into the so-called 'war on terror', which saw US and British forces bombing one country after another, supposedly in pursuit of 'al-Qaeda' and its elusive leaders, the US Defense Science Board published a report confirming that the real goal is to transform the Middle East and North Africa into an integrated market economy for the US. In order to achieve this decades-long goal (a crucial building-block of the American Empire), the enemy of terrorism has been put forward as a motivating commitment:

> [I]n stark contrast to the Cold War, the United States today is not seeking to contain a threatening state/empire, but rather seeking to convert a broad movement within Islamic civilization to accept the value structure of Western Modernity – an agenda hidden within the official rubric of a 'War on Terrorism'.[61]

Some commentators have falsely attributed this quote to how Muslims perceive US policy, but a careful reading clearly shows that the comments were general and made in the paragraphs following the analyses of Muslim perceptions.

This chapter has documented the fact that many people in

positions of power search for and deliberately create enemies for a variety of reasons, the main one being to deflect public attention from themselves so that the public does not challenge the controllers of society. Muslims are the current favoured enemy. If Muslims were not the current enemy, a new one would be manufactured by dominant elites. From this it follows that dominant elites will always find or create an enemy with which they (via the mainstream media) try to manipulate the public. We should therefore ask Islamophobes why they hate and fear Muslims when an entirely different enemy could have been conjured by elites?

Chapter 2

'Attitudes could be changed by an event'

Some policy planners are quite open about the fact that they seek enemies and indeed consider provoking or fabricating events or connecting dots that aren't there. Their aims are specific to their desires. The British Ministry of Defence, for instance, understands the appeal of fear and has written extensively about the various ways in which events could occur in order to work in the interests of the British state. Think-tanks, military academies and Futures documents are a treasure-trove of information and insight into how some elite minds work.

In a 30-year projection sponsored by Goldman Sachs and Shell oil, the UK Ministry of Defence says that '[m]ilitary operations are *likely* to continue to result in casualties and face the challenge of demonstrating legitimacy to sceptical public audiences'. As a result, '[i]nfluence activity, the battle of ideas, and perceptions of moral legitimacy *will* be important for success'. Perceptions of moral legitimacy can take many forms, with humanitarian intervention and self-defence being the most common. Counterterrorism includes so-called self-defence operations, like drone attacks. 'The challenges to legal norms and legitimacy include: the blurring of roles between civilian and military, regular and irregular; the chameleon-like behaviour of groups that switch identity, being concurrently organised criminals, terrorists, insurgents and agents of a state' (emphases in original).[62] Note, '... agents of a state'.

Instilling fear

In 2010, the Royal Institute for International Affairs (Chatham House) held a series of meetings attended by politicians, advisers, businesspeople and military experts concerning the future of British foreign policy in the age of neoliberal globalization. The authors of one report, sponsored by BAE weapons, Barclays bank and BP oil, note that the British public is generally passive: 'Voters will not actively call for a more effective foreign policy'. Therefore, the public has to be motivated to support a violent foreign policy. 'We recommend ... the government should think quite carefully about what its basic international mission is and it should redefine that as managing global risk on behalf of British citizens'. Note, '... managing risks on behalf of British citizens'. It goes on: 'We effectively see this as a bargain struck between government and citizens'. The report explains that '[g]overnment is saying ... we will also do our best to shield you from the fallout of the turbulence [of globalization] ... [I]n return citizens are able to go out and benefit from the opportunities that the global system offers them and possibly generate enough economic wealth to keep the government able to pay its debts'.[63]

Under 'The Psychology of Influence', two PhDs working for the Royal Military Academy Sandhurst write about the 'rather simplistic view' that 'facts inform and emotions inspire'. They explain that 'it is important that the emotions triggered by soft power strategies are the correct ones and targeted at the correct audience'. They cite the government's 1980s' AIDS awareness campaign as an example. Such campaigns are based on 'using fear as the main persuader'. Some PSYOPS specialists say 'that the use of fear requires a specific set of circumstances and needs to be targeted carefully before there is any chance of effective behavioural change'. The authors discuss 'shared values' as a solution to influence operations: the alleged shared value that we all want to live in peace (when clearly war planners do not want peace, otherwise they'd be out of a job). 'We suggest that influence operators need to try and find a win-win approach. To do this', the authors continue, 'influence operators need to target specific audiences and understand the underlying needs of that audience'. Target Audience Analysis Teams can help: 'The [given] message needs to be tailored uniquely to the target population and its mode of delivery needs to be appropriate'.[64]

Another important statement was made in 2011 by the head of

UK Counterterrorism. It sheds light on the attitudes of those in power:

In 2006, the UK, Kenya and Ethiopia organized a terror group called the Transitional Federal Government (TFG) to invade Somalia and overthrow the Islamic Courts Union (ICU) government, which numerous rights groups (including Amnesty) and government bodies (such as the US Congressional Research Service) defined as non-extremist, socialistic and progressive. The invasion in December 2006 triggered a refugee crisis: hundreds of thousands of Somalis fled the country to avoid the terror of the TFG and the resulting war. The armed wing of the ICU, Al-Shabaab (the Youth) broke away to exist as a separate organization as the ICU folded. At the same time, thieving European vessels, which British government inquiries acknowledge are taking fish from Somalia's waters, faced Somali piracy.[65]

In June 2011, the head of UK Counterterrorism, Campbell McCafferty, testified to a committee that '[t]here has not been any evidence of a link between the [Somali] pirates and al-Shabab' (sic). However, such a 'link to terrorism would change entirely the international community's view ... I think people are looking hard for those links'.[66] The inference being that if terrorism doesn't exist, it has to be invented or fostered. The media followed. A few months later, the tabloid *People* reported: 'fears that al-Shabaab will attempt to strike at the [London Olympic] Games, as well as growing concern over piracy and kidnappings'. Providing no evidence, the author, Nick Dorman, said that '[f]anatics from the [Shabaab] group were responsible for 21/7, the botched plot to set off bombs in London in 2005', following the July 7 attacks.[67] There is just one slight problem with this analysis: *Al-Shabaab didn't even exist in 2005.*[68]

False-flags

Another UK Ministry of Defence document, *Future Character of Conflict* (2010), explains that '[a]ll warfare requires the political support and consensus of the people in whose name it is waged ... The use of military instruments will only be viable once events have been correctly attributed through objective evidence, providing a strong basis in public support'. The 'objective evidence' might include civilians or soldiers allegedly killed on the streets of Britain by Muslims, or British aid workers allegedly kidnapped by Islamic extremists in Iraq. It might include statements allegedly emanating from Islamic State websites, claiming to take responsibility for attacks.[69]

The document continues: 'Delays in decision making will impact operational tempo, putting a premium on more agile decision-making structures and processes, both nationally and within the alliance'. It notes that, 'these processes must be routinely exercised if only to demonstrate resolve'. Worryingly, it concludes that 'public attitude to legitimacy could be changed by an event – such as a Mumbai-style atrocity – designed to provoke a reaction'. The inference is that if such an event does not occur or is not likely to occur, the conditions for its occurrence could be established or indeed even provoked.[70]

The Mumbai attack refers to a terrorist event in November 2008, when Pakistan-based Islamic extremists (Lashkar-e-Taiba) were alleged by Indian officials to have conducted 12 simultaneous shooting and bombing campaigns across the Indian city. The group denied responsibility and the Indian government later revealed that the mastermind was a CIA double-agent, David Headley (pseudonym). The Times reports that Headley was a 'double agent [who] masterminded the Islamist terrorist attack ... that killed 166 people ... while he was being used by the CIA to hunt Osama bin Laden'. The paper goes on to say that, '[w]hen India discovered his role, it accused Washington of having sacrificed Mumbai for the prime target of the al-Qaeda leader'. The article concludes: 'Headley, a former drug smuggler, was acting as a "highly prized counter-terrorism asset" for America, according to former officers in the Joint Terrorism Task Force, who said his covert career had run for 11 years'.[71]

Chapter 3

'A small price to pay'

We have seen how elites desire enemies to justify their own positions of power. We have also seen how some are open about considering the use of fear, including terror attacks, to maintain and expand their power. In order to understand how terrorism is manufactured, it is vital to also consider that people in power are aware that hurting and murdering innocents abroad will escalate terrorism. The fact that they continue to pursue their foreign policies, often against the advice of certain deep state actors, is an indication of how little they value human life and the safety of their own populations who suffer the consequences.

After the 9/11 attacks, US President George W. Bush told Americans that the attackers and their supporters were motivated by no other factor than 'they hate our freedoms'.[72] A few years later, a report by the Pentagon's Defense Science Board concluded: 'Muslims do not "hate our freedom," but rather, they hate our policies'. It goes on to say that, '[t]he overwhelming majority voice their objections to what they see as one-sided support in favor of Israel and against Palestinian rights, and the longstanding, even increasing support for what Muslims collectively see as tyrannies'. The tyrannies listed in the report include 'Egypt, Saudi Arabia, Jordan, Pakistan, and the Gulf states'. The report also notes that 'when American public diplomacy talks about bringing democracy to Islamic societies, this is seen as no more than self-serving hypocrisy'.[73]

The implication is that if the US withdrew its support for dictators in the region and for the State of Israel, and stopped bombing the region, Islamic terrorism would cease or decline. Professor Richard Shultz was told by a senior Special Operations Forces officer, whom he chose not to identify, that occasional terrorist attacks in the US and Europe is 'a small price to pay for being a superpower'.[74]

In the long-term strategic pursuit of securing oil, gas and the pipelines that transport them, the United States and its British ally have committed themselves to the Middle East and North Africa. One of many Ministry of Defence documents states in a long-range projection: 'Key natural resources, especially oil, gas and minerals of strategic value, *will* continue to be sourced from unstable areas and unreliable regions'. It also notes that '[m]aintaining access and containing instability risks in these areas is therefore *likely* to increase in importance, alongside wider developmental and stabilization roles'. Propping up dictators and bombing alleged ISIS targets constitute 'stabilization'. The report concludes: 'Where oil and gas sources are located in areas of doubtful security, military intervention *may* be used to protect the integrity of sites and to secure investments' (emphases in the original).[75]

Since 1839, when the first armed trading ships invaded the Tigris and Euphrates rivers, British and subsequent American policy towards Iraq has been particularly cruel. Having armed and immunized from punishment Iraq's dictator Saddam Hussein, Britain and America turned against their ally and imposed 13 years of economic blockade on the peoples of Iraq (1990–2003). According to the British Parliament, 200,000 Iraqis died as a direct result of the sanctions by the year 2000. President Bill Clinton's Secretary of State, Madeleine Albright, acknowledged that 500,000 Iraqi infants had perished. Other estimates, like the UN and its agencies, double that figure. The political situation in Iraq was complicated. Most of the political and military leaders were Sunni. Iraq's Shia population was harshly oppressed. Kurds had struggled for autonomy, following Western-backed genocide in the 1980s.[76]

During that decade, partially US-backed Shia Muslims in Iraq used the weapon of the suicide bomb for the first time. (I say partially-backed because they were betrayed by the US during the 1991 anti-Saddam uprising.) Iraq's Vice-president Taha Yassin Ramadan said: 'The US administration is going to turn the whole world into people prepared to die for their nations ... All they can do now is turn themselves into bombs. If the B-52 bombs can now kill 500 ... I'm sure that some operations by our freedom fighters will be able to kill 5,000'.[77]

After the invasion in 2003, Iraq experienced an unprecedented surge in suicide bombings. Five years into the occupation, 1,121 people blew themselves and others up in Iraq as part of both the civil war (i.e., Sunnis vs. Shia) and as part of the resistance (i.e., Sunnis, primarily, but not exclusively, vs. US-British forces). These bombers murdered 13,000 Iraqis, most of whom were police, politicians and civilians. Iraqi suicide bombers blew themselves up every two or three days, compared to the different factions that committed the one-per-month or fewer bombings during the Lebanese war against Israel in the 1980s. The Associated Press reports that between 2003 and 2005, only 10% of Iraq's suicide and car bombings were carried out by Iraqis. The rest were carried out by foreigners, mainly Saudis and Arabs from the Gulf States, according to Pentagon and Iraqi government officials. Most of the resistance to US-British occupation came from Iraqis, says Kenneth Katzman of the US Congressional Research Service. But the suicide attacks were almost exclusively the purview of Wahhabi/Salafists brought in by the indigenous Sunnis as a weapon against the occupiers. Robert Fisk notes that Iraqi suicide bombers also came from Algeria, Palestine, Saudi Arabia and Syria.[78]

Numerous intelligence organizations warned politicians like Tony Blair and George W. Bush that invading Iraq would increase terror attacks.

In February 2003, shortly before the invasion, the Joint Intelligence Committee told Prime Minister Blair in a top-secret memo: 'Al Qaida and associated networks will remain the greatest terrorist threat to the UK. The risk of attacks will increase following any Coalition attack on Iraq'. It goes on: 'The threat from Al Qaida will increase at the onset of any military action against Iraq. They will target Coalition forces and other Western interests in the Middle East'. It adds that '[a]ttacks against Western interests elsewhere are also likely, especially in the US and UK, for maximum impact'. The

JIC report also notes that '[t]he worldwide threat from other Islamist terrorist groups and individuals will increase significantly'. It says that, '[w]hile individual attacks are likely to be small-scale they may be numerous'. It concludes: 'Al Qaida will not carry out attacks under Iraqi direction ... Saddam's own capability to conduct terrorist attacks is limited'.[79]

Former MI5 Director-general (DG, 2002-07) Eliza Manningham-Buller told the Blair government in no uncertain terms: 'The threat to us would increase because of Iraq'. She later told the Iraq inquiry: 'our involvement in Iraq radicalised ... a few among a generation ... [who] saw our involvement in Iraq, on top of our involvement in Afghanistan, as being an attack on Islam ... Arguably we gave Osama bin Laden his Iraqi jihad'. Manningham-Buller's colleague at MI5, Stella Rimington (also ex-DG), later said to the media: 'Look at what those people who've been arrested or have left suicide videos say about their motivation. And most of them, as far as I'm aware, say that the war in Iraq played a significant part in persuading them'. Rimington concludes: 'you can't write the war in Iraq out of history. If what we're looking at is groups of disaffected young men born in this country who turn to terrorism, then I think to ignore the effect of the war in Iraq is misleading'.[80]

In 2006, the US National Intelligence Estimate (NIE) published a classified report on the future of global *jihad*. Like the Defense Science Board report quoted above, the NIE document says that '[g]reater pluralism and more responsive political systems in Muslim majority nations would alleviate some of the grievances *jihadists* exploit'. It gives four general reasons for the success of *jihadists*: '(1) Entrenched grievances, such as corruption, injustice, and fear of Western domination, leading to anger, humiliation, and a sense of powerlessness; (2) the Iraq jihad; (3) the slow pace of real and sustained economic, social, and political reforms in many Muslim majority nations; and (4) pervasive anti-US sentiment among most Muslims – all of which jihadists exploit'.[81]

With regards to Iraq specifically, the report says: 'The Iraq conflict has become the "cause célèbre" for jihadists, breeding a deep resentment of US involvement in the Muslim world and cultivating supporters for the global jihadist movement. Should jihadists leaving Iraq perceive themselves, and be perceived, to have failed, we judge fewer fighters will be inspired to carry on the fight'. It concludes: 'The jihadists regard Europe as an important venue for attacking Western interests. Extremist networks inside the extensive Muslim diasporas in Europe facilitate recruitment and staging for urban attacks, as illustrated by the 2004 Madrid and 2005 London bombings'.[82]

Turning to other wars: After 'al-Qaeda' networks protected by the British state bombed two US embassies in Africa in 1998, the Clinton administration unlawfully fired missiles at targets in Sudan and Afghanistan. The Sudan target was a well-known medical facility which produced antiviral drugs for the malaria-ridden region. That single act potentially cost the lives of tens of thousands of Sudanese children, who rely on anti-malarial drugs. Clinton neither apologized nor offered reparations. The other bomb killed a dozen Afghans and did little to weaken the alliance between bin Laden's al-Qaeda network and the ruling Taliban government of Afghanistan.[83]

A classified US National Security Agency report into the bombings concludes: 'retaliatory cruise missile strikes did little to help solve the problem posed by bin Laden and may ultimately prove to have done more harm than good'. It goes on to note that 'the root cause of the Islamic militant threat is the widespread and deep-seated discontent among a large segment of the Islamic world'. It also notes: 'Our problems with terrorism are exacerbated by our position and by our image in the world'.[84]

The NSA report's character profile of bin Laden lists him as '[a] former ally: The moral is that our friends today may be our enemies tomorrow'. We shall see in the next chapter how bin Laden served US interests in the 1980s. Bin Laden commanded 3,000 individuals, 'a rag-tag army, than a more traditional urban terrorist'. 'Al-Qaeda's' main goals include 'a withdrawal of American forces from Saudi Arabia'. It also seeks 'to diminish American influence in the world' and seeks 'the overthrow of numerous regimes seen as overly secular or anti-Islamic (e.g., Egypt, Saudi Arabia)'.[85]

After 9/11, which was blamed without evidence on bin Laden and his so-called 'al-Qaeda' network, the US and Britain invaded Afghanistan (2001), where the Taliban government (made up primarily of ethnic Pashtuns) were said to be protecting bin Laden and his 'al-Qaeda' network, which was made up mainly of Arabs and Pakistani Pashtuns. As the occupation continued, ordinary Afghans – most of whom hated all parties: the British, Americans, 'al-Qaeda' and the Taliban – continued to die in US-British airstrikes and drone attacks. The prolonged occupation fed into bin Laden's 'Crusader West' propaganda.

Numerous agencies suggest that the prolonged occupation of Afghanistan (the real aim of which appears to be to prevent Iran, China and India from building energy pipelines to connect their countries) has empowered 'al-Qaeda' and the Taliban. A British MoD report states: 'State actions are *likely* to have a significant impact on the process of radicalisation'. It gives as an example 'stabilisation operations, [where] the over-vigorous application of military power to crush radical groups *may* result in increased public support for them, or drive them to ally with other extremists'. It concludes that such actions '*may* force radical groups to become more extreme, possibly condensing into terrorist cells' (emphases in original).[86]

A UK Defence Committee report noted of Afghanistan: 'there has been an increase in suicide attacks from 18 in 2005 to 116 in 2006 and an increase in attacks from IEDs [improvised explosive devices] from 530 to 1,297 in 2006'. Cameron Scott of the British-American Security Information Council also reported that 'attacks by insurgents have increased in number and lethality, particularly with the rise of previously rare suicide bombings'. The British government and military refused to keep records on civilian casualties and even destroyed the few records it did keep. Nevertheless in 2007, the Defence Committee acknowledged that 'civilian casualties are of increasing concern to Afghans … [S]ince December 2006 civilian casualties had in fact increased and that, as a consequence, public support for ISAF [the International Security Assistance Force] has weakened'.[87]

In 2010 the National Bureau of Economic Research conducted a study of civilian casualties in Afghanistan and Iraq. It found 'strong evidence that local exposure to civilian casualties caused by international forces leads to increased insurgent violence over the long-run ... Minimizing harm to civilians may indeed help counter-insurgent forces in Afghanistan to reduce insurgent recruitment'.[88] Shortly before, US Lt. Gen. Stanley McChrystal told the media: '[i]f defeating an insurgent formation produces popular resentment, the victory is hollow and unsustainable'. The problem, said McChrystal, was in large part due to the high number of civilian casualties caused by the NATO occupation. 'Our willingness to operate in ways that minimize casualties damage ... is essential to our credibility'.[89]

Torture & murder: empowering 'al-Qaeda'

Torture is another grievance that empowered 'al-Qaeda'. Under the Clinton government, the US, with help from European allies, established a network of sites where alleged terror suspects were kidnapped by CIA and related agents, flown to secret locations and tortured by allies and/or special forces. A report written by an anonymous insider published by the *Financial Times* in 2006 noted that '[t]he "ghost prisoners" of the "black sites" are now a grievance to be added to Guantanamo, Abu Ghraib and Bagram'. Guantánamo refers to the prison in Cuba owned and run by the US, where alleged suspects are detained without charge or trial, and tortured. Abu Ghraib was the prison in Iraq where alleged 'insurgents' (i.e., people resisting occupation) were tortured by US forces. Bagram is the US Air Force base in Afghanistan, also a site of torture and death. 'It is getting hard to think of what more we can do to empower al-Qaeda', the report concludes.[90]

Even US President Barack Obama acknowledged that 'Guantanamo continues to be one of the key magnets for jihadi recruits'. Under the pretence of facing a Republican-controlled Congress that wanted to keep it open, Obama refused to close the prison, even though he could easily have done so by signing an Executive Order to bypass Congress.[91]

A report by Human Rights Watch (2014) concludes that most Guantánamo prisoners were innocent: 'Of the 779 detainees' imprisoned by US forces in Guantánamo since 11 September 2001, 'roughly 600 were released without charges, many after being detained for years ... Of the 149 detainees that remain at Guantanamo only six, Abd al-Rahim al-Nashiri, and the September 11, 2001 co-defendants face any formal charges'. The Center for the Study of Human Rights in the Americas writes: 'fifteen children [aged between 13 and 17 years old] were imprisoned, at some time or another, at Guantánamo. This is three more than the twelve the State Department acknowledged to the public after our earlier report on the subject, and seven more than the eight the State Department reported to the UN Committee on the Rights of the Child'. The Center adds that '[f]ourteen of the individuals ... have now been released – one of them being the first child in History to have been convicted of war crimes (Omar Ahmed Khadr). The fifteenth (Yasser Talal al Zahrani) allegedly killed himself in his Guantánamo cell at age 21'.[92]

The use of unmanned aerial vehicles (drones), which unlawfully target alleged, suspected commanders to be killed, cause a high number of civilian deaths and injuries. They are a terrorist-generating machine.

The US runs two drone programmes: military and CIA (civilian). It has been alleged by rights activists that mercenary companies are also involved. European allies, including the UK and Germany, are part of the war crime, supplying information to the US in its operations. According to the Bureau of Investigative Journalists, Barack Obama – who personally signed off the murder of many alleged terrorism suspects – killed 2,464 individuals with drones in the last six years of his presidency. Counterterrorism adviser to the Pentagon, David Kilcullen, estimated in 2009 that 98% of those killed by drones were civilians. He says: 'every one of these dead noncombatants represents an alienated family, a new desire for revenge, and more recruits for a militant movement that has grown exponentially even as drone strikes have increased'. Drones had or have names like Predators and missiles have names like Hellfire. They are used unlawfully by the US (and often Britain) in Afghanistan (beginning 2002), Yemen (2002), Iraq (2004), Pakistan (2004), Somalia (2006), Libya (2011) and Syria (2014).[93]

In 2009, Pakistan's Prime Minister, Yousuf Raza Gilani, said 'missile strikes by US drones on the northwestern tribal areas bordering Afghanistan were in fact strengthening the militants' (*Financial Times*). In 2010–11, the BBC said that '[m]issile attacks by US drones in Pakistan's tribal areas have more than trebled under the Obama administration … The militant backlash over the same period has been even more violent'. The report notes that '[e]xtremists have struck more than 140 times in various Pakistani locations, killing more than 1,700 people and injuring hundreds more'. The BBC report concludes that Pakistanis have 'consistently argued that drone attacks are hindering rather than helping with the battle against extremism, saying they fuel public anger against the government and the US and boost support for militants'. Reuters reports 'mounting resentment from Pakistanis who decry the government for bowing to U.S. wishes'. Pakistan's President, Asif Ali Zardari, said 'drones are radicalizing more people to side with the Taliban'.[94]

After pleading guilty, the so-called Times Square bomber Faisal Shahzad (a Pakistan-born naturalized American) told the US court that he had been trained by the Taliban to make a bomb and acted alone in trying to detonate it in New York. He said: 'unless the US pulls out of Afghanistan and Iraq, until they stop drone strikes in Somalia, Pakistan, and Yemen, and stop attacking Muslim lands, we will attack the US'.[95] Six years later, Emma Manna of *Georgetown Public Policy Review* studied drone attacks and terrorist counterattacks. Manna finds 'a positive correlation between U.S. drone strikes and terrorist attacks in Pakistan'. Manna notes 'a statistically significant rise in the number of terrorist attacks occurring after the U.S. drone program begins targeting a given province'.[96] Ex-head of Obama's Defense Intelligence Agency, Gen. Mike Flynn, says: 'What we have is this continued investment in conflict … The more weapons we give, the more bombs we drop, that just fuels the conflict' (sic). Flynn also says: 'When you drop a bomb from a drone[,] you're going to cause more damage than you are going to cause good'.[97]

This is a tiny sample from a rich record of intelligence reports warning that violence breeds violence, but as the British Ministry of Defence and others acknowledge, the overarching priority is to seek to control the Middle East and North Africa, not keep people safe.

Chapter 4

Al-Qaeda 1: 'A few stirred up Muslims'

So far, we have seen that: 1) elites want enemies, 2) some are open about using fear and even terrorism to justify their actions, and 3) elites ignore the advice of some of their top intelligence analysts. In order to understand the core of manufactured 'Islamic' terror, it is important to recall how the US and Britain created what they later went on to call 'al-Qaeda' and accused its 'members' of all manner of terrorist crimes. 'Al-Qaeda' spread across the world, leading to new generations of jihadis.

It has been well documented by academics and journalists working in the mainstream (many of whom are referenced here) that what is called 'al-Qaeda' is and was a creation of the British and American intelligence services. The tens of thousands of *jihadis* trained, armed and organized by those agencies in the late-1970s and throughout the 1980s never called themselves 'al-Qaeda' or adhered to any centralized structure, with the exception of certain networks like Osama bin Laden's. But even bin Laden never called his group 'al-Qaeda'. Their largely decentralized presence was an ideal whack-a-mole situation for the US, hell-bent on global empire. ISIS is frequently referred to as an offshoot of 'al-Qaeda in Iraq'.

'Al-Qaeda' as a U.S.-invented label

US President Jimmy Carter's National Security Advisor, Zbigniew Brzezinski, admitted in an interview that he helped to create some 'stirred up Muslims', whom the US military referred to as *mujahideen*, or holy warriors. The plan was 'to draw the Russians into the Afghan trap'.[98] The plan worked. In December 1979, in response to growing terrorism in Soviet colonies by *mujahideen*, and to prop up a pro-Soviet regime, the Soviets invaded Afghanistan, launching a brutal decade-long war that killed 1.25 million people and drove three million out of the country.[99] Thousands of refugees living in neighbouring Pakistan went on to become Afghan Taliban when they reached adulthood and returned to their home country in 1994.[100]

In 2005, following the 7 July attacks in London, Britain's former Foreign Secretary Robin Cook explained that 'al-Qaeda' simply refers to the *mujahideen*, whom Britain and America had organized, trained, armed, funded and protected from mid-1979 into the 1980s (and, it turns out, long after), including a wealthy construction magnate named Osama bin Laden, whom the CIA paid to construct tunnels along the Pakistan-Afghanistan border. Cook wrote: 'Al-Qaida, literally "the database", was originally the computer file of the thousands of *mujahideen* who were recruited and trained with help from the CIA to defeat the Russians'. Ergo, when the media mention 'al-Qaeda', what they are really saying is, terrorists whose leaders were at one time armed and trained by Britain and the US.[101]

It is easy for the British secret services to mobilize Muslim extremists because, for much of modern Middle Eastern history, the UK has been the main driver of fundamentalism; directly and indirectly. The eighteenth century saw the rise of political Islam's most brutal deviation: Wahhabism, named after Adbul Wahhab. By the early-nineteenth century, the Saudi dynasty launched a religious cleansing of Shia, including those of Karbala (now in Iraq). Beginning in 1865, Britain subsidized the Saudis to act as a proxy force; a policy that remains unchanged. Muhammad bin Saud converted to Wahhabism, apparently for political reasons, and went on to found Saudi Arabia. In 1916, Sir Percy Cox, Britain's representative of the Persian Gulf India Office, ordered MI6 agent Harry Philby to chaperone Ibn Saud. During the 1920s, the Saud dynasty killed 400,000 Arabs in its regional conquest, executing 40,000 and amputating the limbs of 350,000 people.[102]

The Muslim Brotherhood was established with a grant from Britain's Suez Canal Company in the 1930s to ensure that progressive, socialist elements in Egypt and the region would not jeopardize UK business interests. MI6 financed the Muslim

Brotherhood throughout the 1940s and has maintained links ever since. As the British Empire transitioned to the American Empire, 'America's connection to the Muslim Brotherhood-linked Islamic fundamentalists in Afghanistan began', writes journalist and historian Robert Dreyfuss. The Brotherhood's Said Ramadan met President Eisenhower in 1953. According to a Pakistani government official, the CIA began financing Islamic extremists in Afghanistan in 1973, after a coup that brought Muhammad Daoud to power. The CIA sponsored numerous Islamists through its Asia Foundation front, including Professor Gholam Muhammad Niyazi's Organisation of Muslim Youth (OMY). Using small cells of five, the OMY gradually infiltrated the Afghan Army, laying the groundwork for the coup of 1978.[103]

An associated group was SAVAK. Established by MI6 and the CIA in 1950s' Iran, the SAVAK secret police quickly earned a reputation as 'one of the worst violators of human rights' (Amnesty International), kidnapping and torturing tens of thousands of Iranians from 1953 up to the Shah of Iran's overthrow in 1979.[104]

Drawing on declassified Soviet archives, researchers Cordovez and Harrison write: 'SAVAK and the CIA worked hand in hand, sometimes in loose collaboration with underground Afghan Islamic fundamentalist groups that shared their anti-Soviet objectives ... The Afghan fundamentalists were closely linked' to the Muslim Brotherhood and the Muslim World League. Their funding came primarily from Saudi oil revenues. SAVAK, the CIA, and Pakistani intelligence (the ISI) attempted to depose Daoud in September 1973 and in June 1974. Two of the major players in the coup were Gulbuddin Hekmatyar and Professor Burhaneddin Rabbani: both of whom fled to Pakistan, where they were protected by the Pakistani government.[105]

Afghanistan

In *Unholy Wars*, a book endorsed by both a CIA agent and a former advisor to JFK, author John K. Cooley reveals that Anglo-American preparations for training the *mujahideen* began as early as 1978: 'British intelligence input, and that of GCHQ in particular, was enhanced during the 1978–83 period, when British participation in the jihad was initiated'.[106]

Zahir Shah's cousin, Muhammad Daoud, overthrew the monarchy in 1973. Afghan leftists and communists formed the People's Democratic Party of Afghanistan (PDPA), which split into two factions, Parcham and Khalq. They reunited in 1977. The PDPA killed Daoud in the April Revolution of 1978, bringing Nur Muhammad Taraki to power. The Soviets believed that Taraki was a CIA agent and that the anti-Taraki revolution in Herat was sponsored by Iran. Actually, sponsored by Pakistan's Inter-Services Intelligence (ISI), the Herat coup, led by Ismail Khan, resulted in the hacking to death of over a dozen Soviet advisers, including their women and children.[107]

Taraki and his deputy, Hafizullah Amin requested Soviet assistance in defeating opposition from Pakistan and Iran. The PDPA was opposed by the CIA-funded Muslim Youth Movement, which split into four factions: one (Hizb-i-Islami) was led by Hekmatyar; the other (sharing the same name) by Mawlawi Younis Khalis; the third (Jamayat-i-Islami) by Professor Rabbani; and the fourth (Ittihad) by Professor Abdul Rasul Sayyaf. Hekmatyar, Rabbani and Sayyaf would later help create the Taliban by radicalizing young Afghan refugees.[108]

According to Dreyfuss, Sayyaf was an affiliate of the British-created, MI6-funded Muslim Brotherhood: 'The Islamic right supported by the ISI carried out a countrywide campaign of terrorism, assassinating hundreds of teachers and civil servants in a Pol Pot-style attack against secular and educated Afghanis [sic]'. Many of the terrorists were based in London. A US embassy report from June 1979 says the Afghan government referred to the *mujahideen* as 'made-in-London mullahs'.[109]

The *mujahideen* were funded substantially by 'the drug trade, which the CIA helped to promote ... From the beginning of the Afghan *jihad*, senior Britons and Americans in government consulted about it', writes Cooley. 'When the Soviets invaded Afghanistan in December 1979, Prince Turki', head of Saudi intelligence, which has close links with the CIA and MI6, 'sent [Osama] bin

Laden to Peshawar to scout out the possibilities of raising an Arab volunteer army'.[110]

Cooley notes Prince Turki al-Faisal's 'close association with Osama bin Laden'. Bin Laden, a wealthy Saudi, was also married to Taliban leader Mullah Omar's daughter. Bin Laden's Professor was a Palestinian working as a recruiter for the CIA, Abdullah Azzam. Their money was funnelled through Egyptian- and Saudi-sponsored fronts, including the International Islamic Relief Organization and the Muslim World League.[111]

Probably at the behest of the CIA, MI6 and Pakistan's ISI, an Afghanistan Army unit sponsored by President Hafizullah Amin mutinied in Kabul in June 1979. This was at a time when US President Carter's administration, at the behest of National Security Advisor Zbigniew Brzezinski, began funding, arming, training and directing those whom the CIA would later rename 'al-Qaeda' (led by Hekmatyar, Rabbani, et al). In September, Taraki was killed, presumably in the civil war. The Soviets invaded in December 1979, killing Amin. 'These facts make it clear that U.S. covert operations in Afghanistan were not a direct response to a particular Soviet maneuver', writes historian John Prados in the *Journal of American History*. Because the CIA and MI6 could not sustain a large, permanent presence, 'the secret war was run through Pakistan'.[112]

The majority of the *mujahids* were Saudi. However, the operation was so immense that it drew tens of thousands of Muslims from all over the world, adding to the 300,000 or so indigenous fighters: Algerians, American Muslims, Chechens, Chinese Uighurs, Egyptians, Filipinos, Indonesians, Jordanians, Lebanese, Libyans, Pakistanis, Palestinians, Somalis, Turks and Yemenis. The terrorists were trained by the US Navy SEALS and the Green Berets at Fort Bragg and the JFK Special Warfare Center.[113]

However, we now know from Robert Dreyfuss's research that the preparations were laid in the previous years and decades by the CIA – not in the Summer of 1979 – and that, according to Cooley, the British started preparations as early as 1978.

A CIA official involved in the operation, Gus Avrakotos, said: the British 'have guys who have lived [in Afghanistan] for over twenty years as journalists, as authors or tobacco growers ... [W]hen the Soviets invaded, MI6 activated these old networks ... The Brits', he said, sponsored 'murder, assassination and indiscriminate bomb-ings. They could issue guns with silencers ... [which] implied assassination – and heaven forbid car bombs!' The *mujahideen* used bombs disguised as pens, watches, cigarette lighters, tape recorders and bicycles.[114]

In Afghanistan, 'a shipment of several thousand venerable Enfield .303 rifles, the standard weapon of the Afghan tribals [was sent] to the [*mujahideen*] who were already beginning to snipe at the Soviet invaders', writes the CIA's man in Pakistan, Milton Bearden. 'Its officers in Pakistan kept a low profile, and the weapons it sup-plied to the *mujahideen*, with the exception of the British Enfields, were models manufactured in Warsaw Pact countries'.[115]

According to Jason Burke, '[i]n addition to the military training base (the "seekers of martyrdom" camp) and "University of Da'wa and Jihad" he had built at Pabbi, near Peshawar, Sayyaf constructed another large training facility at Khaldan ... In all camps, particu-larly Sayyaf's, small groups of Arabs trained alongside the muja-hideen'.[116]

In *Ghost Wars*, Steve Coll writes:

> The self-described 'moderate' Afghan rebel leaders with ties to the old royal family or the country's mystical Sufi brotherhood relied more on support from Europe and Washington, parti-cularly from Capitol Hill ... The Islamist radicals tended to cultivate wealthy patrons in Saudi Arabia ... Those Afghans who felt neglected by Pakistani intelligence tended to be most active in Washington ... All this ensured that ISI's Muslim Brotherhood-inspired clients – mainly Hekmatyar but also Sayyaf, Rabbani, and radical commanders who operated along the Pakistan border, such as Jallaladin Haqqanni – won the greatest share of support.[117]

Aid specialist Jonathan Goodhand writes:

> In the 1980s refugee and cross-border programmes were seen by many as the non-lethal component of [the Anglo-American]

aid to the Afghan [*mujahideen*]. The refugee camps became a rear base for the Mujaheddin, and refugees had to register with one of the seven political/military parties approved by the Pakistani government.[118]

Operation cyclone

Cooley writes that the US and Britain secretly 'train[ed the] huge foreign mercenary army; one of the largest ever seen in American military history'. The operations cost over one billion dollars per annum and were sponsored by France, Morocco, Egypt, Saudi Arabia and Israel, which purchased massive amounts of land and developed telecommunications infrastructure for tapping by the US National Security Agency and Britain's GCHQ. Israel directed to the cause weapons captured from Egypt, the Palestine Liberation Army and Syria. It worked with the would-be members of Hamas. US Air Force cargo planes flew Egyptian arms to Pakistan, which were smuggled into Afghanistan. Aid agencies, including Médecins Sans Frontières, Médecins du Monde and Aide Médicale Internationale, allegedly helped the *mujahideen*.[119]

The CIA printed distorted and extremist versions of the Koran from its Langley headquarters and established religious 'schools' to brainwash and train young Muslims. The CIA established fake Muslim charities. The World Muslim League and similar front organizations funded by the Saudi elite, including Osama bin Laden, funnelled money to the cause. Construction giant bin Laden, worth several million dollars, built a cave complex in the Tora Bora mountain range. Britain's Special Air Service (SAS) had a major role in creating 'al-Qaeda'. They were 'the jihad's managers', writes Cooley.[120]

In his partly-censored history of MI6, Dr Stephen Dorril found that 'MI6 sent an annual mission to the rebels consisting of two MI6 officers and military instructors. The most important contribution was help with organisation and communication', including supplying three hundred Blowpipe missiles and radio equipment.[121]

Ken Connor, ex-SAS, revealed (BBC's words):

that he helped train Mujahedin fighters at two secret camps in
Scotland and another in northern England during the 1980s
... [O]ne of the training camps was located in mountains surrounding the Criffel in Dumfries while the other was in the
remote Applecross peninsula in the West Highlands.

Connor himself says:

> The main thing they lacked was tactical knowledge and battle
> planning, so we worked constantly on that. Some helicopter
> training was also arranged for them and they were taught how
> to attack airfields. But the main achievement was to turn them
> from a disorganised mob into a fighting unit.[122]

Unknown numbers of the men were smuggled into Britain disguised as Afghan tourists and trained in three-week cycles. Other
ex-SAS men who trained the *mujahideen* in Britain included Lt. Col.
Keith Farnes and Maj. Brian Baty. The Cheltenham-based GCHQ
intercepted and translated Soviet battle-plan communications and
adjusted *mujahid* training accordingly.[123]

The SAS closely trained Massoud in the use of Blowpipe missiles.
Former Chatham House Fellow Mark Curtis writes:

> Activities included sabotage operations such as rocket attacks
> on villages in Tajikistan ... MI6 funded the leader of Pakistan's
> Jamaat-i-Islami, Qazi Hussain Ahmad – who had close links
> with Massoud and Hekmatyr – to pump money and Islamic
> literature into the Soviet republics of Tajikistan and Uzbeki-
> stan to incite the local religious circles to rebel against their
> communist governments.[124]

The authorized media were able to keep these facts from the British
public, whose tax money paid for the terrorist operations, because
of the Ministry of Defence's state-censorship: the D-Notice system.[125]

MI6's man in Islamabad was Anthony Hawkes. He ran operations
from 1984 to 1988. Monitored by Scotland Yard's Special Branch
and MI5, and green-lighted by the Foreign Office, a multitude of UK

mercenary firms, whose primary members consisted of ex-SAS and ex-MI6, were also involved in the operations.[126]

The company Hogg Robinson was established to advise Lloyds bank on insurance risks. Its subsidiary, Control Risks, began compiling a massive terrorism database, including of *mujahids*. A Control Risks subsidiary, Keenie-Meenie Services (KMS), conducted training operations. With a tax haven in Jersey, KMS was run by former insurance broker, Col. Jim Johnson and ex-SAS Major, David Walker. Both millionaires, Johnson was an aide to the queen and Walker was a Cambridge graduate, a graduate of the Sandhurst Military Academy and a Tory councillor for Surrey. The training operations were conducted through Saladin Security, a KMS subsidiary. The Qaboos dictatorship of Oman, which the British installed, allowed the US to utilize Omani naval ports, RAF air bases, and its own Tamrit and Sib air bases. Cargo planes bringing military equipment and fighters to Pakistan for the *jihad* next door refuelled at the bases.[127]

The training was provided in a pyramid structure. At the capstone were the SAS, MI6, KMS and other mercenary firms. They would train the leaders of around seven large brigades. These included over 700 former Afghan Army officers in one unit alone, the National Islamic Front of Afghanistan (NIFA), led by Brig. Gen. Rahmatullah Safi. Safi lived in England after the coup in Afghanistan, and returned after the Soviet invasion. The NIFA alone trained around 8,000 *jihadis*.[128]

The Pakistan ISI's main proxy was the extremist Hizb-i-Islami, led by Gulbuddin Hekmatyar. 'Hekmatyar's speciality was trafficking opium and throwing acid in the faces of women who refused to wear the veil', writes John Pilger. 'Invited to London in 1986, he was lauded [by Thatcher] as a "freedom fighter"'.[129] *Mujahideen* Commander Hadji Abdul Haq also met with US President Ronald Reagan and British PM Margaret Thatcher.

Bank of Credit and Commerce International (BCCI) was a CIA front that bribed British journalists. It was run by Pakistan's Agha Hassan Abedi and helped finance the *jihad*'s terrorists through the

ISI. Abedi was a friend of British Prime Ministers James Callaghan and Margaret Thatcher. The CIA ran a branch of BCCI in London's Cromwell Road, which paid British informants and agents. The US National Security Agency's Norman Bailey admitted that the BCCI was involved in 'laundering drug money, financing terrorists, arms deals and manipulation of financial markets'.[130]

After the Soviet withdrawal, MI6 worked closely with many of these and other *jihadis* in London, Manchester and Yorkshire, as we shall now see.

Chapter 5

Al-Qaeda 2: 'Londonistan'

Some of the 20,000 or so terrorists organized by the US and Britain to fight the Soviets in the '80s were used by the same agencies to fight proxy wars in Algeria, Bosnia, Libya, Serbia and elsewhere from the '90s to the present. Some top jihadis settled in Britain where they were protected by the state and went on to indoctrinate alienated youths for jihad in Afghanistan, Kashmir, Sudan and, later, Libya (2010–12) and Syria. Some alleged terrorists were radicalized by the protected leaders and went on to attack civilian targets in Britain.

Right-wing columnist Melanie Phillips wrote *Londonistan* (2006, London: Gibson Square), a book documenting the growth of extremism in many parts of the British capital. The epithet originated with French intelligence who kept tracing Algerian terror suspects back to the UK.[131] Phillips conveniently omits that while they have their own agendas, many UK-based extremists are part of a hierarchy of terrorism at the top of which sits MI6.

'Al-Qaeda', the Database of terrorists organized by the US and British secret services, continued to thrive in Britain throughout the 1990s, i.e., after the Afghan *jihad*, sending out alienated and disenchanted young British Muslim men to fight 'holy wars' for 'sacred' causes. With generic racism against ethnic Pakistani and Bangladeshi Britons rampant, Islamophobia rife and levels of unemployment and poverty high among young, ethnic Muslim men, the MI6-linked 'al-Qaeda' recruiters preached on fertile ground.

Al-Muhajiroun

As noted in the Introduction, nearly a quarter of alleged UK terror plots are linked to al-Muhajiroun.

In 1996, a Syrian called Omar Bakri who had been exiled from Saudi Arabia, co-founded a Salafist group in London called al-Muhajiroun (the Emigrants). The organization intended to broadcast a letter already published in the media supposedly written by Osama bin Laden. It was scheduled to be read at a rally for the group Islamic Revival. MI5 knew about and then cancelled the event, says Bakri. He also said, speaking in 2004:

> we were being continuously monitored by Special Branch; they even said this to us on many public functions . . . I cannot really differentiate between MI5, Special Branch or the Police; they all represent the same authority as far as I am concerned – and I have been questioned by these people on at least 16 occasions.[132]

Journalist Ron Suskind says: 'A British intelligence official told me that Bakri had helped MI5 on several of its investigations'.[133]

It would seem that MI6 was connected to al-Muhajiroun in its proxy war against Serbia. US former prosecutor, John Loftus, claimed on Fox News that two British extremists, Abu Hamza and Haroon Aswat, were working with MI6 via al-Muhajiroun. MI6 helped to create the Kosovo Liberation Army to attack Serbia. Bakri said of al-Muhajiroun: 'We used to help mostly in Bosnia and Kosovo as part of a broader humanitarian effort'. Elsewhere, Bakri said he trained terrorists through his UK-based Sakina Security Services: 'some went to Kashmir, and others to Chechnya and to Kosovo before that. Some remained in Britain because they were not fully trained ideologically'.[134] Bakri was allowed to operate and spread his hate until 2005, when he was banned from the UK.

Hamza & Qatada

Osama bin Laden was one of the most notorious *jihadis* to fight in the war against the Soviet Union. His job was building tunnels in Afghanistan and Pakistan in which the *mujahideen* could hide. Abu Qatada was described by the British media as bin Laden's 'right-hand man' in Britain. Qatada had close connections with the

Algeria's Armed Islamic Group (GIA), serving as a recruiter and editor of the organization's newsletter.

Baroness Scotland of Asthal, then-Minister of State at the British Home Office, said: 'the Security Service had three meetings with Abu Qatada during 1996 and 1997'.[135] In 2002, *TIME* magazine stated: 'senior European intelligence officials tell *TIME* that Abu Qatada is tucked away in a safe house in the north of England, where he and his family are being lodged, fed and clothed by British intelligence services'.[136] In 2004, *The Times* of London reported:

> One of al-Qaeda's most dangerous figures [Qatada] has been revealed as a double agent working for MI5, raising criticism from European governments, which repeatedly called for his arrest ... He pledged to MI5 that he would not 'bite the hand that fed him[.]' ... Indignant French officials accused MI5 of helping the cleric to abscond. While he remained on the run, one intelligence chief in Paris was quoted as saying: 'British intelligence is saying they have no idea where he is, but we know where he is and, if we know, I'm quite sure they do.' Almost a year later Abu Qatada was found hiding in a flat not far from Scotland Yard.[137]

From the mid-1990s to 2000, Reda Hassaine, an MI5 double-agent (who was also working for the French and Algerian secret services), monitored Qatada and his colleague Abu Hamza at the Four Feathers Youth and Community Centre and the Finsbury Park Mosque, London. Hassaine told the *Mail on Sunday*:

> At the Fourth Feathers Club, I saw Qatada brainwash young Muslims living in Britain from Africa, Somalia, Sudan, Morocco and my own country of Algeria, by urging them to kill Christians and Jews. Qatada preached that if a Muslim became a suicide bomber, he would go to paradise and be able to make love to virgins.[138]

In 1990, Abu Hamza worked as an engineer at the Royal Military Academy Sandhurst. According to authors Sean O'Neill and Daniel McGrory, Hamza was 'volunteering to help wounded mujahideen receiving treatment in London'.[139] In 1995, he visited Bosnia three times. Former Chatham House Fellow Mark Curtis writes:

> According to Bosnian Muslim military intelligence sources, Britain [and the US, were some of] the main channels through which foreign jihadists entered Bosnia, while London hosted several financiers and recruiters for the cause ... Britain, along with the US, actively encouraged foreign jihadists to go to Bosnia.[140]

In the 1990s, the governments of Egypt and Yemen sought Hamza's extradition, but he was protected by the British government. Between 1997 and 2000, MI5 met with Hamza seven times. O'Neill and McGrory write:

> Special Branch, the intelligence-gathering arm of Scotland Yard, had been talking to Abu Hamza since early 1997, when he was still preaching in Luton. In the classified records of the meetings he is referred to by the codename 'damson berry'. Unknown to the police, MI5 had also begun meeting Abu Hamza at the behest of French intelligence; he was given the MI5 code number 910.[141]

According to *The Observer*:

> Evidence collected by the American [intelligence] agencies shows that, as early as 1997, Hamza was organising terror camps in the Brecon Beacons, at an old monastery in Tunbridge Wells, Kent, and in Scotland, suggesting that he ran a far more extensive training network than has been officially acknowledged until now ... British ex-soldiers, some of whom fought in Bosnia, were recruited to train about 10 of Hamza's followers at the Brecon Beacons camp for three weeks in 1998. The former troops taught them to strip and clean weapons and gave them endurance training and lessons in surveillance techniques.[142]

So far, we have established Qatada and Hamza as UK intelligence assets and recruiters and trainers for 'al-Qaeda'.

In 1992, one Rachid Ramda arrived in the UK from Algeria, 'after police there linked him to terrorist attacks', writes Mark Curtis. In 1994, French intelligence alerted MI5, who chose not to act. In 1995, Curtis continues, 'it is alleged that Ramda led a gang which exploded a bomb packed with nails and bolts on the Paris underground'. The French sought Ramda's extradition, but Ramda was protected by the British until 2006. 'Can you imagine how the British would react if France caught the alleged moneyman behind the July 7 [2005] bombings, and then ten years later he was still fighting extradition?', asked a French intelligence officer.[143]

The murder of Lee Rigby

In December 2006, the US, Britain and Kenya organized a terrorist regime called the Transitional Federal Government (TFG), to destroy the socialistic Islamic Courts Union (ICU) of Somalia. US Congressional reports confirm that the ICU was not an Islamic extremist group. In fact, Amnesty International and the United Nations praised the ICU for reversing Somalia's horrifying socio-economic decline caused by its civil war. The invasion by the TFG was funded by British taxpayers, unbeknownst to them. The TFG's torturing internal police unit received money from the UK's Department for International Development. The ensuing war sparked a refugee crisis of hundreds of thousands of Somalis who became internally displaced, fled to neighbouring Kenya and across the Gulf of Aden to Yemen.[144]

The British public knew nothing of this because it was reported almost nowhere, with the exception of journalist Aidan Hartley.

Al-Shabaab (the Youth) was the military wing of the ICU. After the collapse of the ICU, 'al-Qaeda' members infiltrated al-Shabaab, made the organization pledge allegiance to 'al-Qaeda' and, in the minds of Western warmongers, justified a continued US-British presence in Somalia under the pretext of countering terrorism. Britain's state-terrorism against Somalia alone is greater than all of the terrorism discussed in this book combined: overthrowing the government, triggering a refugee crisis, reversing social gains such as healthcare, fuelling the civil war, recruiting for 'al-Qaeda' (as MI5 informant Qatada did), torturing Somalis via the UK-funded Department of the Interior, and triggering a series of famines by collapsing food stocks and distribution, which wiped out 250,000 people.[145]

One potential recruit for al-Shabaab in Somalia was a British man called Michael Adebolajo.

Above, we examined Bakri's al-Muhajiroun group. Adebolajo was associated with the group from at least 2005, when Bakri was expelled from the UK and Anjem Choudary became its leader. At that point, the so-called security services placed Adebolajo on its watch-list and placed him under investigation.[146] Adebolajo was also involved in al-Muhajiroun's successor, Izhar Ud-Deen-il-Haq. Known to MI5 since 2008,[147] Adebolajo travelled to Kenya in 2010 in an attempt to get into Somalia and join al-Shabaab.[148] Boniface Mwaniki, head of Kenya's anti-terror police, told the Associated Press that Adebolajo and five others were detained after they tried to fight with al-Shabaab in neighbouring Somalia. Kenyan government spokesman Muthui Kariuki said: 'Kenya's government arrested Michael Olemendis Ndemolajo. We handed him to British security agents in Kenya and he seems to have found his way to London and mutated to Michael Adebolajo'.[149]

Adebolajo was allowed to travel freely by MI6 ('it is difficult to understand their passive approach to Adebolajo's arrest', says a government inquiry) and questioned at the behest of MI5 upon his return. Adebolajo was being heavily monitored for his links to two Yemeni extremists, drug-dealing, plans to commit terror-related financial fraud and even potential involvement in the London Riots 2011.[150]

Abu Nusaybah, a friend of Adebolajo, told the BBC: '[MI5] asked him whether he'd be interested in working for them'.[151] A government inquiry says: 'In relation to the allegations that MI5 had been trying to recruit Adebolajo as an agent, MI5 has argued that it would be damaging to national security to comment on such allegations'. About six months before Adebolajo and his friend Michael Adebowale allegedly killed fusilier Lee Rigby, MI5 agents had visited Adebolajo.[152]

CCTV footage obtained by ITV News of Adebowale supposedly being shot by the police also shows two unidentified joggers running to the crime scene, while the police are in action, and throwing down items onto the pavement. Who were they? The government's report into the killing says that unarmed police had cordoned off the area before the armed police arrived,[153] so how did they break the cordon? Why aren't they mentioned in any police report? Why has no police report been made public?

Charlie Hebdo

On 7 January 2015, brothers Saïd and Chérif Kouachi allegedly killed 13 people, including a policeman, Ahmed Merabet, who was shot in the head at point blank range with a Zastava M70 assault rifle, yet appeared to shed no blood. The brothers targeted the offices of the Islamophobic *Charlie Hebdo* magazine.

The Paris Métro bombing of 1995 was connected to Qatada's GIA group and to one Smaïn Aït Ali Belkacem, who was jailed for life in 2002. Via a man called Djmael Beghal, Belkacem is connected to suspects allegedly involved in the *Hebdo* killings.[154] O'Neill and McGrory describe the Algerian-born Beghal as a 'Finsbury Park recruiter'. Beghal moved to London with his French-born wife in 1997, before moving to Jalalabad, Afghanistan, in 2000. He was arrested in Dubai in July 2001 and sentenced to ten years' imprisonment in France for planning to bomb the US embassy in Paris.[155] Beghal's wife, Sylvie, has been allowed to live in Leicester, UK, with her children.[156]

The *Daily Mail* writes that MI5 double-agent and Franco-Algerian spy Reda Hassaine 'described Beghal as a "constant presence" at Finsbury Park Mosque in the late 1990s. He said he was particularly close to extremist preacher' and MI5 asset, 'Abu Qatada, but also mixed in the same circles as Abu Hamza', the MI6 asset.[157] The *Telegraph* quotes Hassaine as saying that Beghal 'was closer to Abu Qatada than to Abu Hamza … He definitely had connections with them. I believe he lived outside London at the time but he was regularly seen at the mosque and at the coffee shops around Finsbury Park'.[158]

Between 2004 and 2006, the so-called Buttes-Chaumont group recruited fighters for Iraq to battle the Anglo-American invaders. One of the gang was Chérif Kouachi, an orphan of Algerian parents and a former pizza-deliverer. In 2005, Kouachi was detained by the French police when he attempted to travel to Iraq's neighbour Syria. *Le Monde* writes: 'During the year and a half he spent in prison, from January 2005 to October 2006 ... Cherif Kouachi met who would become his mentor: Djamel Beghal',[159] whom, as we saw above, is connected to MI5's double-agent Qatada.

The BBC writes: 'In 2008, Cherif Kouachi was jailed [for a second time] for three years for his role in sending militants to Iraq, but 18 months of the sentence was suspended'. Kouachi denied the charges.[160] (Even more unusual is the fact that no pictures show Kouachi, or any of the suspects, wearing a long beard, which is required for the Salafi/Wahhabi 'al-Qaeda' ideologues.) According to *The Guardian*:

> [Beghal] was released in 2009 but put under house arrest in the village of Murat, in the Auvergne, where he appears to have been visited by several aspiring jihadis including Kouachi and [Amedy] Coulibaly. They were all arrested in May 2010, accused of attempting to free Smaïn Aït Ali Belkacem, a convicted terrorist jailed for a 1995 bombing of the Paris metro.[161]

Tunisia beach massacre

From the year 2000, the bearded Seifallah Ben Hassine, who had fought against the Soviets in the 1980s during the US-British led proxy war,[162] used London as a base for his Tunisian Fighting Group. Ben Hassine was a disciple of Qatada. Ben Hassine was recruiting for 'al-Qaeda'. According to High Court documents: 'Abu Qatada appears as a watermark running through the whole of this case as being the mastermind'.[163] In 2011, Ben Hassine established a group called Ansar al-Sharia Tunisia (Supporters of Islamic Law in Tunisia). In June 2015, an alleged Ansar al-Sharia recruit, Seifeddine Rezgui, allegedly murdered 38 holidaymakers on a beach in Tunisia.

Despite media claims of a 'lone-wolf' killer, there were at least two gunmen involved in the Sousse beach massacre. It was a military operation: the men landed on the beach by boat, armed with rifles and grenades. Witnesses reported seeing at least one gunman wearing a police uniform. Here's the evidence:

Rezgui was described by friends and family as a rap-listening, football-loving, breakdancing moderate who showed no more interest in Islam than others in his wide social circle. Was this a cover for his extremism or was his extremism a media fabrication? Was he playing the role of a *jihadi* for the state? It has been alleged that shortly before lunchtime on 26 June, Rezgui attacked the Imperial Marhaba Hotel, Sousse. However, early reports (BBC) said: 'Gunmen' – plural – 'have attacked a beach hotel at a tourist resort in Tunisia, killing at least 27 people. Officials' – officials, no less – 'said one of the gunmen was shot dead by the security forces, and that the other was being pursued'.[164]

British and other witnesses said: 'They came on a boat. From the beach they ran to the Hotel Imperial Marhaba'. *Metro* reports that 'Tunisian radio Mosaique FM interviewed eyewitnesses of the attack who said they saw gunmen, some of whom were carrying grenades, exiting the inflatable boat before unleashing their attack'. The story was then changed by Tunisia's Secretary of State, Rafik Chelli, who informed local media 'that the gunman' – singular – 'hid his Kalashnikov machine gun under a parasol before opening fire'.[165] The BBC reported that Tunisia's Interior Ministry claims the gunman killed by police, apparently Rezgui, 'was acting alone … The Interior Ministry had previously said two attackers were involved, including one who had fled the scene'.[166] Tunisia Live said: 'Local media reports claim that one of the attackers was wearing a police uniform'.[167]

The second gunman arrived at the Imperial Marhaba Hotel and opened fire on the crowd. Witness Tom Richards described the assailant as having 'long black hair and a beard'. Ergo, not Rezgui, who was clean-shaven and had short hair. A second, bearded man was seen being carried away by armed police.[168] Sky News reported: 'Local radio said police captured a second gunman, but officials did not confirm the arrest or his role in the attack'.[169] Was the second gunman working for the deep state?

The allegation that the Islamic State claimed responsibility for the attack comes for Search for International Terrorist Entities (SITE), a private US-based corporation run by a woman (Rita Katz) who served in the Israeli Defence Forces; in other words, from a Pentagon-linked Israeli outfit.[170]

Scholars agree that Islamic State adopts the Wahhabi/Salafist forms of Islam. Under these, 'shaving of the beard ... [is] forbidden'.[171] The French *Journal of African Studies*, describes Wahhabism as 'a purification of practices inscribed in the bodies through the wearing of the beard or specific dress codes (such as wearing black dress and integral veil for women) practices such as praying crossed arms'.[172] Yet Rezgui, like many other alleged terrorists (e.g., Coulibaly), is clean-shaven, meaning that he was likely not an Islamic extremist. The BBC explains this anomaly: Rezgui 'had his beard shaved off, presumably the better to make his way onto the beach without arousing suspicion'. How would a bearded man in a Muslim-majority country arouse suspicion? His uncle Ali al-Rezgui points out: 'He didn't even have a beard, and I've never seen him with anyone with a beard. We have extremists like that in Gaafour, but never have I seen him with them'.[173]

Also in 2015, Rezgui's mentor, Ben Hassine, was supposedly killed in Libya in a US drone attack. It is important to remember that if he was really the – or a – perpetrator, Rezgui was recruited via an organization called Katibat Al-Battar, Al-Libi's Tunisia offshoot.[174] This organization is indirectly funded by MI5, as we shall see, and linked to the Bataclan bombers and the Manchester Arena bomber.

The Bataclan

The second major attack in France in 2015, the Bataclan massacre, in which 130 people died, is also linked to Britain's deep state. On 13 November, three gunmen, Foued Mohamed-Aggad, Samy Amimour and Omar Ismaïl Mostefaï, opened fire in the Bataclan theatre, Paris, during a rock concert. The terrorists murdered people at random and took hostages. After police stormed the theatre, two of the three reportedly blew themselves up and the third was killed by the police.

Mohamed-Aggad was born in France to a Moroccan mother. He had tried to work for the French police and army, but was apparently rejected by both. In 2012, age 20, he started attending a mosque where he was allegedly radicalized and recruited by Mourad Fares. Mohamed-Aggad and his brother travelled to Syria in late 2013.[175] At the same time, one Amr al-Absi declared himself leader of the Islamic State in Aleppo, Syria, where the US-British-French-organized terrorists, the Free Syrian Army, were fighting the regime of Bashar al-Assad. The foreign arm of the Islamic State in Aleppo was Katibat al-Muhajireen (KAM), which specialized in recruiting French and Belgian Muslims.[176] Fares seems to have been linked to KAM before defecting to 'al-Qaeda's' breakaway group, Jabhat al-Nusra. Fares further defected and turned himself in to the Turkish authorities, which in turn deported him to France, where he was later put on trial for recruiting for the Islamic State.[177] After a short stint in Aleppo, Mohamed-Aggad returned to France.

Samy Amimour was born in France to Algerian parents. In 2012, as Mohamed-Aggad was becoming radicalized, Amimour also showed signs of extremism, reportedly praising bin Laden. Arrested for plotting to travel to Yemen in support of terrorism in 2012, Amimour was under police surveillance and free to move, except to report at the local police station once a week.[178] Amimour had a licence for the police shooting club in Paris, the *Association nationale de tir de la police*.[179] In 2013, he travelled to Turkey and then on to Syria to fight for ISIS. His father was allowed to fly there, and somehow found out where his son was, in an effort to persuade him to return. When Amimour did return alone, he was not stopped by French border officials.[180]

Little is known about Omar Ismaïl Mostefaï. He was born in France to an Algerian-French father and placed under surveillance. It is believed that he also fought for Islamic State in Syria.[181]

The financing of the Batalcan operation appears to have originated partly in Britain. Two men, Mohamed Abrini and Abdelhamid Abaaoud, are alleged to have financed the terror attack. Their funding came from a paid MI5 informant called Zakaria Boufassil, who gave £3,000 to Abrini.[182] Abaaoud helped run a recruitment organization for Franco-Belgian *jihadis* to fight in Libya, Katibat Al-Battar Al-Libi (KBL). One contact was the alleged Manchester bomber, Salman Abedi.

The Manchester Arena bombing

In May 2017, 22 people were murdered when one Salman Abedi allegedly detonated a suicide bomb in the foyer of the Manchester Arena as people were leaving a pop concert. Abedi's father, Ramadan, was a paid MI6 operative who was allowed to live in the UK under successive governments, including under then-Home Secretary Theresa May, who was PM when the bombing occurred. He left the UK in 2011, in the same year that MI6 had helped organize a terrorist takeover of Libya.

In 1994, after fighting in Afghanistan, one Abd al-Baset Azzouz left Libya, his home country, to live in London, where he was protected by the British government. In 1995, MI6 learned of a coup plot against Libya's leader, Muammar Gaddafi. The plot appears to have been readied for February 1996 and devised by secular colonels within Gaddafi's military circle.[183] A leaked MI6 report says: 'It would begin with attacks on a number of military and security installations including the military installation at Tarhuna. There would also be orchestrated civil unrest in Benghazi, Misratah and Tripoli'. The report notes that '[c]oup plotters are not associated with Islamic fundamentalists', like Azzouz, 'who were fermenting unrest in Benghazi'. However, the coup plotters 'had had some limited contact with the fundamentalists, whom [MI6 informant "Tunworth"] described as a mix of Libya veterans who served in Afghanistan', i.e., old CIA-MI6 contacts, 'and Libyan students'.[184]

There were two coup plots: a secular one led by Gaddafi's inner circle and an Islamic one led by extremists in Benghazi. The MI6 report on the 1996 coup said that the plotters wanted to see Libya decentralized and federally run.

Richard Bartlett and David Watson were MI6 agents involved in the operations. Watson worked with the Libya contact, 'Tunworth', who provided information from within the Libyan Islamic Fighting Group (LIFG), the organization referred to in the MI6 report as the Benghazi-based extremist group. Manchester bomber Abedi's father was associated with the LIFG. In 1995, MI6 chose to work with the extremists in Benghazi, who had close connections with Osama bin Laden through their leaders, Abu Abdullah al-Sadiq (a.k.a. Belhaj) and Anas al-Liby.[185] The British government protected al-Liby, who is described by the US Congress as 'the builder of al-Qaeda's network in Libya'.[186] In 1992, al-Liby trained with a CIA operative, Ali Mohamed, in Osama bin Laden's house in Hyatabad, Pakistan.[187] In 1996, MI6 financed the anti-Gaddafi LIFG to the tune of £100,000.

In 2013, Salman Abedi travelled to Libya and met the Islamic State-linked KBL, mentioned above. The KBL, as noted, was indirectly getting money from MI5 via informants.[188] It quickly emerged that Abedi was Ramadan's son. It later transpired that: British police did not believe he acted alone;[189] America's FBI had warned the UK about Abedi;[190] that Abedi had been on an MI5 watch-list as he travelled from Manchester to Libya and back;[191] and that police very quickly dropped investigations into co-conspirators.[192]

London Bridge attack

On 3 June 2017, Khuram Shazad Butt, Rachid Redouane and Youssef Zaghba reportedly murdered three people in a van by deliberately running them over before stabbing to death five more.

Butt and Redouane were notorious members of al-Muhajiroun (the organization linked to MI6 which supplied *jihadis* for Kosovo, mentioned above, and MI5 via its informant leader, Bakri). A counterterrorism source told CNN that Butt was known to the state and believed to be 'one of the most dangerous extremists in the UK'; which contradicts the official claim that the monitoring of him was deprioritized. Redouane fought in Libya for the Liwa al-Ummah brigade,[193] headed by Irish-Libyan, Mahdi al-Harati, who was reportedly paid €200,000 by the CIA.[194] The third attacker,

Zaghba, was on a European Union watch-list, yet was able to enter the UK as part of Home Secretary Theresa May's 'open door' policy for *jihadis*, circa 2011 to 2012, when Britain was facilitating the wars in Libya and Syria.[195]

Part II

MANUFACTURING TERRORISM IN SIX STEPS

Chapter 6

Step 1: Blowback

The first step in the manufacture of terrorism is the state harming innocent people via war. Angry responses will be evoked from the victims and some responses will include terrorism. This chapter examines how many countries, from Israel and Pakistan to the British in Northern Ireland, have either created or tolerated certain organizations which go on to attack their interests or simply cause widespread harm to civilian populations. The chapter also explores what bombing does to the human organism.

As noted in Chapter 3, a significant number of official sources warn that bombing innocent men, women and children to death in Muslim-majority nations fuels support among certain sectors of the population for *jihadis*. Blowback is a CIA rather than a military term, coined in the mid-1950s when that organization, together with British intelligence, orchestrated a coup to depose Iran's secular leader, Mohamed Mossadeq. Chalmers Johnson writes: 'It is a metaphor for the unintended consequences of covert operations against foreign nations and governments ... [9/11 was] blowback from American clandestine operations in Afghanistan' in the 1980s.[196] Many, of course, dispute this, arguing that 9/11 was an inside-job.

Today, blowback can refer to any negative consequence for the perpetrator. Take the case of drones. Many believe, whilst others question, the idea that murdering alleged, suspected terrorists and wiping out innocent people nearby might provoke some people into taking revenge in the form of *jihadi* terror against US and British interests. For example: 'Drone blowback is real' (*Salon*, Sep. 2012), 'Drone strikes could cause "blowback"' (*Business Insider* Mar. 2013), 'Drone blowback in Pakistan is a myth. Here's why'

(*Washington Post* May 2016), 'Drone blowback: Hi-tech weapons come home to roost' (*New Scientist*, Jun. 2017), 'Blowback: How U.S. drones, coups, and invasions just create more violence' (*The Intercept* Jan. 2018). And so on.

Different forms of blowback

The first step in manufacturing terrorism is bomb, bomb, bomb. This will stir the pot of extremism and result in occasional counterattacks against US and British interests. Of course, governments do not necessarily bomb other countries in order to create terrorists. They bomb for a variety of reasons: to intimidate poor countries, support ground-based military operations (their own or in support of rebel groups) and to demolish infrastructure in the hope of winning rebuilding contracts for their domestic corporations. It is also important to remember that although opposition to bombing is a main driver of terrorism directed against Western interests by diasporas, it is not the only reason. Consider the motivations of Nigeria's Islamist group, Boko Haram (Western Education is Forbidden). The US Subcommittee on Counterterrorism and Intelligence on Homeland Security said in 2011:

> A number of factors have been attributed to fueling Boko Haram's violence and fanaticism, including a feeling of alienation from the wealthier, Christian, oil-producing, southern Nigeria, pervasive poverty, rampant government corruption, heavy-handed security measures, and the belief that relations with the West are a corrupting influence. These grievances have led to sympathy among the local Muslim population despite Boko Haram's violent tactics.[197]

Pakistan: Secret services around the world have connections to terrorists for a number of reasons. Pakistan's Inter-Services Intelligence, for example, has connections with the terror group, Lashkar-e-Taiba (LeT). LeT was banned in Pakistan in 2002 but is allowed to operate as Jamaat ud-Dawa. LeT has been encouraged to attack Pakistan's rival, India. Yet, Pakistan, being a US ally at the time, had to control LeT to some degree in order to appease the US in its so-called 'war on terror'. The upper echelons of LeT enjoy a degree of protection from Pakistan, which allegedly aided LeT in its attack on Mumbai in 2008.[198] Things get even murkier when we learn that one of LeT's operatives, David Headley, was on the CIA payroll (as noted in Chapter 2). By 2016, several LeT members defected to the Islamic State,[199] which has attacked Pakistan: an example of 'blowback' for the Pakistani government and, worst of all, a tragedy for the innocent Pakistanis murdered.

Israel: In the Middle East in the 1970s, it looked as though the secular Palestine Liberation Organization (PLO) might accept peace with Israel (which has occupied the Palestinian West Bank and Gaza Strip since 1967) on the terms of UN Security Council Resolution 242 (as they formally did in 1988-89), which demands both an Israeli military and settler withdrawal from the occupied Palestinian territories and the cessation of violence on both sides. Israel wants to conquer the land of Palestine and has been slowly expanding its illegal colonies ever since. A Palestinian government accepting conditional peace with Israel might prevent Israel from continuing to justify its gradual annexation of Palestine.[200]

To prevent this, 1980s' Israel supported Hamas, the Islamist Palestinian faction of the Muslim Brotherhood, 'to use it as a counterbalance to the PLO', says Anthony H. Cordesman of the Center for Strategic Studies. Speaking on the condition of anonymity, a CIA official told Richard Sale of United Press International: Israel's aim was 'to divide and dilute support for a strong, secular PLO by using a competing religious alternative'. A US government official (again speaking on condition of anonymity) said that Israel's political right-wing hoped that Hamas 'would refuse to have any part of the peace process and would torpedo any agreements put in place'.[201] (Hamas did accept peace with Israel under the same terms as the PLO in 2006, with the signing of the so-called Prisoners' Document,[202] leaving Israel with the serious problem of justifying its continued occupation and annexation.) Hamas started carrying out suicide bombings in Israel in 1993; blowback for the Israel government: more importantly, a tragedy for the innocent Israelis murdered.

Most Muslims oppose terrorism

It is important to reiterate that most Muslims are against the Islamic State, 'al-Qaeda' and other extremist organizations for a variety of reasons. Among them are at least these: 1) Muslims are human beings and most human beings agree that killing in any situation other than direct and immediate self-defense is immoral, 2) 'al-Qaeda' et al.'s leaders are Wahhabi/Salafist Muslims, a far-right fringe of Islam rejected by most imams and scholars, 3) supporting terrorists only makes Muslims more of a target for Western forces, 4) their own governments introduce increasingly oppressive laws under counterterror pretexts, 5) terrorists often kill fellow Muslims, so Muslims tend not to support them.

A November 2001 *Sunday Times* poll of 1,170 British Muslims found that 40% believed that, 'bin Laden has cause to wage war against the US'. But 'has cause' does not translate into support. Indeed, only 11% agreed that there was some justification for the 9/11 attacks.[203] However, in 2005, 34% of British Muslims were 'very' concerned about Islamic extremism in Britain. A year later, after the bombings in London, 42% were 'very concerned'.[204]

In 2011, Pew reported that Muslim Americans were less likely than other groups to support violence against civilians. The percentages of persons who say that terrorists killing civilians is 'never' justified is as follows: Muslim 89% (to 11%), Mormon 79% (to 19%), No religion/atheist/agnostic 76% (to 23%), Jew 75% (to 22%), Protestant 71% (to 26%) and Catholic 71% (to 27%).[205] In 2012, Pew conducted a poll. Associated Press reported: 'The poll found overwhelmingly unfavorable views of al-Qaida in Egypt at 71 percent compared to 21 percent who held favorable views; Jordan, 77 percent to 15 percent; Turkey, 73 percent to 6 percent; and Lebanon, 98 percent to 2 percent. The areas of Pakistan polled found 55 percent negative, and 13 percent positive'.[206]

In 2013, majorities and pluralities of Muslims across 11 countries expressed concern about the rise of extremism: 67% in total were concerned, compared to 27% who were unconcerned. The following percentages had unfavourable views of the following groups: 'Al-Qaeda' 57%, Taliban 51%, Hamas 45% and Hezbollah

42%. The following countries – Jordan, Palestine, Egypt, Pakistan, Nigeria, Malaysia, Tunisia, Lebanon and Senegal – expressed concern ranging from 54% (Jordan) to 75% (Senegal); only majorities or pluralities in Indonesia (48%) and Turkey (51%) were not concerned.[207]

Pew reported on Muslims who hold favourable views of 'al-Qaeda' in 2013: Palestine 35%, Indonesia 23%, Egypt 20%, Malaysia 20%, Tunisia 15%, Jordan 13%, Pakistan 13%, Nigeria 9%, Senegal 9%, Turkey 7%, Jordan 13%. The report also notes: 'Only 3% of Muslims in Pakistan, where bin Laden was supposedly living for most of the years after the 9/11 attacks, said suicide bombing was often or sometimes justified to defend Islam from its enemies. And less than two-in-ten Muslims said this in Indonesia (20%), Nigeria (8%), Jordan (12%), Tunisia (12%), Turkey (16%) and Senegal (18%)'. It adds: 'substantial minorities of Muslims in Lebanon (33%) and Egypt (25%) said that suicide bombing is an acceptable tactic in defense of Islam. And in the Palestinian territories, 62% of Muslims said this'.[208]

Muslims are often slandered because while the majority oppose terrorism, significant minorities to majorities (depending on the poll and specificity of questions) suggest that they feel that the US and Europe are partly to blame for terrorism due to their foreign policies. What is seldom reported is that after 9/11, a majority of British non-Muslims agreed. A YouGov poll suggested that 62% of respondents agreed that the US was partly responsible for the attacks and 70% agreed that 'the US has been far too arrogant and selfish in the way it has treated the world's poorest countries'.[209]

Most Britons & Americans oppose bombing civilians

The British and American publics tend to support war only when they are convinced by media propaganda that they are under threat or when media atrocity propaganda is so extreme that they are made to feel guilty.

Afghanistan: An Ipsos-MORI poll from late-2001 found that nearly 70% (depending on the month) of Britons supported the US-British bombing of Afghanistan.[210] Gallup reported that eight out of ten Americans supported the invasion.[211] Obscured in media reporting was the fact that of the four out of five polls taken in the month after 9/11 which specifically asked about civilian casualties, majorities or pluralities opposed bombing if it risked civilians. Eighty-two percent of respondents to another Gallup poll said that bombing 'should only be [under]taken after the identity of the perpetrators was clearly established, even if this process took several months to accomplish'. A YouGov poll found that 60% of respondents opposed 'massive air strikes', meaning carpet bombing (which is what actually occurred).[212]

Iraq: In the US, a Chicago Council on Foreign Relations poll in June 2002 found that only 20% of Americans agreed that the US should invade Iraq without UN approval.[213] By January 2003, 68% of Americans polled by the Program on International Policy Attitudes/Knowledge Networks (PIPA/KN) wrongly believed that Iraq was linked to the 9/11 attacks; which is a credit to the power of propaganda. PIPA/KN also found that '[o]verwhelming majorities believed that Iraq had [weapons of mass destruction]'; again, a lie.[214] By the time of the invasion, however, a majority of Americans appeared to support bombing, though it is not clear whether they understood that the UN had not approved.

Also in January 2003, two months before the invasion, an Ipsos-MORI poll found that only 15% of Britons supported a US-British invasion 'without UN approval', which is what happened; but people wouldn't know it because the media bent over backwards to portray the invasion as lawful or at least legally questionable.[215] In the run-up to the invasion of Iraq in 2003, an ICM poll put support among Britons at 38%, 'but this probably reflects difference in question wording', says Ipsos-MORI. The ICM poll asked, simply, if respondents approve or disapprove of military action 'to remove Saddam'. The Ipsos-MORI poll (in an article citing ICM) found that by 2 March, 67% were opposed, but by 16 March, just a few days before the invasion, opposition had declined slightly to 63%. Only 24% and 26%, respectively, supported the invasion.[216] By May 2007, 77% of respondents disapproved of PM Tony Blair's 'handling' of the occupation (as noted).

Libya: The US, Britain, France and Italy began demolishing Libya in March 2011 under the fraudulent pretext that its dictator Muammar Gaddafi was going to initiate an 'ethnic cleansing' in the Benghazi region. A March post-invasion poll found that 47% to 37% approved of the US bombing of Libya, but Gallup acknowledges: 'The poll did not ask Americans specific reasons for approving or disapproving of the efforts against Libya'.[217] Americans were not told that the bombing was illegal (UNSCR 1973 did not authorize the use of force, as many believe, because it was adopted under Article 7 of the UN Charter, which does not reference alleged or actual atrocities committed by governments against domestic populations). Americans were also not told that their government was working with 'al-Qaeda' in Libya.

By the end of March, Gallup reported that despite a majority or plurality supporting bombing, only 39% thought the US should take a lead or major role in the operations, compared to 58% who thought the US should either withdraw or play a minor role.[218] By June, as the bombing continued and it became more clear that the US was using 'al-Qaeda' as a proxy, approval shifted from a 47% plurality in March to a 39% minority (with 46% disapproving) by June.[219]

In the UK by April 2011, Reuters/Ipsos-MORI reported that 63% supported 'the removal' of Gaddafi, but fewer, 50%, supported the bombing. An additional 51% thought that 'we should not interfere'. As the poll could not possibly equal 101%, many of those who approved the bombing therefore also thought it was not our business (double-think) and conflated bombing with 'removing' Gaddafi; which is a tribute to the confusing media narrative.[220] In the same month, another Ipsos-MORI poll found that 40% were 'satisfied' with the way in which the government was handling the bombing compared to 40% who were not.[221] YouGov found mixed results. A poll for *The Sun* suggested support was 45% to 36% against, but ComRes suggested only 35% support to 43% opposition. Interestingly, only 4% of British people believed that Libyans supported Gaddafi, when in fact Gaddafi was quite popular among Libyans.[222] From the limited evidence available, no questions were asked about what Libyans thought of Gaddafi, but only 29% of people in Tripoli and 33% in Benghazi said they were 'dissatisfied' with freedom in their lives.[223]

Syria: The public does not realize that the US, Britain, France and Israel, with support from Turkey and Jordan, trained and organized a terrorist force, in violation of international law, to launch a war in Syria, as they had in Libya, to overthrow Bashar al-Assad. The public also does not realize that according to then-Foreign Secretary William Hague, speaking in Parliament, Britain supplied Assad with the chemicals and manufacturing components which he might have used in his alleged chemical weapons attacks.[224] Despite this, Parliament voted against bombing Assad's forces in Syria in 2013, but as rights-group Reprieve discovered, the UK was bombing anyway.[225]

According to Britain's YouGov: 'surveys in recent months have shown consistent support for humanitarian aid for the victims of Syria's civil war, but strong opposition to any form of military involvement'.[226] In the USA, 51% to 36% opposed Obama's bombing.[227] Most Americans even opposed arming the anti-Assad terrorists, which is what the US did. Even those Americans who said they are following the situation on the news opposed arming the terrorists (who were described as 'moderate rebels'): 51% to 44%.[228]

Iraq: In 2014, after enduring nearly a year of atrocity-propaganda against the Islamic State, the British public finally relented and supported more bombing, supposedly against ISIS targets. By August 2014, 37% approved bombing to 36% who disapproved. When journalist James Foley was allegedly beheaded, support rose above 40%. (A private forensic team hired by Britain's Metropolitan Police, said that Foley was murdered and then beheaded, and that the execution video was staged.)[229] When it was reported that Steven Sotloff and David Haines were murdered, support crept up, peaking at 57% by the end of September.[230] In the US, by the end of September, 60% approved the bombing of ISIS.[231]

Syria: In 2015, Britain started bombing Syria; this time under the pretext of bombing the Islamic State. Data are limited for the US, but in November at 2015 at the start of the bombing, 59% of Britons approved of bombing ISIS in Syria, specifically as part of a 'coalition'. By December, that was down to 44% (with 36%) approving.[232]

What bombing does

The above results suggest that until they are brainwashed, the public does not generally support war. When it does, it is usually within the context of what people regard as 'multilateral' actions, which usually means cooperating with France and the USA. Excluded from the equation is the inevitability of killing civilians. Respondents to polls are not reminded that civilians will be destroyed in bombing operations. Like their counterparts in the UK and USA, a majority of Muslims around the world oppose violence against civilians in the form of terrorism. Interestingly, most Muslims oppose terrorism without qualification (as noted above), unlike majorities of Britons and Americans, who can support war with qualifications. Be they the relatively small, home-made bombs of terrorists or highly-destructive explosives manufactured by arms companies, all so-called High-order Explosive devices follow the same basic principles. The bombs we drop tend to be far more destructive than the bombs detonated by terrorists.

Blast-waves: In bomb blasts, primary injuries come from the blast-wave. A blast wave occurs when air molecules are rapidly compressed and changed into a gas. The molecules are pushed out before oscillating (supersonic). As they travel, peak overpressure is reached faster than the inverse square of the distance relationship (suction wave). Depending on the explosive yield, type of bomb and environmental conditions, the blast waves of the tens of thousands of bombs dropped by the US and Britain on Afghanistan, Yemen, Iraq, Pakistan, Somalia, Libya and Syria have the following effects on millions of men, women and children: 'high-order' explosives are more susceptible to over-pressurization, so victims can experience trauma to one or more of their organs, including the lungs ('blast lung', or pulmonary barotrauma, being the most common fatal injury), stomach perforation and bleeding, and eye and ear trauma.[233]

Studies from the early-'60s suggest that humans can withstand overpressure of 15 pound-force per square-inch (psi) before 50% of eardrums will burst. When standing within 50ft of a landmine, 500-lb aerial bomb or 3-inch mortar shell, ear drum rupture occurred in 52% of cases. These explosions create an overpressure of 17 psi. In over 300 cases of temporary deafness induced by acoustic trauma, 78% of victims had no ear drum perforations.[234]

Debris and shrapnel: Secondary injuries come from debris, such as shrapnel. The Centers for Disease Control (CDC) in the US cites blast-induced structural collapse as the most common killer in explosions. In addition, the CDC says that around 10% of all bomb-blast victims have some form of eye injury. Injuries are usually perforations caused by the high-velocity projectiles that result from the blast-wave. 'Symptoms include eye pain or irritation, foreign body sensation, altered vision, periorbital swelling or contusions'. Other symptoms, temporary or permanent, can include sight loss, hyphaemia (red eyes), globe perforation, subconjunctival bleeding and eyelid laceration.[235]

The perpetrators of the Boston Marathon bombing in April 2013 allegedly used pressure cooker bombs, murdering three and injuring over 260. Thirty-two of the 43 Boston Marathon bombing victims analyzed by Singh et al. had a total of 189 shrapnel fragments, including ball bearings, nails, metal, screws, gravel and glass, some buried deep in their flesh and bones. Aged between 19 and 65, the victims sustained injuries to the legs, pelvis and thigh.[236]

Tertiary injuries: These result from falling or being pushed by the blast-wave.

Quaternary injuries: These are caused by, for example, resulting fires. When it comes to terrorist bombings, 10% of victims are likely to experience burns, which can cover 9% to 90% of the body, depending on the incident. 'Increased severity' of burns is caused by several factors including, crucially, '[g]reater weight of explosive material'. As we know, the military drop and fire heavier bombs and missiles than their terrorist counterparts tend to do, meaning that military operations are far more likely to kill civilians 'accidentally', and do to them far greater physical damage than a terrorist bomb, depending of course on the size of the device and the environmental conditions.

During the Falklands War (1982), 100% of the injuries sustained by troops on ships were burns, with 45% being serious. Burns are more common in urban fighting than in open spaces, which is bad news for civilians and the moral legitimacy of the West because Western forces having increasingly shifted from state-on-state combat to fighting pockets of resistance in towns and cities. Kauvar et al. write: 'the extent of flame burn-induced injury will be greater if the force of the blast itself rips off or ignites clothing'.[237]

Thermobarics: Starting in the 1970s, various US weapons companies began to build helicopter-launched Heliborne, Laser, Fire and Forget (Hellfire) missiles. Weighing 100 pounds (45kg), the bombs were intended as anti-tank munitions, but are now launched from drones to destroy human beings. Thermobaric weapons use surrounding oxygen to create high-temperature explosions whose blast-wave is longer in duration than non-thermobarics. One variety of thermobaric missile, the AGM-144N, was field-tested on human beings in Fallujah, Iraq in 2004; a city resisting the US-British occupation. The reason that so many Fallujan children are severely deformed and the rate of cancer is so high is due to the use of radioactive uranium in the Hellfire thermobarics. Alaani et al. write:

> Thermobaric weapons use high temperature/high pressure explosives as anti-personnel incendiary weapons. They char or vaporise victims in the immediate target location, or suffocate and collapse internal organs with their extended blast/vacuum effects. These weapons use a new generation of reactive metal explosives, some of which are suspected of using Uranium for the high temperature and increased kinetic blast effects.[238]

Now, imagine thousands of people, including hundreds of children and babies, enduring this fate. Is it any wonder that a small minority of Muslims are enraged enough to commit terrorism? As noted in Chapter 3, the security services know the answer.

U.S. & British drones

With programme names like Widowmaker,[239] US and British ground-based 'pilots' operate drones such as Predator and Reaper from which they launch Hellfire and other missiles. We have seen above what high explosives do to human beings. The greater the explosive potential, the worse the effects on men, women and children.

The UK has a single drone operation programme, as far as we know. It is run by the Ministry of Defence (MoD) and involves murdering alleged, terrorist suspects in Iraq and Syria. The MoD is reportedly working through a 'kill list', which includes British citizens, like Reyaad Khan, in Raqqa, Syria.[240] The US has two drone operations, one run by the CIA (a civilian organization, which, curiously, or not so curiously, is an organization equipped with its own military) and another run by the military.[241] Due to a legal loophole – that alleged, suspected terrorists are civilians, not enemy combatants under the Geneva Conventions – they cannot be killed by the US military without the US violating international human rights law, and thus potentially putting legal pressure on the executive.[242] Apparently for this reason, the CIA gives the military thin cover to murder alleged suspects.

The US military is conducting drone operations in Syria under the slim legal pretext of attacking the Islamic State, as well as in Afghanistan and Iraq. The CIA's operations, which, in reality, are blurred with the Air Force (as the CIA relies on Air Force technology) include Iraq, Libya, Pakistan, Somalia and Yemen. Beginning November 2001 in Afghanistan, the US has targeted 'al-Qaeda' in each of those countries, as well as the Taliban in Afghanistan and Pakistan, al-Shabaab in Somalia, the Haqqani network in Afghanistan, 'al-Qaeda in the Arabian Peninsula' in Yemen, and the Islamic State in each of those countries. British drone operators have murdered alleged suspects and innocent civilians in Afghanistan, Iraq, Libya (for the US) and Syria. In addition, the British produce signals and communications intelligence for US drone operations elsewhere.[243]

All deadly drone operations to date are illegal. The UN Special Rapporteur on Extrajudicial, Summary or Arbitrary Execution, Philip Alston, settled the issue in 2010, writing: 'A State killing is legal only if it is required to protect life (making lethal force *proportionate*) and there is no other means, such as capture or non-lethal incapacitation, of preventing that threat to life (making lethal force *necessary*)' (emphases in original).[244]

Between late-2001 and early-2018, US-British drone strikes have killed: Afghanistan 3,923 (137 civilians, 26 children); Pakistan 2,515 (424 civilians, 172 children); Somalia 524 (10 civilians); and Yemen 988 (166 civilians, 44 children). These figures are minimum casualties or confirmed deaths (i.e., with physical evidence). The actual toll is likely double.[245] By 2014, the US had targeted 41 alleged terror suspects for death, but wiped out 1,147 by mistake: a 'success' rate of 3.57%.[246]

Consider what drone and other air strikes do to human beings (these are scattered examples):

On 4 September 2009, a NATO strike ignited fuel tanks in the village of Eissa Khail, Kunduz, Afghanistan. At least 70 people were killed. The head of the village, Omar Khan, said: 'We didn't recognise any of the dead when we arrived ... The villagers were fighting over the corpses. People were saying this is my brother, this is my cousin, and no one could identify anyone ... The smell was so bad. For three days I smelled of burned meat and fuel'. The elderly Jan Mohammad said: 'I couldn't find my son, so I took a piece of flesh with me home and I called it my son. I told my wife we had him, but I didn't let his children or anyone see. We buried the flesh as if it was my son'.[247]

On 24 October 2012, 68-year-old Mamana Bibi was gathering vegetables in Ghundi Kala village, northwest Pakistan, when, according to Amnesty International, which interviewed one of her grandchildren, Mamana 'was blasted into pieces before her eyes'. Her granddaughter Nabeela (age eight at the time) said: 'I saw her shoes. We found her mutilated body a short time afterwards ... It had been thrown quite a long distance away by the blast and it was in pieces. We collected as many different parts from the field and wrapped them in a cloth'.[248]

Mohammed Tuaiman of al-Zur village, Yemen, was thirteen-years old when a CIA drone operator murdered him on 26 January 2015 in Hareeb, near al-Zur. 'A lot of the kids in this area wake up from sleeping because of nightmares from them [the drones] and some now have mental problems', he said before his death. Mohammed lost his brother and father in an earlier strike. His surviving brother Maqded said: 'I saw all the bodies completely burned, like charcoal ... We couldn't move the bodies so we just buried them there, near the car'.[249]

On 17 March 2017, 200 Iraqis were murdered in an airstrike on Aghawat Jadidah, Mosul. The strike included the deaths of nine of Munatha Jasim's relatives, including her son Firas (seven) and daughter Taiba (4). Of Firas, Jasim said: 'We recovered half his body ... The other half is still there ... [B]ecause one Islamic State [fighter] was on our house, the aircraft bombed us'.[250]

This generalizes across the Middle East and North Africa.

Blowback: what terrorists say

Northern Ireland is the territory that Irish Republicans failed to win back from the British in their wars of independence. Following decades of Catholic oppression on the part of the British state and its Protestant allies, a new struggle for independence was born in the 1960s. Former Irish Republican Army (IRA) leader and later deputy First Minister of Northern Ireland, Martin McGuinness, told *The Journal* (Ireland): 'I come from a community that was discriminated against for far too long – not just treated like second class citizens, but third class citizens in our city. As a result of that there was a conflict'.[251]

Tony Doherty's 31-year-old father, Patrick, was murdered by a British soldier on Bloody Sunday 1972, the infamous murder of 14 civilians. Patrick was shot from behind as he crawled from the scene. The soldier who killed him claimed he had been carrying a pistol.[252] In 1981, aged 18, Tony Doherty joined the Irish Republican Army and served time in prison for planting a bomb. Reflecting on Bloody Sunday, he says:

> My journey towards the IRA happened on that day ... [It's] not that surprising to find that as an 18-year-old I ended up walking down a street in my own city with a bomb in my hand... It changed the discourse even among children in that we started talking about murder ... It was all about how you oppose the Brits, it was all about rioting, and even though we could only throw small stones with small hands. That's what you did.[253]

Breige Brownlee says: 'I was 11 years old. The house has been getting wrecked with British soldiers in. My fathers, brothers, were arrested and going through general harassment in the home. And, seeing what was happening on the streets, I ... joined the IRA in the late '70s'.[254]

British Grenadier Guard Mick Corbett served two tours of Northern Ireland. He told the *Derry Journal*: 'It gave me a lot more understanding and a different perspective and empathy. If I had been born in Creggan I know I would have joined the IRA'.[255] Bloody Sunday and the Hunger Strikes (1981) 'are seen by many as the two seminal watershed moments in the Northern Ireland conflict that increased passive and active support for PIRA [Provisional IRA] activities', write two researchers, Gill and Horgan.[256] These and many other examples demonstrate that violence begets violence. From a purely self-interested point of view, Britain's (Northern) Ireland policy created 'blowback' for the state and civilians.

The same thing is happening today in Muslim-majority countries.

The US-British carnage and misery imposed on the Middle East and Central Asia via its combination of carpet bombing, drone attacks and so-called counterinsurgency operations is difficult to comprehend. Physicians for Social Responsibility co-authored a report on the death toll in Afghanistan, Iraq and Pakistan. By 2015, they estimated 1.3 million deaths.[257]

Thanks to media propaganda, we are familiar with what terrorism, including suicide bombing, does to civilians, but we are generally not familiar with the effects of carpet- and 'precision' bombing. The rights group Medact wrote in 2012: 'The deaths and injuries suffered by innocent civilians who happen to be in the vicinity of a drone's target go largely unreported. These men, women and children remain statistics: anonymous and nameless'.[258]

Media outlets act as filters to shape opinion and perceptions of reality. But what do terrorists actually cite as their motives for committing and attempting to commit criminal and immoral actions, namely murdering innocent civilians? Most of their actions are in response to much bigger and more immoral criminal acts committed by states. State actions are bigger and more immoral because states are more powerful than terrorist organizations and individuals. What follows are examples of failed and 'successful' terrorists who explain their motivations. If we take at face value that certain terrorists and potential terrorists are genuine and not being handled by the intelligence services, their motives are clear.

Osama bin Laden: In 1998, former CIA associate Osama bin Laden allegedly turned against his former colleagues (this is an example of the CIA's understanding of blowback) and issued a *fatwa* against the US and its supporters. Bin Laden gave his alleged reasons (one of many examples):

> [F]or over seven years, the United States has been occupying the lands of Islam in the holiest of places, the Arabian Peninsula, plundering its riches, dictating to its rulers, humiliating its people, terrorizing its neighbors, and turning its bases ... into a spearhead through which to fight the neighboring Muslim peoples ... The best proof is the Americans' continuing aggression against the Iraqi people ... [T]hey come here to annihilate what is left of this people and to humiliate their Muslim neighbors.[259]

Bin Laden errs in claiming that US motives are religious and driven by support of Israel ('the Jews' petty state', as he calls it); though of course he is mainly addressing his followers.

Ayman al-Zawahiri: Bin Laden's second-in-command was Ayman al-Zawahiri, formerly of the Egyptian Islamic Jihad, which merged with 'al-Qaeda' (i.e., bin Laden's group) in 1998. After the 7 July 2005 bombings in London, Zawahiri said:

> After long centuries of [the enemy's] taking the battle to our soil and after his hordes and armed forces occupied our lands in Chechnya, Afghanistan, Iraq and Palestine, and after centuries of his occupying our land while enjoying security at home ... [T]aste some of what you have made us taste ... [W]hy didn't you gather in front of the British parliament when the sanctions murdered a million children in Iraq? Why didn't you gather in front of the British parliament when the mosques in Afghanistan were bombed with the worshippers inside?[260]

The Times Square Bomber: Faisal Shahzad was born in Pakistan and moved to the US in 1997 to study business. In 2004, he married a woman in Pakistan, herself a graduate of a US university. By 2006, he had become more devout and his wife left to live in Saudi Arabia. In 2009, he left the US for Pakistan, where he trained with the Taliban. Shahzad made at least one more trip there before attempting to detonate a car bomb in May 2010. In 2006, he wrote to a friend:

> It is with no doubt that we today Muslim [sic] followers of Islam are attacked and occupied by foreign infidel forces ... Friends with peaceful protest! Can you tell me a way to save the oppressed? And a way to fight back when rockets are fired at us and Muslims blood flows? In Palestine, Afghan [sic], Iraq, Chechnya and else where [sic] ... [T]here is a force out there that is fighting the west and is defeating them ... And fight them on until there is no more tumult or oppression, and there prevail justice and faith in Allah altogether and everywhere.[261]

The Little Rock Killer: In 2009, Carlos Bledsoe (a.k.a. Abdulhakim Mujahid Muhammad) shot and killed a US soldier, wounding another, outside a recruiting centre in Little Rock, Arkansas. Before the shooting, he travelled to Yemen to study the Qur'an, where he married a Yemeni woman and was imprisoned, allegedly for out-staying his visa. Whilst in prison, he was interviewed by an FBI agent who then visited him when he returned to the USA. The agency then claims to have ceased monitoring him. He was only deported from Yemen due to US embassy pressure. Bledsoe later claimed to have been a member of Yemen's newly-formed 'Al-Qaeda in the Arabian Peninsula' (whose top command consists largely of Saudi exiles who oppose the corrupt Saudi royal family). The judge barred the FBI from saying more about the case.[262]

After the shooting, Bledsoe wrote a letter to the judge, stating: 'I wasn't insane or post traumatic [sic] nor was I forced to do this act, which I believe and it is justified according to Islamic Laws and the Islamic Religious Jihad — to fight these who wage war on Islam and Muslims'.[263]

The Underpants Bomber: Umar Farouk Abdulmutallab's father, Alhaji Umaru, is a wealthy Nigerian banker with political connec-tions. His son, Umar, studied at the British School in Lome, Togo (Africa) where he allegedly became radicalized. Alhaji warned US authorities of his son's radicalization. Yemeni officials claimed that 'al-Qaeda' recruited Umar when he studied engineering at Uni-versity College London in 2008. Umar was on a US watch-list but allowed to fly, when he allegedly tried to detonate a bomb hidden in his underwear on a flight to Detroit, USA.[264] He gave his reasons in court:

> ... in retaliation for U.S. support of Israel and in retaliation of the killing of innocent and civilian Muslim populations in Palestine, especially in the blockade of Gaza, and in retaliation for the killing of innocent and civilian Muslim populations in Yemen, Iraq, Somalia, Afghanistan and beyond, most of them women, children, and noncombatants.[265]

Fort Hood Shooter: Nidal Hasan was born in Arlington County, Virginia. He became more devout after the death of his Palestine-born parents. By 2003, Hasan was studying to become a psychia-trist in the Walter Reed Army Medical Center. Before he was transferred to Fort Hood, the FBI had been alerted to Hasan's increasingly radical views when he corresponded with US citizen Anwar al-Awlaki, who was allegedly preaching *jihad* in Yemen.[266]

In 2013, Hasan allegedly murdered 13 colleagues. He was not indicted on terrorism charges. His stated reasons were as follows:

> ... the illegal and immoral aggression against Muslims ... their religion ... and their lands. It has resulted in the death ... destruction. and deception of many innocent men ... women ... and children. As a United States Army Psychiatrist ... my job was to 'conserve the fighting strength of military armed forces personnel' and by deceit to 'win the hearts and minds' of Muslims throughout the world. Using American Muslim soldiers such as myself to help win the hearts and minds of naive and desperate Muslims around the world is a powerful strategy. I am too ashamed to even mention the clandestine and covert operations that have already occurred ... or are still in progress about the Muslim world [sic].[267]

The Subway Bomber: Najibullah Zazi was born in Afghanistan during the Soviet war against the *jihadis* organized by the US and Britain (*mujahideen*, later called 'al-Qaeda', the database, by the CIA). After the Soviet withdrawal, the Afghan warlords supported by the US and Britain − Hekmatyar, Rabbani, Sayyaf and others − killed tens of thousands of Afghans in their bloody power struggle. The Zazi family moved to Pakistan, seeking asylum.

The family moved to the USA in 1999. Najibullah attended a mosque run by Hekmatyar's representative in the US, Saifur Rahman Halimi. (By then, Hekmatyar was on a proscribed list, raising questions about how and why his representative was allowed to operate in the US.) In 2008, he was recruited in Pakistan by 'al-Qaeda'. Supposedly as part of Operation Pathway (a British counterterrorism operation), Zazi's emails to senior al-Qaeda's members were intercepted, which allowed the FBI to move against the plot. Zazi told the court:

> During the training, al-Qaeda leaders asked us to return to the United States and conduct martyrdom operation [sic]. We

agreed to this plan. I did so because of my feelings about what the United States was doing in Afghanistan ... ['Suicide bomber'] meant that I would sacrifice myself to bring attention to what the United States military was doing to civilian in Afghanistan by sacrificing my soul for the sake of saving other souls.[268]

Chapter 7

Step 2: Proxies

The second step in the manufacture of terrorism is the creation of proxy forces, as seen in '80s Afghanistan. After examining the use of terrorists by the US in Cuba, Iran and elsewhere, and of the British in Northern Ireland, this chapter explores how the US and Britain organized jihadis to invade and fight in Syria against a regime both countries supported and then turned against when it would not privatize the economy and open it to US businesses.

As noted in the previous chapter, Israel helped to create Hamas to act as a proxy against the PLO. In Pakistan, Lashkar-e-Taiba was allowed to operate freely by the government as a proxy against India. But what about the US and Britain? The US and Britain have worked with a number of terrorists and terrorist groups in opposition to sovereign states.

Some examples: secular & religious
Cuba: Ever since the Cuban Revolution (1953-59) brought Fidel Castro to power, the US has used a variety of methods, including punishing Cuba with a 50-year illegal embargo (a violation of the IV Geneva Convention which prohibits collective penalties), allegedly seeking Castro's removal from power. The anti-Castro CIA operative, Dr Orlando Bosch, admitted being 'the chief' of several consulate bombings in the 1960s and '70s (Castro held him responsible for 90 alleged crimes. 'Some of them [are] true', said Bosch).[269] He was allowed to live openly in the USA and even granted a presidential pardon. Luis Posada Carriles is considered a terrorist by the FBI but is a CIA operative. Posada was considered by the US State Department to be responsible for the Cubana Airlines atrocity in 1976, in which 73 individuals were murdered.[270]

Iraq: In the mid-1990s, with Iraq being literally and slowly destroyed via a cruel and illegal US-British siege, the Clinton administration was financing the secular Iraqi National Accord (INA) to oppose the Saddam Hussein regime. According to one of its members, the INA was, 'heavily sponsored by the US and under the influence of the CIA', particularly through bomb-maker Abu Amneh al-Khadamai ('[my job was] to buy clocks ... and turn them into timers'). One of the leaders, Adnan Mohammed al-Nuri, was a defector. Amneh says: 'We blew up a car and we were supposed to get $2,000 but Adnan gave us $1,000'.[271] The INA also worked with the CIA and MI6 in joint operations to oust Saddam. Patrick Cockburn says: 'Despite its dubious reputation among Iraqis, the Accord was favoured not only by MI6, but by the London station of the CIA, according to former agency officials', which tells us something about Britain's real attitude towards the promotion of democracy.[272]

Iran: The secular 'Marxist' People's Mujahideen of Iran, also known as Mujahiddin e Khalq (MEK) consists of exiled Iranians. Seymour Hersh found out that beginning 2005, members of MEK were being trained by the US Joint Special Operations Command (JSOC) with the aim of overthrowing the government. By 2007, MEK members, with Israeli financing, were murdering Iranian civilian scientists, 'to affect Iranian psychology and morale' (according to one Obama official). Energy pipelines have also been attacked by MEK operatives. A JSOC adviser told Hersh: 'Everything being done inside Iran now is being done with surrogates'. A senior Pentagon consultant told Hersh: 'M.E.K. was a total joke ... now it's a real network inside Iran'.[273]

Overruling the wishes of Britain's then-Home Secretary Jacqui Smith, the High Court ordered the British government to remove MEK from its list of terrorist organizations in 2008. A year later, the European Court of First Instance ruled that the European Union must also remove the MEK from its list of proscribed organiza-tions.[274] MEK has even attacked US interests inside Iran, including General Motors, PanAm and PepsiCo. The US State Department described MEK as 'claim[ing] responsibility for murdering thous-ands of Iranians they describe as agents of the regime'.[275]

Another terror group once supported by the US is Jundullah (Soldiers of God). It is a Sunni group opposed to the Shia regime of Iran. It operates on the border of Iran and Pakistan in the Sistan-Baluchestan region. Wikipedia has an entry for Jundullah which claims that reports into US-Jundullah collaboration were 'debunked' (no citations or evidence necessary, 21 April 2018). The entry might be referring to a Reuters report which quotes a CIA official as saying that a particular source (ABC, cited below) was 'not accurate', though it did not deny CIA involvement (Reuters 4 April 2007).

The facts are that: 1) then-US Vice President Dick Cheney referred to the terrorist organization as a 'guerilla' — not *terrorist* — force when he met Pakistan's President Musharraf, signalling US support for the organization;[276] 2) The *Sunday Telegraph* quotes a US CIA official speaking on the condition of anonymity, who said that CIA black budget support was 'no great secret'. It also quoted US State Department counterterrorism agent, Fred Burton: 'The latest [Jundullah] attacks [in 2007] inside Iran fall in line with US efforts to supply and train Iran's ethnic minorities to destabilise the Iranian regime';[277] 3) ABC news also quoted US intelligence officials (and Pakistani officials) confirming support for the group. Money was indirectly funnelled via European and Gulf contacts;[278] 4) The *New York Times* (NYT) confirmed that the CIA (via its Iranian Operations Division) and FBI had infiltrated the group via an informant called Thomas McHale (no suggestion McHale was involved in terrorism). The NYT says: 'Contacts with informants did not end when Jundullah's attacks led to the deaths of Iranian civilians, or when the State Department designated it a terrorist organization';[279] 5) Ex-CIA agent Robert Baer said: 'you can also describe [Jundullah] as Al Qaeda ... These are guys who cut off the heads of nonbelievers ... [W]e're once again working with Sunni fundamentalists, just as we did in Afghanistan in the nineteen-eighties'.[280]

Modus operandi: The deep state manufactures terrorism by creating terrorist groups and using them as proxies to fight wars on its behalf. We have already seen how 'al-Qaeda' was created (Chapter 4) to 'draw the Russians into the Afghan trap' (as Brzezinski put it). The major proxy wars of today are Libya and Syria. By paying poor people a pittance,[281] Western agencies have a cheap supply of cannon fodder, particularly of young, desperate men, many of whom have political grievances and who are desperate for respect, inclusion and 'adventure' (i.e., fighting). Using the Afghan *mujahideen* model (1978-89), the agencies usually apply the formula of collaborating closely with the *jihadis'* top commanders behind the scenes, who then go on to recruit lower-level fighters. When domestic police forces in Western countries want to arrest the top commanders, the secret services call off any investigations.

Violating international law (the UN Charter which forbids interference in the domestic affairs on other nations), the US and Britain have succeeded in creating the most awesome terrorist network since the 1980s in an effort to depose regimes in the Middle East and North Africa. When governments use their legitimate right to prevent foreign-organized terrorists from overthrowing them, the West uses its propaganda arm (the mainstream media and, increasingly, some online sites) to plead for 'humanitarian intervention' to stop the regimes from hurting 'rebels' (who are terrorists in reality) fighting for democracy (who, in reality, want to impose an Islamic state on the given country whose regimes they are trying to overthrow). It is an old technique pioneered in Kosovo, when the US and Britain organized the Kosovo Liberation Army to attack targets in Serbia, before claiming that the regime was committing ethnic cleansing.

Regime change

'Regime change', getting rid of governments the West doesn't like, is a violation of international law.[282] It is beyond dispute that many regimes opposed by the West are dictatorships, but this has nothing to do with why the West wants them deposed. There is no moral consistency in the appeal to 'humanitarian intervention' (meaning getting rid of a regime because it is brutal) because:

1) Often the West supports regimes (including Assad and Gaddafi) until they have served their purpose. 2) The West enables their crimes against humanity by supplying them with weapons, training,

financial investments and diplomatic immunity. 3) There is no indication that the publics of those countries (except a small minority) want their regimes overthrown, especially by violent Western-back *jihadis* (though, of course, many want democratic reforms). 4) The Hippocratic principle, first do no harm, is violated because using violence to depose a regime results in the regime using even greater violence to suppress the rebellion. 5) As noted, the given rebellion is often not supported by the majority and is thus immoral for the West to support. 6) Universality; would Western publics want to see an invasion of their country by largely foreign rebels (terrorists), dominated by right-wing elements, seeking to depose their governments and wrecking the country while doing so? 7) The selectivity of expressed moral 'concern' about oppressive regimes is so hypocritical as to render it meaningless, given that the most brutal regimes and groups (e.g., the Saudis, Colombian armed forces) are close allies. 8) Domestic publics who fund these proxy wars often don't support them; they feel that their governments should keep out of international affairs unless they are directly threatened. And, 9) often the terrorists supported by the West are as bad, in terms of violating human rights and wanting to impose regressive policies, as the people they are trying to overthrow.

But none of this matters to giant war machines such as the US Pentagon and its energy company and banking allies, and the same institutions in the UK.

The importance of energy: Regime change is mostly, but not entirely, about oil and gas. Sticking with the post-9/11 period alone: US officials had worked with the Taliban regime in Afghanistan (which the US and Britain invaded after 9/11). Just before 9/11, the US threatened the Taliban: 'either you accept our offer of a carpet of gold', referring to the Turkmenistan-Afghanistan-Pakistan pipeline Unocal had contracted the Taliban to lay in the mid-1990s, 'or we bury you under a carpet of bombs'.[283] Referring to Iraq in 2002, US Colonel William J. Bender informed students at the US Army War College: 'A primary US interest has been to maintain access to the vast supplies of inexpensive and readily available oil from the Gulf, a critical commodity to the economies of all industrialized nations'.[284] While the SAS were training Gaddafi's forces in 2009 (two years before the NATO bombing), then-UK Foreign Secretary David Miliband told Parliament: 'With the largest proven oil reserves in Africa and extensive gas reserves, Libya is potentially a major energy source for the future. We work hard to support British business in Libya, as we do worldwide'.[285] In 2007, four years before the Syrian Arab Spring, policy specialist Andrew Tabler wrote: 'the Syrian state is releasing controls on the Syrian economy. This opens a new arena for American influence in Syria'.[286] But neither Libya's Muammar Gaddafi nor Syria's President Bashar al-Assad fully 'liberalized' their economies, hence the need to depose them.

Syria as a case-study[*]

The US State Department's Middle East Partnership Initiative finances the California-based Democracy Council. The Initiative spent $12m in Syria between 2005 and 2010. In 2006, a US Embassy cable read: 'no bona fide opposition member will be courageous enough to accept [US] funding', hence the decision on the part of the US to support grassroots, or astroturf opposition. In 2007, more cables showed support in the US for establishing an anti-Assad satellite channel, Barada TV. The channel airs programmes featuring Syrian exiles, including the UK-based Ausama Monajed and the US-based dissidents who produced the show First Step.[287]

Tamara Wittes of the State Department's Bureau of Near Eastern Affairs acknowledged in 2009: 'There are a lot of organizations in Syria and other countries that are seeking changes from their government. That's an agenda that we believe in and we're going to

---

[*] I have documented the use of proxies in Libya in *Britain's Secret Wars* and how they spill over into Syria and Iraq (2018, 2nd Ed., Clairview Books, Chapters 1–3). See also the latest edition of Mark Curtis (2018) *Secret Affairs: Britain's Collusion with Radical Islam*, London, Serpent's Tail, which also includes information about Libya and Syria).

support'. In the context of Syrian intelligence agencies' awareness of US government (USG) knowledge of expenditures in Syria, a US Embassy cable from 2009 actually uses the word proxy: 'USG money enters Syria and through ... proxy organizations'.[288]

As noted, no political opponents had the bravery to tackle the brutal Assad regime and its murdering and torturing secret police, with which the US and Britain were happy to ally as part of the 'war on terror' when they wanted alleged suspects tortured. As a result, it was essential for the US and Britain to use as proxies psychopathic thugs as bad as the Assad regime, hence the reliance on *jihadis*. At some point, a decision was made within the upper political and deep state echelons to create an 'al-Qaeda' 2.0 in Libya and Syria, as they had in Afghanistan in the 1980s. The only consequence was the creation of the triggering of an Assad-led counterinsurgency war which has taken 400,000 lives, created 11 million refugees, cost the tiny economy $200bn, bolstered the failing Islamic State, created blowback for innocent Europeans and Americans and threatened a nuclear apocalypse when Russia got involved in the war.

In early-2010, the British Ministry of Defence published *The Future Character of Conflict*, which predicted that troops would soon be fighting in littoral regions and in urban centres (both Syria and Libya have coasts): 'We must adjust capabilities for operations in the urban and littoral environment, where the people live; operations will be about influencing people'.[289]

Also in 2010, the MoD published the 4th edition of its *Strategic Trends Programme: Out to 2040*. The document acknowledges the use of 'proxies' to fight wars. It also acknowledges that proxies will use non-conventional, meaning terroristic, tactics to achieve their objectives. Even worse, it states that terrorist proxies will be hard to control, which is what happened; the US and Britain organized a *jihadi* force to depose Assad and Gaddafi and ended up boosting Islamic State with weapons and defectors.

The document states: '[w]hen intervention becomes unavoidable, actors *will* seek to distance themselves by use of proxy forces, cyber attack, as well as covert and clandestine methods'. It goes on to say that, '[m]any of these proxy forces are *likely* to employ irregular tactics including terrorism, while concealing and refuting links to state sponsors in order to preserve their freedom of action and maintaining a degree of deniability for the state'. It concludes that '[p]roxies are *unlikely* to follow predictable paths and are *likely* to prove difficult to control over time' (emphases in original).[290]

According to the former French Foreign Minister, Roland Dumas, Britain was organizing an invasion of Syria with a terrorist proxy army as early as 2010. Dumas was approached by MI6 and asked for assistance from the French. Dumas said he declined, but he was covering for France (there is no suggestion that Dumas was directly or indirectly involved), because the French secret services were as involved as the British in creating the proxy force. Dumas said:

> I went to England almost two years before the start of the hostilities in Syria [i.e., in 2010 – TJC]. I was there by chance on other business, not at all for Syria [sic]. I met British officials, some of whom are friends of mine. They confessed while trying to persuade me that preparations for something were underway in Syria ... Britain was preparing rebels to invade Syria [sic]. They even asked me, under the pretext that I was a former foreign minister, whether I wanted to participate ... [T]his operation goes way back. It was prepared, conceived, and planned ... [v]ery simply for the purpose of overthrowing the Syrian government.[291]

The statement was made on French television and the translation reads 'gunmen' instead of rebels, but Dumas clearly says '*rebelles*' (rebels).* Dumas then claims, ridiculously, that the plot to topple Assad was at the behest of Israel.

In early-2011, peaceful, pro-democracy demonstrators were murdered by Assad's regime, as were pro-democracy demonstrators in Britain's Middle Eastern allies, most notably Egypt. The US, Britain and France hijacked the Syria Arab Spring and transformed

---

* I have made slight changes to the translation that appears on the video, changing 'pretence' to 'pretext' and 'another' to 'other', for instance.

it into an opportunity to push for regime change, which as we have seen was the goal all along. By October 2011, the UK was helping Syrian opposition groups to form an alternative government. The UK's Middle East Minister Alistair Burt said:

> The establishment of the Syrian National Council [SNC] marked a positive step in bringing together a broad range of Syrian opposition [sic] representatives. I was therefore pleased to meet SNC members Dr Burhan Ghalioun, Basma Kadmani [sic – Bassma Kodmani] and Nibras el-Fadel ... [.] Dr Ghalioun out the importance of establishing a shared vision for the future of Syria and a credible plan of how to move peacefully to an alternative political system. I welcome this, and his belief that any change should be Syrian-led and non-violent. It is crucial for all Syrian groups to be represented in any future opposition body in Syria.[292]

Firstly, the UK had no legal or moral right to help establish a group opposing the very regime it had been supporting. Secondly, the talk of 'non-violen[ce]' was nonsense. Not only do we have the statement of Dumas and the statements of the UK MoD, but a month later Elite UK Forces, a semi-official website for the British Special Forces, said:

> Reports from late November [2011] ... state that British Special forces have met up with members of the Free Syrian Army (FSA), the armed wing of the Syrian National Council. The apparent goal of this initial contact was to establish the rebel forces' strength and to pave the way for any future training operations.
>
> More recent reports have stated that British and French Special Forces have been actively training members of the FSA, from a base in Turkey. Some reports indicate that training is also taking place in locations in Libya and Northern Lebanon. British MI6 operatives and UKSF (SAS/SBS) [UK Special Forces Special Air Service/Special Boat Service] personnel have reportedly been training the rebels in urban warfare as well as

supplying them with arms and equipment. US CIA operatives and special forces are believed to be providing communications assistance to the rebels.[293]

Who were the leaders of the political opposition, with whom Burt met in 2011? None of them are *jihadis*. However, the SNC's armed wing, the Free Syrian Army, counted *jihadis* in its ranks, so the lines between each opposition group grew increasingly blurred as factions merged and fell apart with equal intensity.

Nibras al-Fadel (or el-Fadel) had long been working for the US in pushing its Five-Year Plan on Syria's economy: 'Private banks and a stock exchange opened' in Syria, writes specialist Christopher Philips: 'A marked increase in foreign direct investment ... prompted growth in luxury construction and tourism'.[294] The Paris-based Dr Bassma Kodmani was a major spokesperson for the SNC. She works for Arab Reform, an organization which in turn works with the US Council on Foreign Relations' offshoot, Middle East Project, along with other institutions.[295] Army defector and SNC chair, Dr Burhan Ghalioun, started out as a legitimate democratic reformer working with the Muslim Brotherhood in '70s Syria. But by late-2012, he was openly supporting the use of force by the Free Syrian Army: 'We need arms and until now we haven't had what we need. We need new arms, anti-aircraft arms'.[296] It is simply not true that the FSA had no weapons:

MI6 facilitated the armament of anti-Assad terrorists. '[A] secret agreement reached in early-2012 between the Obama and [Turkish Prime Minister] Erdoğan administrations ... was responsible for getting arms from Gaddafi's arsenals into Syria', says veteran investigative reporter, Seymour Hersh. '[F]unding came from Turkey, as well as Saudi Arabia and Qatar'. Hersh says the so-called ratline was organized by 'the CIA, with the support of MI6 ... A number of front companies were set up in Libya, some under the cover of Australian entities'. Hersh also notes that '[r]etired American soldiers, who didn't always know who was really employing them, were hired to manage procurement and shipping. The operation was run by [CIA director] David Petraeus'. Hersh concludes: '[t]he involvement of MI6 enabled the CIA to evade the law by classifying the mission as a liaison operation'.[297]

In March 2013, then-UK Foreign Secretary William Hague told Parliament that the UK was training Syrian opposition fighters – in neighbouring Jordan's King Abdullah II Special Operations Training Centre, it turns out. In addition, a British Foreign Office source told the *Guardian*: 'at some point Assad is going to fall, and the opposition are going to need help to provide governance in areas they control'. The US provided the terrorists with portable anti-aircraft missiles (previously impounded in Turkey), as well as rations and medical kits.[298] The UK provided the terrorists with mini satellites, 4 × 4s, radios, body armour and solar-powered batteries. The *Independent* reports that 'France was instrumental, alongside the UK, in lifting the European arms embargo on Syria'.[299]

By 2013, there were 100,000 opposition fighters and terrorists in Syria: 20% of whom are foreign, spread over 1,000 discrete groups.[300] According to the UN, 20,000 foreign fighters poured into Syria between 2011 and 2016 to fight with different groups, including the FSA (which the US and Britain backed), 'al-Qaeda's' offshoot al-Nusra (which they tolerated) and the Islamic State (which they initially tolerated as a weapon against Assad). FSA's Southern Front consisted of 58 factions and 25,000 members, while the Northern Front had 14 factions and 20,000 members.[301]

A heavily-redacted US Defense Intelligence Agency report from 2012 suggests blanket support for the opposition. It states (all capitalized in original): 'The Salafist, the Muslim Brotherhood, and AQI ['al-Qaeda' in Iraq] are the major forces driving the insurgency in Syria ... The west, the Gulf countries, and Turkey support the opposition; while Russia, China, and Iran support the regime'. It further states that 'AQI supported the Syrian opposition from the beginning, both ideologically and through the media'.[302] By 2014, it was impossible to pretend that the FSA was not dominated by *jihadis*. Veteran correspondent Patrick Cockburn cited 'strong evidence that the Syrian armed opposition are, more than ever, dominated by jihadi fighters similar in their beliefs and methods to al-Qa'ida'. He noted an attack near Latakia, northern Syria, 'led by Chechen and Moroccan jihadis'.[303]

Just how moderate is the moderate FSA and its affiliates? Between January 2012 and April 2014, Human Rights Watch (HRW) documented 17 car bombings conducted by US-British-backed opposition groups in just a handful of locations alone. 'Initial attacks targeted state security forces and outposts, but the groups soon began to carry out bombings in populated areas without evident military targets'. HRW says it received reports of car bombings long after it stopped investigating.[304] In September, the FSA admitted to carrying out at least one car bombing, which reportedly murdered 17 people.[305]

In November 2012, the FSA became an umbrella group backed by the National Coalition for Syrian Opposition and Revolutionary Forces, making it harder to confirm which terrorist group was backing which.

In December 2012, just in time for Christmas, FSA moderates beheaded Andrei Arbashe, a Christian taxi driver, and fed his corpse to dogs. His remains were found in Ras al-Ayn, on the Turkish border.[306] In July 2016, it was reported that the 'moderate' (Associated Press) Nureddine al-Zinki, a faction of the FSA, beheaded a 12-year-old boy, believed to be Mahmoud Issa, filming it for good measure. Mahmoud was murdered for allegedly being a spy for the Palestinian al-Quds Brigades.[307] In February 2018, it was revealed that 'moderate' FSA terrorists had killed four Kurdish female fighters of the Women's Protection Units in Afrin. In one case, the corpse of Barin Kobani was mutilated by the male FSA 'moderates'.[308]

This is a small sample of innumerable atrocities, most of which will never see the light of day. By October 2017, the British taxpayer had spent £14m assisting these so-called moderates.[309]

Syria, Libya & the CIA's definition of blowback
In Chapter 6, it was argued that blowback has now come to mean any kind of consequence of supporting violence abroad. The CIA uses the term specifically to refer to being double-crossed by terrorists they train who then attack US or allied targets.

Quite apart from the appalling humanitarian catastrophe of wrecking a country, the British NATO destruction of Libya created, 'political and economic collapse, inter-militia and inter-tribal warfare ... [,] the spread of Gaddafi regime weapons across the region and the growth of ISIL in North Africa', says the House of Commons Foreign Affairs Committee.[310] Aaron Y. Zelin of the Washington Institute for Near East Policy and US Vice Admiral Michael T. Franken (Ret.) say (summary of speech): 'Libya's influx of foreign fighters has become the fourth-largest mobilization in jihadist history, behind only the Syria war, the Afghan jihad of the 1980s, and the 2003 Iraq war'. This amounted to at least 2,600 foreign fighters entering Libya, spread over 41 nations.[311]

According to the BBC: 'Counter-terrorism officers in the Metropolitan Police are increasingly concerned that so-called Islamic State's foothold in Libya could become a second springboard, after Syria, for attacks on the UK and the rest of Europe'.[312]

Alastair Crooke CMG is a former MI6 officer and security expert. 'When the US and British militaries were working with the Turks to train various Syrian rebel groups, many military officers knew that among those we were training was the next round of jihadists', he said. 'But the CIA was fixated on regime change. We knew that even if at any moment ISIS was eventually defeated, these Islamist groups would move against secular and moderate forces'.[313] The US Defense Intelligence Agency report confirms that the US-British support for *jihadis* revived the fading Salafist presence in Iraq: 'There was a regression of AQI in the western provinces of Iraq during the years 2009 and 2010; however, after the rise of the insurgency in Syria, the religious and tribal powers in the region began to sympathize with the sectarian uprising'.[314]

Trained by *jihadis* directly or indirectly supported by the US, Britain, France and Israel, terrorists are returning to their home countries across Europe and North America. In 2014, MI5 warned that perhaps 500 *jihadis* who had fought with 'al-Qaeda' could return to the UK and act as sleeper cells. MI5 Director-general Andrew Parker said: 'there is good reason to be concerned about Syria. A growing proportion of our casework now has some link to

Syria, mostly concerning individuals from the UK who have travelled to fight there or who aspire to do so'. Richard Walton of Scotland Yard's counterterrorism command said: 'Syria is a game-changer. We are seeing it every day. You have hundreds of people going to Syria, and if they don't get killed they get radicalised'. An ISIS defector spoke to the *Telegraph* about British *jihadis* coming home to roost:

> They talked often about terrorist attacks. The foreigners were proud of 9/11 and the London bombings. The British, French and American mujahideen . . . in the room started talking about places that they wanted to bomb or explode themselves in Europe and the United States. Everyone named a target. The American said he dreamed of blowing up the White House.[315]

Warnings were sounded again in 2017. Professor Tahir Abbas of the Royal United Services Institute said:

> These returning fighters pose a number of threats in relation to security here. They've been through a lot of very traumatic conflict and engagement, often involved in street-to-street fighting . . . Now, having made their way back to Britain, they pose a particular threat because of their capacity – and perhaps they've been instructed to return, hold fire and wait for the go ahead to launch attacks. They are likely to be traumatised, but also extremely experienced and well trained individuals who pose a serious risk. (See note 316.)

Ex-Scotland Yard Specialist Firearms Officer Tony Long says: 'they've seen more close quarter conflict and more urban fighting than probably most members of the British Armed Forces and you have to respect that. Of course they're bringing that knowledge back with them to the UK'.[316]

Chapter 8

Step 3: Provocateurs

The third step in manufacturing terrorism is to act as a provocateur, to goad individuals or groups into committing acts they would not or might not have otherwise done. When it comes to provocateurs operating abroad, there is absolute proof in the form of declassified documents and sometimes interviews with provocateurs or their handlers. This chapter focuses primarily on the bombing of the World Trade Center in 1993, when the FBI set up a terror cell and, it was reported, deliberately allowed the bombing to go ahead.

So far, we've seen how state actions abroad can come home to roost in the form of a) domestic terrorism as revenge acts for foreign policies (blowback) and b) how terrorists are created for use as proxies against sovereign states and who may then attack their facilitators (the CIA's definition of blowback). But what about manufacturing terrorism specifically aimed at domestic targets? Would the deep state ever do such things and if so, why?

When it comes to the use of provocateurs at home, 100% proof in the form of confessions or declassified documents is much harder to come by. This is partly due to a reluctance on the part of political leaders to authorize terrorist attacks at home. It is also due to the lack of hard evidence. As deep state-actors seek to hide their traces at home (few care about what they do abroad), they produce little in the way of written documents, such as memos.

One of the few documented exceptions is the FBI's COIN-TELPRO. In its attack on women's groups, the Civil Rights movement, Native American groups, the Black Panthers, unions and the so-called New Left, as well as far-right groups including the Ku Klux Klan, the FBI's counterintelligence program (COINTELPRO) involved mass surveillance, smear campaigns, infiltration, assassination in some cases and, according to a book review included in a CIA document available on the organization's website, '[p]rovocateurs ... sent into organizations, to prod them into breaking laws'.[317]

The work of provocateurs tends to be under the onus of special operations forces, according to the CIA's forerunner, the Office of Strategic Services, whose *Special Operations Field Manual* (1944) discusses provocateurs, sabotage operations and much more.[318] Before looking at the few 100% provable provocateur cases in the US, let's examine a few examples of proven cases abroad.

Iran: In 1953, the governments of the US (Eisenhower) and UK (Churchill) authorized a coup (Operation TPAJAX) to depose Iran's secular Prime Minister, Mohammed Mossadeq, who had nationalized the Anglo-Iranian oil company (later BP) two years earlier. A book review posted on the CIA's website says that TPAJAX 'comprised propaganda, provocations, demonstrations, and bribery, and employed agents of influence, "false flag" operatives, dissident military leaders, and paid protestors'.[319] One of the individuals involved in the coup was described by US Air Force Captain Wolfgang K. Kressin as the 'CIA provocateur, Kermit Roosevelt [Junior]'.[320] The coup led to the worst period of Iran's post-war history, the rule of the Shah, Reza Pahlavi, and his murderous SAVAK secret police. The Shah was deposed in the Iranian Revolution (1979), which brought Ayatollah Khomeini to power. The Ayatollah had played a part in deposing Mossadeq in 1953 ('blowback').

Chile: After years of influence operations, including funding antigovernment elections, the CIA finally succeeded in 1973 in overthrowing the government of Salvador Allende in Chile and supporting Augusto Pinochet (who was protected from prosecution by the UK in his later life). Pinochet's men murdered over 3,000 people, tortured tens of thousands and privatized large parts of the economy. 'There is typically no attempt made by the CIA officer to influence the actions of the "asset[...]"', says a US Senate report into covert operations in Chile. 'Yet even that kind of covert relationship may have political significance. Witness the maintenance of CIA's and military attaches' contacts with the Chilean military after the inauguration of Salvador Allende', it continues. '[A]lthough the purpose was information-gathering, the United States maintained links to the group most likely to overthrow the new president. To do so was to walk a tightrope'. The Senate explains how information-gathering inevitably led to provocateuring. '[T]he distinction between collecting information and exercising influence was inherently hard to maintain. Since the Chilean military perceived its actions to be contingent to some degree on the attitude of the U.S. government, those possibilities for exercising influence scarcely would have had to be consciously manipulated'.[321]

Northern Ireland: In 1982, the British Army set up a secret organization called the Force Research Unit (FRU), in part to penetrate the pro-independence Irish Republican Army which it was fighting in an undeclared war. The late Brian Nelson, a British soldier working for FRU, was told by his handlers (one of whom was a Sergeant Margaret Walshaw of Scotland Yard) that they wanted to take control of the pro-British loyalist gangs and paramilitaries who were murdering Republicans. Nelson posed as a taxi driver and operated in Republican areas. The British police force operating in Northern Ireland, the Royal Ulster Constabulary, gave Nelson 'a considerable number of files' (BBC) on Republican targets. In addition, Nelson infiltrated the Loyalist Ulster Defence Association and encouraged the Loyalist Ulster Volunteer Force (UVF) to carry out assassinations. In exchange for information, the UVF gave him explosives. Nelson developed an index of 1,000 Republican targets the British and Loyalists wanted dead, including their photos and addresses.[322]

Nelson helped loyalists murder Terry McDaid, a civilian. They were after his brother. To boost Nelson's morale, the British handlers lied and told him that McDaid had connections to the IRA. Michael Power was also murdered by loyalists who claimed to believe that he was a member of the IRA. Nelson recruited Ken Barrett, a key Ulster Defence Association figure, to murder IRA member and later Sinn Féin politician, Alex Maskey. Barrett admits murdering 10 individuals and was convicted of murdering the solicitor Pat Finucane in 1989, which he denies. Finucane got the charges dropped against the alleged IRA killer of two Army corporals. Northern Irish (British) detectives working for Belfast's Police Interrogation Centre allegedly told Brian Gillen, who was being represented by Finucane, 'We'll have him [Finucane] taken out'. This was done by the detectives releasing young loyalists and urging them to murder him.[323]

Detective-Sergeant Nicholas Benwell, who worked on the Stevens Inquiry, agrees that Nelson was a 'provocateur': 'Nelson went around North Belfast trying to recruit an assassination team, and when one unit were unable to assist, he moved on until he found another one'. Benwell was also tasked with interviewing Nelson's handler, Sgt. Walshaw. Lochlan Maginn was also murdered at the behest of Nelson. Fearing exposure, the British sent Cambridge-based Deputy-Constable (later Sir) John Stevens to 'investigate'. Scotland Yard, Special Branch, MI5, the British Army and its units, as well as the Northern Ireland police and the RUC, each obstructed the inquiry in their own ways, even denying the existence of special agents like Nelson.[324]

USA: As part of the 'war on terror' at home, Trevor Aaronson documents multiple cases of FBI provocateuring in his book, *The Terror Factory: Inside the FBI's Manufactured War on Terrorism* (New York: Ig Publishing). Most of the cases documented by Aaronson and others involve the FBI setting up patsies via informants and handlers and then stepping in at the last minute to save the day. But in 1993, agents actually allowed a terror cell working under their surveillance to detonate a truck bomb at the base of the North Tower of the World Trade Center, murdering six and injuring over 1,000.

The 'blind sheikh'

Omar Abdel Rahman (the 'Blind Sheikh') and Yusuf al-Qaradawi were major investors in the Faisal Islamic Bank of Egypt. The bank had investments in the CIA front, the Bank of Credit and Commerce International, which, as noted, laundered drug money, financed terrorists and bribed journalists. In the 1980s, Rahman and his Egyptian Islamic Jihad were 'helpmate[s] to the CIA in recruiting young zealots' (author John K. Cooley) for the war in Afghanistan, in which two of Rahman's sons were fighting.[325]

Although Rahman had been implicated in Egyptian President Anwar Sadat's murder (Sadat was a former Muslim Brother) and arrested in one of the sweeps, Rahman 'escaped – or was allowed to escape – from detention in mysterious circumstances', says Cooley. Al-Gama'a al-Islamiya (the Islamic Group) included Rahman's disciple, Lt. Khaled al-Islambuli. After Sadat's murder in October 1981, the people of the Assiut territory, in which Rahman's men had trained militias, revolted. The revolt was led by the Islamic Group. Al-Islambuli and Rahman were tried over their involvement in Sadat's murder, as well as for their involvement in the uprising. Rahman was acquitted on both counts.[326]

Abdel Moneim Said, a scholar of the Al Ahram Center, Cairo, writes: 'Abdul Omar Rahman was being harbored in the United States, having escaped in between trials and going to Sudan. The United States was not cooperating' with Egypt in apprehending him. '[Y]ou', meaning Egypt, 'are not making reforms', US officials would reply. The 'reforms' are those of the Broader Middle East and North Africa Initiative. 'So they [the US] were creating a worldwide terrorist network, and we were practically on our own', says Said.[327]

In 1984, bin Laden and Abdullah Azzam (assassinated in 1989) established the Maktab al-Khadamat (Services Office) to raise funds for the US-British proxy war against the Soviets in the 1980s. The Maktab al-Khadamat established a mosque, al-Farouq, in Brooklyn, New York. Sergeant Ali Mohamed of Fort Bragg (US) provided members of the mosque with training manuals. Mohamed was a CIA agent who had, as part of his infiltration work connected to the Egyptian Islamic Jihad (EIJ), sworn allegiance to bin Laden's future second-in-command, Zawahiri. (The report revealing his allegiance to the CIA claims that at heart he was a radical *jihadi* who was as much using the CIA as it was using him. Be that as it may, Mohamed was clearly protected from arrest or prosecution by higher sources until 1998.) An al-Farouq mosque attendee was El Sayyid Nosair. It is likely that Nosair was also working for the deep state because he was acquitted of murdering Meir Kahane, founder of the terrorist group, the Jewish Defense League.[328]

CIA double-agent Mohamed met with the CIA-protected 'blind Sheikh' Omar Abdul Rahman in New York and stayed with al-Farouq mosque attendee Nosair. According to the report by the Combating Terrorism Center (CTC) at West Point, Mohamed's job included 'provid[ing] training to an EIJ cell'. By 1989, the FBI's New York-based Operations Group had ceased monitoring the cell, despite its fairly open activities, which included target practice. Mohamed's role went far beyond monitoring and informing. The CIA was using him as a provocateur. By 1991, Mohamed was trying to facilitate bin Laden's move to Sudan. 'Over the course of numerous trips to South Asia during the 1990s, Mohamed provided training of various kinds to virtually the entire al-Qa'ida leadership structure', says the CTC: 'including Bin Ladin, Zawahiri, Abu Ubaydah al-Banshiri and Muhammad Atef'.[329]

One Marcus Dwayne Robertson, a.k.a. Abu Taubah, was a US Marine in the elite Joint Special Operations Command. He claims to have had 'training in radiotelegraphy, scuba diving, marksmanship, parachuting, terrorism counteraction, surveillance, infantry patrolling and finance'.[330] He spent 15 years working undercover in Egypt for the FBI. He was closely linked to Rahman, spending time as Rahman's bodyguard. Allegedly linked to organized crime, Robertson financed several mosques across the USA, where he and others recruited terrorists. Robertson was also working for the CIA.[331]

Sent on espionage missions to Mauritania, which borders Mali, Algeria and other African countries, a defence memo states that Robertson was a 'confidential source in domestic terrorism investigations from Atlanta to Los Angeles, wherein he was provided with actual authority to, inter alia, possess firearms in order to maintain his cover and fulfil the objectives set for him by the [FBI Joint Terrorist Task Force] JTTF'.[332]

World Trade Center 1993

Richard A. Clarke, America's national coordinator for counter-terrorism, made the bin Laden-Rahman connection: 'We'd see C.I.A. reports that referred to "financier Osama bin Laden," and we'd ask ourselves, "Who the hell is he?" The more we drilled down, the more we realized that he was not just a financier – he was the leader. John [O'Neill, the late chief of the FBI's counterterrorism section,] said, "We've got to get this guy. He's building a network. Everything leads back to him" '.[333]

In 1993, Rahman sought asylum in the United States, where he was protected by the CIA and preached at the bin Laden-funded al-Farouq mosque. The FBI used an Egyptian Army Colonel, Emad Salem, as an agent provocateur to frame Muslim extremists or to apprehend them in a sting. Rahman set up meetings between the terrorists. Khalid Sheikh Mohammed, a bin Laden associate and alleged mastermind of the 9/11 plot, financed the operation.

Rahman was eventually sentenced for his role in the bombing and imprisoned for life without parole. The other bomb plotters were as follows: Ramzi Yousef, bomb-maker and fuse-lighter; El Sayid Nosair (the man linked to CIA asset Ali Mohamed), initiator of the plot; Mohammed Salameh (an FBI informant);[334] Musab Yassin and Abdul Rahman Yasin (who was never caught, interviewed by the FBI after the bombing and allowed to 'walk out the door', according to his lawyer, Stephen Somerstein);[335] Mahmud Abouhalima (met Rahman in Egypt in the 1980s and was a friend of Nosair);[336] Mohammad Salameh (another Nosair accomplice who, according to the LA Times, seemed to have learning difficulties); Nidal A. Ayyad (better-educated friend of Salameh, both of whom met at the mosque where Rahman was preaching);[337] Ahmed Ajaj (worked with Yousef and trained in Pakistan); and Eyad Ismoil (who drove the truck).[338] Nosair was never convicted.[339]

Conspicuously absent from most media reporting and the Wikipedia entry for the WTC bombing of 1993 is any serious exploration of the connection with the Egyptian Army Col., Emad Salem, whom the FBI was using as an informant/provocateur. Salem was part of the cell and tasked with making the bomb by the imprisoned Nosair. Rahman infiltrated the Jersey City mosque, where Rahman also preached. Salem rented the cell an apartment, which the FBI bugged.[340] Salem suspected that he was being set up. Unbeknownst to the FBI, Salem began taping the telephone conversations with his handlers, John Anticev and Nancy Floyd (no suggestion that either played a part in the bombing). He told agent Anticev: '[The bomb] was built by supervising supervision [sic] from the Bureau and the DA [District Attorney] and we was all informed about it [sic] and we know that the bomb started to be built [sic]'.[341] According to the *New York Times*: '[Salem] planned to thwart the plotters by secretly substituting harmless powder for the explosives ... but the plan was called off by an F.B.I. supervisor'.[342] Who?

Chapter 9

Step 4: Green-lighting

The fourth step towards manufacturing terrorism is allowing ('green-lighting') terrorists to strike when the possibility of capturing or killing them exists. This chapter presents two case studies: Northern Ireland and Osama bin Laden. The study of Northern Ireland is a chronology of bombings and shootings by the IRA and pro-British Loyalist forces. In many cases, infiltrators and informants warned their British handlers of impending attacks. The CIA's head of the unit responsible for tracking bin Laden revealed that the White House repeatedly let him live.

Northern Ireland

Until independence, the whole of Ireland was occupied by Britain. Sinn Féin ('We ourselves' or 'Ourselves alone', *Sinn Féin Amháin*) was founded in 1905. The Sinn Féin-linked Irish Volunteers evolved into the original Irish Republican Army (IRA, *Óglaigh na hÉireann*, Irish volunteers or warriors) founded in 1919 to fight in the Irish War of Independence (1919–21). The Anglo-Irish Treaty (1921) led to the partition of the country, creating the Republic of Ireland and the British territory of Northern Ireland. The IRA split because most wanted full independence. A brief civil war (1922–23) saw the anti-treaty IRA fight the Free State Army. The IRA never abandoned their goal of full independence.

The Catholic minority in Protestant-dominated Northern Ireland experienced various forms of increasing oppression, including disenfranchisement, high unemployment and mounting poverty. The British-controlled Royal Ulster Constabulary (RUC) played a role in social oppression by targeting Catholics. Oppression continued into the 1960s until Catholic groups, many of which supported independence, began armed resistance against British-sponsored oppression. These protests and forms of armed resistance are known as the Troubles (1963–1999, also dated 1968–85). The IRA split in two in 1969, creating Sinn Féin's armed wing, the Provisional IRA, and the so-called Official IRA.

The so-called Troubles were a disaster for civilians, at least until the Good Friday Agreement (1998), which finally led to some minimal rights for the Catholic minority. Between 1969 and 2010, 3,558 people on all sides were killed and murdered in the Troubles.[343] Of these, 1,879 were civilians, of which 650 (approx.)[344] were murdered by the IRA.

The anti-British[*] IRA ended up as a quasi-proxy of the British state which played a deadly divide and rule game with the people of Ireland and Northern Ireland. Documents seen by the *Belfast Telegraph* emerged concerning the killing of two men working for the RUC. Within those documents, it was said that by the late-1990s 25% of all Provisional IRA (PIRA) members were informants for the British, and fully half of PIRA's top leaders secretly worked for the British. 'PIRA was extensively penetrated at all levels, most sources of the information to PIRA were readily identified (by military intelligence) but seldom compromised'.[345] Anthony McIntyre of the IRA said: 'they know everything about the IRA. They are like an electrical junction box through which every wire must flow. If the British put somebody in there, the British must really have their wedding tackle [genitals] firmly in their hands'.[346]

The Defence Advisory Committee confirmed that military intelligence had kept activist and later Sinn Féin president Gerry Adams alive by sabotaging bullets used in assassination attempts. Then-head of the Metropolitan Police (now) Lord Stevens is quoted in the document as saying that 207 out of the 210 arrested suspects in a terror probe were working for MI5, the British Army, the RUC or multiple agencies. Though he denies it, one Sergeant Owen Corrigan of the An Garda Síochána (Irish Police) was named in the British Parliament as allegedly being an informer working for the Irish. Ian Hurst worked in military intelligence between 1981 and

---

[*] 'Anti-British' in the sense of anti-British establishment and wanting an end to the British occupation of Ireland via its pene-exclave, Northern Ireland.

1990, spending much of the time in the secret British Force Research Unit. Hurst claims that the RUC, Ulster Defence Regiment and British Army passed information on to the IRA about the pro-British loyalist groups.[347] It is alleged that An Garda Síochána Sergeants Leo Colton and Finbarr Hickey were also informants, though they deny it.[348]

The BBC reports: 'British security forces had thousands of agents and informants working inside Northern Ireland para-military groups ... The undercover operatives were recruited by the Army, MI5 and Special Branch and many were involved in criminality and murder'. Lord Stevens says that a single infor-mant alone, named as the late Brian Nelson, was linked to 'dozens and dozens' of murders. Nelson was paid by the British Army and provided target lists for the pro-UK Ulster Freedom Fighters, Ulster Volunteer Force and Red Hand Commandos. Another, Mark Haddock, worked for Special Branch, ran a gang for the Ulster Volunteer Force and was paid £79,000. He has been linked to 20 murders. Until 2015, the police refused to pro-vide evidence requested by Northern Ireland's police ombuds-man, Baroness Nuala O'Loan.[349]

The 'troubles'

In 1974, three car bombs exploded in Dublin and Monaghan. Thirty-four died, including an unborn. The IRA was blamed, but in 1993 the pro-British Ulster Volunteer Force admitted responsi-bility. In a defence case, the Court of Criminal Appeal refused to publish information given to an inquiry into the bombings.[350]

Patrick Daly informed on the IRA for Special Branch from Bristol in the mid-1970s, before moving to Galway and joining the Irish National Liberation Army, where he became an MI5 agent. He denies charges of being a provocateur.[351]

In 1976, the Provisional IRA murdered 10 workmen near Whitecross, South Armagh. Sole survivor Alan Black claimed that the IRA group behind the massacre (supposedly the Republican Action Force) included at least one informer for the British in the group that murdered his colleagues: 'did they sacrifice us to protect an informer?', he asks. No one was convicted for the murders and '[t]he police just turned their backs on us'.[352]

In 1982, the British Army established a Force Research Unit (FRU, later renamed the Joint Support Group). The FRU worked with Britain's Royal Ulster Constabulary (Special Branch) in Northern Ireland and MI5. Sean Rayment of the *Telegraph* writes: 'By targeting and then "turning" members of the paramilitary organisation with a variety of "inducements" ranging from blackmail to bribes, the FRU operators developed agents at virtually every command level within the IRA'.[353]

Martin Ingram (Ian Hurst), an FRU officer, writes: 'The FRU recruited and ran agents within [pro-British] paramilitary organisations'. Ingram denies that politicians were directly involved, preferring to murder by proxy.[354] Ingram also says that the FRU was used to prevent the loyalists from killing a top-ranking IRA official allegedly working secretly for the British, codenamed Stakeknife (Freddie Scappaticci). Historian Ed Moloney (who denies that the FRU provided a kill-list to the loyalists) revealed that the FRU saved the life of Gerry Adams, the leader of the IRA's political wing, Sinn Féin. Adams was targeted for death by the loyalist Ulster Defence Association.[355]

Alfredo (Freddie) Scappaticci of the IRA was kidnapped by the British and imprisoned (internment). In jail, he met Gerry Adams whom he befriended, eventually becoming his bodyguard. After a colleague beat him up in 1978, he offered his services to the British Army. The UK's Force Research Unit arranged for Scappaticci to get a senior position in the IRA, which is no small indication of the FRU's influence on or within the IRA. The *Guardian* reported (writing in 2003) that: 'he is credited with involvement in nearly every big security operation in the past 25 years'. Scappaticci (Scap)'s job in the IRA was to identify, torture and kill informants, including fellow FRU informants – the ultimate way to gain credibility. Scappaticci, linked to the murder of 40 individuals, was paid £80,000 a year by the UK. A security official told the *Guardian* that '[i]f there was an IRA man they needed to get rid of, or another agent past his sell-by date, Scap did the dirty work'.[356] Scappaticci denies working for British intelligence and said he cut all ties with the IRA in 1990.

Kevin Fulton (Peter Keeley) worked for the First Battalion Royal Irish Rangers. He appeared on the radar of the British Intelligence Corps, a regiment which included the FRU. Fulton allegedly became an MI5 and FRU informant, the latter under Brig. Gordon Kerr. He was 'friends' with IRA officer and later Real IRA officer Patrick Joseph Blair, who was alleged to be responsible (with others) for the Omagh bombing (1998). Blair mentored Fulton. By the late-1980s, Fulton was reportedly travelling to the US to develop light-sensitive bombs activated by photo flashes, which overcame the IRA's problem of having the signals of remotely-detonated bombs jammed.[357]

PM Margaret Thatcher supposedly knew about these activities because, as chair of the Joint Intelligence Committee, she was informed about the FRU's activities – though to what extent we will never know. After the IRA bombed the Enniskillen Remembrance Day (1987), murdering twelve, Thatcher increased funding for the FRU.[358]

Intelligence Officer Colin Wallace says of terrorism in general:

> A number of those involved [in killings] were informants of the security services, who must have had advance warning ... There never has been a case before or since where Loyalist terrorists have been able to carry out bombings of such complexity. It's my belief that the explosives were supplied by the security forces or were recycled from explosives they'd captured ... The British Government spent millions on the Bloody Sunday inquiry, but there was much greater loss of life here while there has been a complete apparent lack of interest in finding out what happened ... In 1984, along with Captain Fred Holroyd, I sent a complete file to [then Prime Minister] Margaret Thatcher – which then went missing. This is a jar of worms which nobody wants to open up – because it will reveal why these people who were connected to other killings were allowed to roam free for so long.[359]

D Company was the Belfast IRA's 2nd Battalion. Two of its members, Seamus Wright and Kevin McKee, confessed to being informants for Britain's early-1970s' Military Reaction Force and were subsequently murdered.[360]

In 1987, a shipment of weapons, some of which were used in the murders, arrived in Belfast. One of the dealers alleges that arms-supplier Armscor (which provided weapons for Apartheid South Africa) struck a deal via a British agent working for the pro-British Ulster Defence Association (at the behest of MI5 and the British Army) to supply the UDA. Within weeks, Michael Stone threw grenades and shot at a funeral, murdering three people. Pro-UK groups killed 230 people in the six years that followed the arrival of the weapons shipment, compared to 70 in the previous six years. In 1994, Loyalists murdered six people in a pub in Loughinisland, County Down, with weapons from the shipment.[361]

With regards to the so-called Troubles more generally: Ex-Irish PM Bertie Ahern established two judicial inquiries, which were denied access to the events by UK PM Tony Blair. It wasn't until June 2015 that the An Garda Síochána was ordered to hand its files on the case to the Irish government.[362] *Irish News* saw documents that were allegedly stolen and confirm that one of the FRU's operatives was Fulton (a.k.a., Kevin Fulton). Keeley alleges that on several occasions, he passed information on to his British handlers concerning IRA attacks, but the attacks were allowed to happen.[363]

In 1990, Eoin Morley was murdered, allegedly by the IRA's splinter group, the Irish People's Liberation Organisation. Eoin's mother Eilish alleges that Britain's Special Branch withheld intelligence and that Britain's Royal Ulster Constabulary failed to investigate. The murder was one of many cases where, according to a lawyer's statement, the Chief Constable 'failed to effectively investigate th[e] incidents or ... [Keeley's] involvement in them, because it was regarded as too important not to terminate his cover'.[364]

The IRA bomb outside the department store Harrods was planted with the involvement of a former British Army Royal Signals Corps corporal and UN peace medal recipient, Jan Taylor, who was later jailed. Taylor's colleague was Patrick Hayes who plotted the bombings at Canary Wharf, Tottenham Court Road and Woodside Park tube station in 1992. The *Independent* reported 'huge gaps in detectives' knowledge of the bombers' lives'. The report says '[p]olice sources have no idea how or when either made the transition from being "weekend Socialist Workers" in the 1970s to working for the IRA in the 1990s'.[365]

Also in 1992, double-agent Fulton informed his handlers that then-IRA officer Blair was going to fire a mortar at the police. The handlers refused to act, leading to the death of policewoman Colleen McMurray and causing another officer to lose his legs.[366]

Stolen documents confirm that Special Branch was working with an IRA informant, a commander known only as agent AA, who was directly responsible for the Frizzell's fish shop bombing in 1993, which intended to kill loyalist paramilitaries, but ended up murdering nine civilians. Agent AA had been a snitch for ten years.[367] It was also revealed that Agent AA's information passed on to his handlers at Special Branch could have prevented the atrocity, but the handlers or their superiors chose not to act. The pro-British Ulster Defence Association retaliated by murdering eight civilians.[368]

In 1994, double-agent Fulton was reportedly shopped by his handlers because they now had Freddie Scappaticci, whom they were protecting. This story makes little sense because Fulton started acting against the British Ministry of Defence in 1995, yet he was supposedly an informant working inside the Real IRA as late as 1998, when the Omagh bomb went off. Either this account is unreliable or some disinformation is being deliberately weaved into the narrative. Military records seen by the *Sunday Herald* (Scotland) appear to confirm that he was working for the FRU.[369]

The so-called Real IRA was founded in 1997 by Michael McKevitt, who quit the IRA in protest over the peace process and disarmament. The Real IRA was infiltrated by British-Irish and US agents. Paddy Dixon was a crook who procured cars for Real IRA bombings throughout 1998, i.e., while working for MI5. David Rupert was working for the FBI and then for MI5 via a handler called Norman. Norman instructed Rupert not to give information to the Garda (the

Irish police) but to use a secret PO Box and phone number and pass information to MI5. Dixon, conversely, was encouraged to share intelligence. These alleged failings led to the Omagh bombing, partly on account of the British refusal to act on intelligence.[370]

Fulton alleges that he told both his handlers and the RUC (confirmed by intelligence sources speaking on the condition of anonymity) but they refused to act on his warnings about the Omagh bomb (1998), which murdered 29 people. Fulton alleges that the agencies didn't act because stopping the bombing would have blown his cover. This suggests that the British authorities had higher priorities than stopping terrorism, which is the reason they give the public for having informants in the first place. (It wasn't as if the Real IRA was as big or significant as its rival, the IRA.)[371]

To date, no one has been convicted for the Omagh bombing.

The Herald (Ireland) reports that, 'the garda has very close links to a man that was arrested in relation to the 1998 Omagh bombing in which 29 people were murdered including a woman pregnant with twins'.[372]

Now we will turn to the Middle East and Central Asia.

How Bill Clinton saved Osama bin Laden

The CIA knew of bin Laden's whereabouts. The Agency's head of the Counterterrorism Center, Cofer Black, had been monitoring his activities in Sudan.[373] As he was apparently setting up terror networks in Albania in preparation for *jihad* against Serbia (in which Britain played a role) bin Laden visited London, where he established the Advice and Reformation Committee (ARC), a front organization set up to finance terrorism through London and European banks.[374]

Sudan's despot, Omar al-Bashir, offered to extradite bin Laden to the US from Sudan, but the US refused. After being expelled from Sudan by al-Bashir in 1996, bin Laden moved to Afghanistan and supposedly lived in caves.[375] In August 1996, bin Laden personally issued a *fatwa* calling for attacks against US interests: 'Terrorising you, while you are carrying arms on our land, is a legitimate and morally demanded duty. It is a legitimate right well known to all humans and other creatures. Your example and our example is like a snake which entered into a house of a man and got killed by him'.[376] President Bill Clinton's Department of State did not add 'Al Qaeda' to the list of proscribed terrorist organizations.

Bin Laden's telephone records show that he made 238 calls to his London agents from 1996 to 1998, one of whom was Khaled al-Fawwaz, head of bin Laden's Advice and Reformation Committee.[377] CIA agents later confirmed that bin Laden lived in a palace in Kandahar and in the nearby Tarnak Farms, Afghanistan, which was close to the Kandahar Airport. (The word 'farm' has been a traditional intelligence euphemism for training camp.) At both the palace and 'farm', bin Laden was monitored by the CIA.[378]

In February 1998, bin Laden issued his second personal *fatwa* against the US, stating: 'To kill Americans and their allies, both civil and military, is an individual duty of every Muslim who is able, in any country where this is possible, until the Aqsa Mosque [in Jerusalem] and the Haram Mosque [in Mecca] are freed from their grip and until their armies, shattered and broken-winged, depart from all the lands of Islam, incapable of threatening any Muslim'.[379] Again, 'al-Qaeda' was not designated a terrorist group by the US State Department.

In March 1998, Interpol issued an arrest warrant for bin Laden. According to two French intelligence experts, Guillaume Dasquié and Jean-Charles Brisard, MI6 and the CIA leaned on Interpol to retract the warrant.[380] At that time, MI6 was working with the bin Laden-linked Libyan Islamic Fighting Group, whose membership included Anas al-Liby. Egypt sought al-Liby's extradition for the plot against President Hosni Mubarak. Al-Liby had been living in Sudan where he trained *jihadis* in surveillance techniques. He moved to Nairobi, Kenya, where he developed pictures of the US Embassy. In 1995, he was granted asylum in Britain, whose government, led by John Major, protected him from extradition.[381]

Bin Laden's inner circle in Afghanistan was penetrated by US intelligence assets. The CIA watched his movements in real-time, with overhead drones feeding live footage to its headquarters in Langley, Virginia. Agent Hank Crumpton told the BBC: 'There were occasions where you would drive into CIA headquarters and you would get the live video feed from the Predator. On one occasion we were able to position the drone over Tarnak Farm [sic] and see bin Laden arrive'.[382] Michael Scheuer, head of the CIA's Osama bin Laden Unit (which President Bush closed in 2006), says:

> Between May of 1998 and May of 1999, we had, by my count, ten opportunities to either kill or capture Usama bin Laden. Not only clear opportunities, but easy opportunities ... When we briefed [CIA Director George] Tenet – when Mr. Tenet examined the information himself – on each of these ten occasions, he said he was convinced by it and said that he would tell the White House that the information was as good as it's going to get. And on each occasion the government decided not to shoot.[383]

By 1998, EIJ had merged with bin Laden's so-called 'al-Qaeda' network. CIA asset Ali Mohamed had written an 'al-Qaeda' manual (*Military studies in the jihad against the tyrants*) which made its way to the Manchester, UK, home of Anas al-Liby,[384] a key operative in the Libyan Islamic Fighting Group which had been paid £100,000 by MI6 to kill Muammar Gaddafi in 1995–96, and whose member, Ramadan Abedi, had a son, Salman, who went on reportedly to murder 22 pop concert-goers in May 2017.

In 1998, EIJ instigated the bombing of two US Embassies in Africa: one in Nairobi (Kenya) and the other in Dar es Salaam (Tanzania). Earlier that year, MI6 agents George and Anthea Temple were stationed in Nairobi and, Anthea claims, knew of an impending attack. MI6 'had under close surveillance Bin Laden's ... frontman in London, Khalid Al-Fawwaz, who had bought him a satellite phone'.[385] On 5 August, EIJ's London branch, run by Abdel Bary, sent a fax to Egypt's newspaper, *al-Hayat*, warning the world that American interests would be attacked. The faxes were sent from bin Laden's London-based Advice and Reformation Committee, run at the time by al-Fawwaz. The fax was traced to Baku, Azerbaijan.[386]

According to the *New Yorker*, 'nearly a year before [the two US embassy bombings in Africa], a member of Al Qaeda had walked into the American Embassy in Nairobi and told the C.I.A. of the bombing plot'. No action was taken. 'In the spring of 1998, one of [FBI counterterrorism chief John] O'Neill's New York friends, a producer at ABC News named Christopher Isham, arranged an interview for a network reporter, John Miller, with Osama bin Laden'. An ABC reporter can find and interview bin Laden – the man who declared war on America – but a military special ops team can't find him and take him out? 'Miller's narration contained information to the effect that one of bin Laden's aides was coop- erating with the F.B.I. The leak of that detail created, in Isham's words, "a firestorm in the bureau." '[387]

Ibrahim Eidarous of EIJ was living in London, having left Azer- baijan.[388] The CIA was monitoring the correspondences of bin Laden's Azerbaijan-Egypt-London-Afghanistan network because the Agency tried to extradite the ARC and EIJ members on terrorism charges, based on those correspondences.[389] The latter's members, including Harun Fazil, Abdullah Ahmed Abdulla, and Abdul Rah- man (not the above-mentioned Rahman), who trained the two US Embassy bombers, made the bombs and gave them instructions over the phone. The US Embassies in Nairobi and Dar es Salaam were destroyed simultaneously, murdering 214.

The bombers – X, Azzam X, Mohammed Odeh, and Mohammed al-Owhali – were to die in the attacks. Al-Owhali survived, however, and was later arrested and interrogated by the Federal Bureau of Investigation.[390] The US sought the extradition of Anas al-Liby, Abdel Bary, Khaled al-Fawwaz and Ibrahim Eidarous on terrorism charges: at least three in connection with the Embassy bombings. Until 2012, Britain protected them all.[391] In the US, one Ali Mohamed was jailed for training the bomb-makers in the Nairobi cell. Mohamed was a double-agent for Egyptian intelligence (who are allies of the US) and was living in North Carolina. He had previously been trained by US Army Special Forces.[392]

Finally, bin Laden was added to the FBI's most wanted list. Again, 'al-Qaeda' was not proscribed by the State Department. Michael Scheuer says: 'On the Sunday before Christmas [1998], we certainly

could have killed him [bin Laden]. He had gone up to Kandahar
from his farm. We happened to have information from a human
asset about which wing of the palace he was in and which room'.
Again, the effort to kill or capture bin Laden was blocked by Clinton's White House, which ordered CIA Director George Tenet, who
then ordered bin Laden Unit director Michael Scheuer, not to move
on the target.[393] It was as late as 1999 that US Secretary of State
Madeleine Albright designated 'al-Qaeda' a Foreign Terrorist
Organization.

Chapter 10

Step 5: False-flags

The most direct state crime against domestic publics is the false-flag. It is the fifth and perhaps most controversial step towards manufacturing terrorism. The most conclusive example of false-flag attacks is NATO's post-WWII stay-behind network, euphemistically called Gladio. Within Italy's Gladio were far-right terrorist networks who used weapons and training to attack civilians and blame left-wing groups. This chapter's Gladio segment mainly focuses on the links between Britain, the US and military networks (including post-war Nazis) across Europe and their blurred lines with terrorists.

'False-flag' derives from naval terminology. A vessel would raise the flag of its enemy and attack either the enemy or its own ships for strategic reasons.[394] Typically, false-flags occur in other territories during times of war. There is a reluctance in many but not all special forces and security service circles to use false-flags at home, as getting caught incurs a higher penalty than getting caught abroad. At home, there are parliamentarians and congress members who are compelled by constituents to ask questions. There is some measure of exposure and accountability. There is also a quasi-functioning media, of which precious few reporters, but some nonetheless, are willing to ask awkward questions and do some digging.

Let's look at some proven false-flag cases throughout recent history before going on to look at Gladio, the most definitive case of a series of major false-flag/proxy operations directed at European citizens, particularly in Italy. Because it was never implemented, we shall discount Operation Northwoods (1962). Northwoods was a Joint Chiefs of Staff plan to frame Castro's Cuba for a wave of attacks against US interests.[395] In this chapter, we shall look only at

a) false-flags that actually occurred and b) where there is near-unanimous agreement about them. Again, 9/11 is not included because there is no agreement on how it was done.

For example: The Gulf of Tonkin incident is often cited as a false-flag operation. The evidence is still murky, but the clearest picture so far is painted by the US Naval Institute. Drawing on declassified records, a publication notes that Tonkin was the result of provocation more than false-flag. The CIA was working with South Vietnamese allies under Operations Plan 34A to provoke opposition forces in the North. The US Navy was conducting reconnaissance and signals intelligence-gathering in the Gulf of Tonkin. The US ship *Maddox* was unaware of this, apparently, and in the area when an OPLAN 34A raid was conducted on Hon Me Island, prompting the North Vietnamese to attack the *Maddox*. All of this context was omitted by President Johnson, who claimed that the US was under attack. This elicited support in Congress to escalate the US war in the North.[396]

To give another example: Some who believe that 9/11 was an inside-job think that the planes were hijacked and crashed into the World Trade Center by US military assets who died in the attacks.[397] Others believe that the planes were remotely controlled.[398] Others believe that there were no planes and that holograms were projected to confuse onlookers.[399] In addition to this lack of agreement (some of which may be disinformation to confuse the issue), it is still not widely accepted in scholarship that it was an inside-job.

In order to make an air-tight case, therefore, we look in this instance only at unanimously agreed upon cases.

False-flags in recent history

Unless you are working for the deep state as a disinformation agent, it is cheap and lazy to smear researchers or people with alternative ideas about certain events as 'conspiracy theorists'. The state and the deep state, as well as corporations, are run on the principle that the general public should know as little about them and their operations as possible, lest the public push for change, as history proves:

Germany: In August 1939, the Nazis staged an invasion of Germany by Polish forces. A German radio station in Gliwice (Gleiwitz) was invaded by seven of Hitler's SS men posing as Polish Army officers. Karl Hornack of the SS made a fake broadcast claiming that the station was in Polish hands. The next day, Hitler withdrew from the non-aggression pact and declared war on Poland, telling the Reichstag: 'Polish Army hooligans ha[ve] finally exhausted our patience'.[400]

Soviet Union: In November 1939, the Soviets under Artillery Marshal Grigory Kulik shelled the Russian village of Mainila, close to the border of Finland. The authorities claimed that the Finns were responsible and withdrew from the Soviet-Finland nonaggression treaty. Stalin then launched the Winter War with Finland.[401]

Israel-Palestine: In 1946, at the request of Labour's first post-war Prime Minister, Clement Attlee, MI6 blew up Jewish refugee ships heading to Palestine as part of its divide and conquer strategy in the post-war Middle East. As part of this so-called Operation Embarrass, Sir Stewart Menzies, head of MI6, suggested inventing a terrorist group, the Defenders of Arab Palestine, on which to blame the murders. It is not clear how many Jews were murdered as a result of the operation.[402]

Northern Ireland: The northeast of Ireland is the one part of the country that Britain retained after the Irish wars of independence. By the late-1960s, the pro-British protestants and London-based political system imposed on the North had oppressed Catholics and/or Republicans to the point that riots and demonstrations broke out. As we have seen in Chapter 6, the British responded with more violence and oppression, which led to the so-called Troubles: an undeclared war waged by the British against Northern Irish republicanism, particularly against the Irish Republican Army (IRA).

The Military Reaction Force (MRF, 1971–73)[*] was secret, a plain-

---

[*] In other books, *Britain's Secret Wars* (2016, Clairview Books, amended for 2nd edition,) and *Human Wrongs* (2018, Iff Books, initial circa 100 copies) I erroneously identified several civilians 'murdered' by the MRF, including Eugene Devlin and Aiden McAloon. They were in fact shot at by the MRF, but fortunately survived.

clothes unit of the 39th Infantry Brigade of the British Army, founded as part of Operation Banner. The infiltration and death squad consisted of around 40 individuals, some ex-Parachute Regiment, Royal Marines, SAS and SBS.[403] It operated mainly in Belfast and used tactics honed in Britain's colonies, including Cyprus and Malaya, says Lt. Col. Tony Le Tissier, formerly of the British Royal Military Police.[404] Operatives later disclosed to the BBC that the British allowed the MRF to murder (Northern) Irish people, including alleged IRA suspects. The MRF used Tommy guns, a weapon of the IRA. A former MRF soldier says: 'We were not there to act like an Army unit, we were there to act like a terror group'.[405]

Both loyalists and republicans set up physical barricades in their areas, partly in response to drive-by murders committed by both sides. The MRF would shoot both unarmed and armed guards ('give 'em a blast', as one MRF soldier said). Because the MRF soldiers wore plain clothes, communities on both sides blamed the other. As the MoD put it in declassified files: 'There can be no useful purpose in admitting the existence of any such organisation ... There seems to be considerable advantage in maintaining as much confusion as possible'.[406]

South Africa: Under Apartheid, the white minority dominated the black majority. By the 1980s, the African National Congress (ANC) was the leading anti-Apartheid political organization. Various state actors working in favour of Apartheid sought to blame the ANC for various acts of terrorism. According to Charles Alfred Zeelie, one-time head of the Bomb Disposal Unit at Witwatersand, the July 1989 bombings of Joubert Park and the J.G. Strydom Hospital were, according to Zeelie's counsel 'false flag operations ... aimed at discrediting the [ANC] ... by creating the impression that the organisation was responsible for the explosions'. Zeelie was tasked with 'submitting false statements supporting the impression that the explosives [sic] were caused by operatives of the ANC'.[407]

In another incident in 1989, Zeelie 'was ordered by his superiors to participate in a false flag attack upon the headquarters of the Flying Squad in Brixton, Johannesburg. The objective was to create the impression that the ANC was responsible for the attack ... and the intention was to discredit the ANC among the white electorate'. Hand grenades and AK47s were used in the attack. In the Charles Landman incident, Zeelie was asked to help blow up the police car of the former, eponymous Murder and Robbery squad chief. The organization behind the false-flag was a covert group within the South African Defence Force, the Civil Cooperation Bureau. Again, the aim was 'discrediting the ANC by bombing the police vehicle of the investigating officer into the [high-profile] murder[s]' at Eikenhof, for which ANC members were charged.[408]

Algeria: The Algerian Civil War ran from 1991 to 2002. The counterinsurgency war was launched by the government and consisted of groups including the main FLN political party, the Army and the Département du Renseignement et de la Sécurité (DRS). Their opposition was the popular Islamic Salvation Front, which had assistance from many groups, including the Armed Islamic Group (GIA).[409] As we have seen, the GIA was partly led by Abu Qatada, who was protected by the British, and linked to the Paris Métro bombing whose alleged perpetrator was also protected by the British. Over 100,000 people died in the war. The DRS not only tortured and murdered, it also committed false-flag operations to further demonize the Islamists. Habib Souaïdia was a DRS officer for six years (1989–95).[410] His book exposes what went on, and he was vindicated when he won a libel case brought against him in France by Algeria's former Defence Minister, Khaled Nezzar.[411]

In 1996, seven Christians were kidnapped and beheaded. The Qatada-linked GIA was blamed by the French and Algerian authorities. Gen. François Buchwalter (Ret.) says it was a false-flag: that the Algerian military murdered them by mistake during a raid and then covered it up by blaming the GIA. Bishop Pierre Claverie was murdered in a car bombing shortly afterwards. Father Armand Veilleux of the Cistercian Order in Rome was sent to investigate the kidnappings. He says Veilleux was murdered, 'probably [because] he knew too much'. Neither the French nor the Algerian governments launched any inquiries into the deaths.[412]

The USA: In 2001, shortly after the 9/11 attacks, the US was hit with a wave of anthrax packages delivered to journalists and to congressmen Tom Daschle and Pat Leahy – both of whom opposed the Patriot Act 2001, which, as we saw in the Introduction, expanded state powers over Americans. Five people were murdered by the anthrax in the following months. The letters that accompanied them were written in block capitals and read, in part: 'Death to America. Death to Israel. Allah is great'.[413] The anthrax was traced to the Department of Defence biological warfare laboratory at Fort Detrick, Maryland.[414] In November, the FBI announced that it was looking for a rogue agent.[415] But the executive wanted the FBI to blame Muslims. Then-FBI director Robert Mueller says that President George W. Bush pressured him to blame the attacks on 'al-Qaeda' and Iraq. 'They really wanted to blame somebody in the Middle East', said Mueller.[416]

The FBI tried to pin the blame on scientist Steven J. Hatfill. They later tried to blame scientist Bruce E. Ivins. Ivins worked for the American Red Cross and had been awarded the DoD's highest civilian award in 2003, the Secretary of Defense Medal for Valor. The Defense Secretary at the time was Donald Rumsfeld, PNAC member (see Chapter 1) and Bush administration official. Ivins supposedly committed suicide during the investigations.[417]

Gladio

Details are sketchy as to precise dates, but starting circa 1947, based in part on a plan devised by British PM Churchill, the British MI6 and the newly-founded US CIA established a network of guerrilla 'armies' across Europe to repel any potential Soviet invasion; at least that was the stated aim of the secret operations. The Italian version was called Gladio, after *gladius* the double-edged sword. The 'double-edge' was that the networks could repel the Soviets but also act against left-wing elements within their own countries. Gladio became an informal term for the loose network of operations, many of which were eventually run out of a NATO office in Belgium.

But Gladio quickly became a proxy weapon against politicians and left-wing groups that the CIA and MI6 opposed. By committing false-flag attacks against civilians, US-British-trained operatives created a climate of fear across Europe. As a BBC documentary of the early-1990s put it: 'For 40 years, secret terrorist organisations, many trained by Western intelligence agencies, have manipulated the political control of European sovereign states by a campaign of terror and murder'.[418] In November 1990, Nigel West (real name Rupert Allason, a Tory and editor of *Intelligence Quarterly Magazine*), told the Associated Press: 'We [the British] were heavily involved and still are', helping to 'finance and run' the networks.[419]

Senior British military sources speaking on the condition of anonymity told the *Guardian* that by 1940, British guerrilla networks had placed weapon caches all over Europe, following the fall of France. Drawn from the Special Force Ski Battalion of the Scots Guards, members included Brigadier 'Mad' Mike Calvert.[420] Former NATO Commander in Northern Europe, Sir Anthony Farrar-Hockley confirmed that after WWII networks of arms were established in the UK, but he refused to confirm Gladio's contemporary existence.[421] As further proof of the UK's deep involvement: In 1991, Belgian Col. Jean Bodart of military intelligence collected a list of Gladio members working in Belgium from British intelligence agents who met him at RAF Northolt.[422]

According to a US Senate report, the CIA established stay-behind networks in Eastern Europe, including Ukraine, in 1947. 'The CIA assumed the espionage task, running agents and organizing "stay-behind networks" in the event the Soviets rolled west. Agents, mostly refugees, were sent into the East to report on Soviet forces and, in particular, any moves that signalled war'.[423]

The stay-behind units were coordinated from 1948 onwards under the Clandestine Committee of the Western Union, later the Clandestine Planning Committee (CPC, 1951) and overseen by the Belgian-based SHAPE, Supreme Headquarters Allied Command. Ganser writes: 'Only officers with the highest NATO security clearances were allowed to enter CPC headquarters'. They were reportedly 'under the guidance of CIA and MI6 experts'. The chiefs of the Western European Secret Services 'met at regular intervals during the year in order to coordinate measures of non-orthodox warfare in Western Europe'.[424]

In 1953, CIA director Allen Dulles authorized the expansion of stay-behind networks across Europe.[425] The networks gradually operated in: Austria (ÖWSGV), Belgium (SDRA8), Britain (Operation Stay Behind), Denmark (*Absalon*), Finland (?), France (*La Rose des Vents* and *Arc-en-ciel*), Germany (KIBITZ), Greece (Red Sheepskin), Italy (Gladio), the Netherlands (Operatiën en Inlichtinge), Norway (ROCAMBOLE), Portugal (Aginter Press), Spain (where under General Franco, 'Gladio was the government' – former Defence Minister Alberto Oliart),[426] Sweden (Sveaborg), Switzerland (Projekt-26) and Turkey (Counter-Guerrilla). The US denies any links to terrorism, citing the *Westmoreland Field Manual*, which it says was a Soviet forgery. Forgery or not, the fact remains that Gladio networks did commit terrorism across Europe.

Future director of the CIA William Colby was tasked with establishing Scandinavia's network in 1951. Colby acknowledged that the CIA funded the right-wing Christian Democrats and other anti-leftist parties in Italy during the Cold War. The plot also involved paying Italian agent provocateurs, such as Robert Cavallaro, a businessman who was paid to demonstrate against the Soviets.[427] What follows is a small sample of Gladio activities in post-War Europe. In addition to those, Gladio operatives and rightwing extremists connected to them played a role in coups and terrorism in Algeria, Greece and Turkey:

Austria: The British Imperial War Museum's *Secret Wars* exhibition describes an '[e]xplosives pack developed by MI6 to be hidden in potentially hostile territory. It could remain buried for years without any deterioration of its contents'. A booklet reads: 'In the British zone of occupation in Austria, junior Royal Marine officers were detached from normal duties to prepare supply caches in the mountains and liaise with locally recruited agents'. At Fort Monckton, Portsmouth, the SAS and Royal Marines trained officers Michael Giles and Simon Preston, who in turn trained and recruited Austria's Gladio operatives.[428]

Belgium: Britain's involvement began in 1948, when PM Paul-Henri Spaak authorized the secret service (the *Staatsveiligheid*) to contact Britain's MI6, headed by Sir Stewart Menzies (the same

Menzies who had authorized the murder of Jewish refugees and tried to blame it on Arabs in 1948). Between 1982 and 1985, apparently deranged, masked gunmen murdered 28 people in a murder and robbery spree across Belgian supermarkets (the Brabant killings). NATO's Gladio networks used planned robberies as training exercises. The far-right Westland New Post was led by Paul Latinus, who claims to have been involved in a Belgian Gladio unit responsible for the Brabant killings. The job of Latinus and his second-in-command Michel Libert was to pass surveillance information on to the Gladio unit.[429]

There is no evidence connecting the UK to the murders, but the British were training Belgian Gladio units as late as 1989 (at the least). Col. S. Schwebach of the Belgian intelligence service told the Defence Minister that an exercise called Waterland had occurred that year, in which the Royal Marines Special Boat Service landed in Flanders and was guided by Belgian civilians. As late as October 1990, weapon caches were spread across Belgium, according to a former army intelligence officer, speaking to the Associated Press.[430]

France: In 1947, the CIA and British SAS under Plan Bleu established France's stay-behind network, followed by the Western Union Clandestine Committee (WUCC) to coordinate the other networks. The WUCC was then integrated into French NATO under the name Clandestine Planning Committee. In 1958, NATO founded the Allied Clandestine Committee. The French Gladio was established with help from the Service de Documentation Extérieure et de Contre-Espionnage and the 11e régiment parachutiste de choc (11th Shock Parachute Regiment). By 1959, the somewhat anti-US French President and former leader of the Resistance, Charles de Gaulle, was in power. Despite de Gaulle's expulsion of NATO, the French Gladio networks continued to operate. Agent Philip Agee said at the time that the CIA 'want to stop the left from coming to power, and want even more to stop Communist participation in the government. For the CIA this is evidently the priority and priorities'.[431]

Germany: One of the earliest Gladio operations was the CIA's organization of KIBITZ networks. These involved working with Nazi *SS* officers and members of the German Wehrmacht.[432] A declassified CIA report from September 1951 notes, 'the impracticability of our previous concept of small one- and two-man stay-behind teams. We therefore have directed KIBITZs 6 and 10 to flesh out their units to fuller operating strength'.[433] In the early-1950s, a group of CIA-trained *SS* and Waffen-*SS* officers, together with the far-right Federation of German Youth, were primed to assassinate the opposition Social Democratic Party, supposedly in the event of a Soviet invasion.[434]

The Nazi Gladio networks had loose and frequently changing associations with other pan-European fascist groups. For example, the Belgian Jean-François Thiriart established the Mouvement d'Action Civique, which was funded by the Algerian OAS (Organisation armée secrète, which opposed independence from France) and the Portuguese secret police; the former, as we shall see below, was connected to Gladio. Thiriart met with Adolf von Thadden, the neo-Nazi leader of the far-right German National Democratic Party.[435] Von Thadden turned out to be an MI6 agent working undercover.[436] Thitiart also met with the fascist Oswald Mosley of the Union Movement in an effort to create a National Party of Europe. Other groups included the Nouvelle Ordre Européen/ Europäische Neuo-Ordnung (NOE/ENO). An NOE/ENO offshoot was the Junge Europäische Legion (JEL, Young European League). JEL members were connected to the Bund Heimattreuer Jugend (BHJ, Homeland Youth Federation).[437]

In 1980, a bomb at a festival murdered twelve. After the blast, German media received calls from people claiming to be Italians taking responsibility for the bombing. The bomb fragments and detonator went missing. The bomber, Gundolf Köhler, who died in the blast, was carrying a suitcase which disappeared from the crime scene. Before the blast he was seen arguing with two men. Although police said he acted alone, a witness said she saw two men standing over Köhler's body, one of whom shouted: 'I didn't want it! It's not my fault! Just kill me!'. Seemingly by coincidence, another key eyewitness named Frank Lauterjung was regional commander and deputy national leader of the BHJ, another organization with loose connections to the German Gladio, as noted above. Lauterjung was inspired by the Nazi, Hans-Ulrich Rudel,[438] who was linked to Thiriart.[439] BHJ colleagues believed Lauterjung to be a provocateur: After being expelled from the BHJ he joined the Socialist German Student Union.

Portugal: In 1966, the CIA established the fake publishing agency Aginter Press, led by Captain Yves Guérin-Sérac, who had previously co-founded the OAS, which fought on the side of the French during the Algerian War (1954–62). Aginter Press operated in Italy under the acronym OACI. Guérin-Sérac had links to Guido Giannettini of the Italian Gladio. Via the extreme right Ordine Nuovo and Avanguardia Nazionale groups, Giannettini was connected to the 1969 Piazza Fontana bombing in Italy (more below). According to the Italian judge Guido Salvini, Guérin-Sérac, along with an American called Jay Salby and rightists from France, Italy and Spain, planted bombs in the Algerian embassies of Britain, France, Germany and Italy. The bombers left markings indicating that the Algerian opposition was responsible.[440]

Switzerland: Until as late as 1988 (at least), according to Swiss court documents and admissions by Swiss colonels, the UK was training Projekt-26 guerrillas, led by Efrem Cattelan, in combat, communications and sabotage without the knowledge of the Swiss government.[441] Cattelan told *The Observer*: 'English colleagues … instructed [Swiss Gladio operatives] in general training, like covert operations and parachute jumps at night in which England has had exceptionally good experience since the war [i.e., WWII]'. Exercises included Targum (annually from 1973 to 1979) and Cravat and Susanne every few years between 1976 to 1988. Swiss judges revealed that some Swiss agents were trained in Britain and some were using false identities to obtain fishing permits (presumably to train in survival skills).[442]

Gladio Italy

Italy is a special case because it would appear that the most Gladio-related terror occurred there. Italy's Gladio reportedly began in

1958. General Pietro Corona headed the so-called R office from 1969–70 and told the Venetian judicial inquiry that 'parallel to Gladio' there existed 'an alternative clandestine network ... which knew about the arms and explosive dumps and who had access to them'.[443] In late-1969, 16 were killed when four car bombs exploded in Milan and Rome. The attacks were blamed on communists and leftists, but covered up by the state. A judge found that the right-wing Ordine Nuovo organization had collaborated closely with the Italian military's secret service, SID. They carried out the Peteano car bombing in 1972, which killed three police officers, blaming the extreme left Red Brigades (*Brigate Rossa*, founded in 1970).[444]

General Gerardo Serravalle told the Italian parliament that Gladio units were trained in the UK in 1974, during a spate of right-wing terror attacks in Italy. Gladio operatives not connected with terrorism, including Army doctor Decimo Garau, visited the UK for parachute and other training with the SAS in Poole in the Southwest, and in Hereford.[445]

One convicted Gladio terrorist, Vincenzo Vincegeurra, told the BBC that via his network the state was engaged in a 'strategy of tension': 'You were supposed to attack civilians, women, children, innocent people outside the political arena. For one simple reason: To force the Italian public to turn to the State. To turn to the regime and ask for greater security'. He goes on: 'This was precisely the role of the Right in Italy. It placed itself at the service of the State which created a strategy, aptly called the "Strategy of tension"'. The Strategy operated from the 1960s until the mid-1980s, says Vincegeurra.[446] Elsewhere, Vincegeurra stated that one of the goals of the parallel Gladio was 'preventing a slip to the left in the political balance of the country. This they did, with the assistance of the official secret services and the political and military forces'.[447]

In 1978, Italy's former PM and head of the Christian Democracy party, Aldo Moro, was kidnapped and murdered by the supposedly extreme left Red Brigades. Moro had written that the 'secret services of the West ... might be implicated in the destabilisation of our country'.[448] CIA Colonel Oswald Le Winter, a Gladio liaison officer, said the Red Brigades were run by intelligence agents.[449]

In 1980, Italy's Bologna train station was bombed, killing 82 people. It was blamed on left-wing groups, but two Italian secret agents were later convicted. Without mentioning the bombing, General Nino Lugarere, head of Italy's military intelligence agency the SISMI from 1981–84, testified that 800 or so individuals made up a Super Gladio unit responsible for 'internal intervention'.[450] Indicative of the extent of Britain's role, the UK refused to extradite from London the suspect Roberto Fiore who was wanted for questioning about the Bologna bombing, in which at least two British citizens were killed.[451]

Gladio in the Courts: Gladio was exposed in Italy's Parliament during the Presidency of Francesco Cossigo by PM Giulio Andreotti. The CIA translated an article which appeared in *Rome La Repubblica*, which says: 'Every time the legitimacy of the "stay-behind structure" is called into question, the head of state has "hit the ceiling." And he has reviled, one after the other, those who have voiced their doubts'. The Venetian judge Felice Casson called Gladio a 'political conspiracy'.[452] In response to Andreotti's revelations, a US government official 'familiar with Operation Gladio ... would not comment on allegations that Gladio was part of a broad resistance network throughout Western Europe'.[453]

The British parliamentary record on Gladio is remarkably sparse, even for the UK, which is notorious for its secrecy. In 1992, Labour MP Paul Flynn asked the Secretary of State for Defence, Archie Hamilton (Tory), to comment 'on the public disclosure of information on the activities of and United Kingdom support for Operation Gladio since its inception'. Hamilton replied: 'It has been the policy of successive Governments not to comment on matters of this nature. This remains the policy'.[454]

According to the European Parliament's *Resolution on the Gladio Affair* (1990): 'for over 40 years this organization has escaped all democratic controls and has been run by the secret services of the states concerned in collaboration with NATO'. The resolution calls on member states, 'to monitor their links with the respective state intelligence services and their links, if any, with terrorist action groups and/or other illegal practices'.[455]

Chapter 11

Step 6: Simulations

The sixth and final step towards manufacturing terrorism is to simply fake an event. Secret agents are actors by nature: they have to pose as people they are not in order to set traps and get information. It is not difficult, with the kind of resources that the deep state has, to use its agents to act out a 'terrorist' event that never happened. The rise of digital image manipulation, military cyber commands and real-world counterterrorism/crisis exercises and drills, with very realistic props, only serve to further blur the line between reality and simulation. Some drills are included here to illustrate the frequency of exercise/real event coincidences.

Elements of the deep state can get away with fakery because there is no culture of absolute incredulity in the media. Even the best-intentioned journalists and editors will not dig deep into a fake terrorism story; even after the event has been exposed as a hoax, as in the case of the Iraq car bombing below. Overwhelmingly, media take at face value the information given to them by the police and secret services, including unnamed 'security officials'. This is a general problem for the public, not just when it comes to reporting terrorism and inadvertently covering up for the state. Researcher Katrin Voltmer, whose chapter appeared in a book on governance by the World Bank Group, notes: 'Research into news and journalism indicates that for various structural reasons, the media's ability to fulfill their democratic roles often does not live up to textbook ideals. One important reason is the reliance of the media on official sources'.[456] A dialectic exists in which buffoonish online personalities like Alex Jones of InfoWars rave that everything is a conspiracy. Journalists do not want to lose credibility by association and are thus even less inclined to ask questions about the possibility of simulated events.

For their part, the British police are lower in the power hierarchy than MI5 and MI6. (We've already examined cases in Ireland where the secret services directed the police to green-light terrorists.) Those agencies can deny the police evidence and even present them with fake evidence. In this closing chapter, we look at digital fakery, counterterror exercises (and how they often coincide with real events) and at least one event (a car bombing in Iraq) that proved to be entirely fake yet was reported as real by mainstream western media.

Ones & zeros: 'Launch fake terrorist operations'

Increasingly realistic digital productions raise serious questions about the authenticity of certain events and statements attributed to terrorists.

The digital revolution: In 1999, ex-US Army soldier and journalist, William Arkin, wrote in the *Washington Post* an exposé of military advances in digital fakery. US General Carl W. Steiner announced: '[W]e are going to overthrow the United States government'. Or so it sounded. Steiner actually said something entirely mundane, but US military voice morphing specialists fed his statements into a computer and altered them to say something entirely new: a conspiracy to overthrow the government. At Los Alamos National Laboratory in New Mexico (home of the atomic bomb), a team of scientists led by George Papcun developed technology, 'to clone speech patterns and develop an accurate facsimile ... in near real time'.[457]

Daniel T. Kuehl of the US Defense University's Information Operations department told Arkin: '[o]nce you can take any kind of information and reduce it to ones and zeros, you can do some pretty interesting things'. Arkin writes: 'Digital morphing ... has come of age, available for use in psychological operations [PSYOPS]'. As noted in the Introduction, PSYOPS are a core part of the Pentagon's P2OG strategy. 'Being able to manufacture convincing audio or video', says the US military, 'might be the difference in a successful military operation or coup'. Kuehl says: 'We already know that seeing isn't necessarily believing ... [N]ow I guess hearing isn't either'.[458]

The Hollywood movie *Forrest Gump* (1994) pioneered the use of digitally altering old stock footage (e.g., of President Lyndon B. Johnson) and adding new footage (e.g., of actor Tom Hanks playing Forrest Gump) to make it look as though fictional characters were involved in real events. 'For Hollywood, it is special effects', says Arkin. 'For covert operations in the U.S. military and intelligence agencies, it is a weapon of the future'.

By 1990, US military digital video manipulation was sophisticated enough for US PSYOPS units to consider using it in anti-Iraq propaganda. The units considered using 'computer-faked' video of Iraq's dictator (and former US-British ally) Saddam Hussein acting in 'unmanly' ways (such as crying) in order to damage his credibility. Others suggested staging footage of Saddam in sexually compromising situations. Videotapes of the footage would then be distributed throughout the region.[459]

Since the 1970s (as part of Project Pandora), the US has had the power to implant direct sounds (including voices) into people's heads at a distance, using electromagnetic waves as sound carriers: voice-to-skull (V2K). The US military also claims to have developed 3D holographic technology. As part of Gulf War PSYOPS, units considered beaming a 3D image of Allah, which would have to be invented as there are no images of Allah, combined with directions to Iraqis to surrender via V2K technology. Until the 2003 invasion, Iraq was not a particularly religious country by the standards of the region. The idea was therefore abandoned as unrealistic.[460]

Saddam and Osama: The CIA planned to make fake videos of Osama bin Laden drinking alcohol and bragging about sexual conquests with boys. CIA employees would play fellow 'al-Qaeda' members in the videos, according to agents involved. The CIA Operations Division leaders, James Pavitt and Hugh Turner, reportedly rejected the idea. In the run-up to the Iraq invasion (2003), the CIA's Iraq Operations Group plotted to make a fake video of Saddam having sex with a teenage boy.[461] Another idea included getting 'Saddam' to cede power to his son, Uday. The CIA's Office of Technical Services has the capacity to hack into live TV broadcasts and insert spoof information. They planned to insert crawls — messages on the bottom of the screen — into Iraqi news-casts.

Although the CIA allegedly had no luck selling these ideas to the top decision-makers, the Army's PSYOP units at Fort Bragg reportedly considered them, as they had the budget to conduct such operations.

In 2002, following rumours of his demise, an audio tape of Osama bin Laden emerged in which he (or an impostor, or a digital morph of his voice) refers to then-current events. In a study for France 2 television, Swiss researchers at the Dalle Molle Institute for Perceptual Artificial Intelligence ran hours of genuine bin Laden audio and compared it to the 2002 bin Laden audio. The software they used was developed for bank security. In 19 out of 20 tests, it correctly recognized bin Laden's voice. It then tested the 2002 audio and concluded with a 95% certainty that it was not bin Laden.[462]

In 2004, video of bin Laden emerged in which he threatened more terrorism. But controversy arose over the fact that the grey bin Laden was sporting a black beard. Soon, a debate raged on the internet about whether it was in accordance with Islamic law to dye one's hair during battle. (The fact that the man in the video looked nothing like bin Laden should have been enough of a clue.) In a 2007 video released by al-Qaeda, bin Laden delivers his latest *fatwa*. But according to NBC News, a private computer security consultant called Dr Neal Krawetz says: 'Here is Bin Laden in the same cloth-ing, same studio, same studio setup, and same desk THREE YEARS LATER' (emphasis in original). This time, bin Laden has a grey beard, leading some to suspect that the audio was real but the images had been altered by 'al-Qaeda' to make bin Laden look healthier than he was. However, when Krawetz layered the videos over one another, the forgery became apparent. Because of pauses in the video, Krawetz reckons that 'al-Qaeda' layered old video over new sound. But this is implausible because the voice and mouth movements are in synchronization, except for long instances of video freezing.[463]

Blurring the lines: George W. Bush's Deputy Assistant Attorney

General, John Yoo (notorious for drafting the 'torture memos'[464] and now a Professor at UC Berkeley) wrote an article for the *LA Times* (2005) in which he advocated 'new ways to go on the offensive' against what he claimed was a non-hierarchical 'al-Qaeda'. '[T]he U.S. could give Al Qaeda some competition', wrote Yoo: 'cause its nodes to switch allegiances, much in the way that competitors in the computer market seek users to switch products'. Yoo concludes:

> Another tool would have our intelligence agencies create a false terrorist organization. It could have its own websites, recruitment centers, training camps and fundraising operations. It could launch fake terrorist operations and claim credit for real terrorist strikes, helping to sow confusion within Al Qaeda's ranks, causing operatives to doubt others' identities and to question the validity of communications.[465]

In 2007, the UK Ministry of Defence published the 3rd edition of its *Strategic Trends Porgramme*, predicting events out to the year 2036. 'Advances in social science, behavioural science and mathematical modelling *will* combine, leading to more informed decision making', it says. 'Advanced processing and computational power *will* permit a new level of pattern recognition (Combinatronics) enabling the decoding of previously unrecognised or undecipherable systems and allowing the modelling of a range of biological to social, political and economic processes'. It does not go into what these processes are or may be. 'As a result, simulation and representatives *will* have a significant and widespread impact on the future and *will* become an increasingly powerful tool to aid policy and decision makers'. The emphasis on economics and politics brings to mind Yoo's idea quoted above, to set up fake terror networks in the digital world to discourage recruitment in the real world. The proof that the simulations mentioned by the MoD will have real-world effects and not be limited to cyberspace, is evidenced in the final line of the report: 'It will also blur the line between illusion and reality' (emphases in original).[466]

Fake 'al-Qaeda' videos: From 2006 to December 2011, the Pentagon paid Britain's Bell Pottinger PR company $500m to make fake 'al-Qaeda' video segments from the Baghdad Camp Victory base under the command of the US Information Operations Task Force and the Joint Psychological Operations Task Force. (Financial records start from May 2007. There is no suggestion here that the company engaged in illegal activity.) The company hired 300 staff for these operations alone. Documents unearthed by the Bureau of Investigative Journalism verify the claims. Video editor Martin Wells, who worked for the company, blew the whistle.[467]

According to Wells, these so-called information operations consisted of making fake TV commercials, 'portraying al Qaeda in a negative light'. Others included filming news items as if they were made by 'Arabic TV' (whatever that means). Finally, low-definition videos of 'al-Qaeda bombings' were also staged and sent out to TV stations around the world. Turning to black ops, Wells confirmed that special units would make mock 'al-Qaeda' videos for him to edit. The files would be burnt to CDs and planted on targets during raids on Iraqi houses. Wells would encode the CDs, linking them to a Google Analytics account to provide lists of IP addresses. Thanks to the internet, uploads of the fake videos could be watched anywhere in the world and traced to the homes of viewers. These included Iraqis who might be sympathetic to 'al-Qaeda'.[468]

Fake accounts: The Joint Threat Research Intelligence Group (JTRIG) is a unit of Britain's Government Communications Headquarters, the listening agency. JTRIG was exposed by the US private contractor Edward Snowden, who was working for the US National Security Agency. JTRIG specializes in online provocations and false-flags against all manner of targets.

One leaked JTRIG report from 2011 states: 'JTRIG staff use a range of techniques to, for example, discredit, disrupt, delay, deny, degrade, and deter'. Techniques used by JTRIG operatives include: 'uploading YouTube videos containing persuasive messages; establishing online aliases with Facebook and Twitter accounts, blogs and forum memberships for conducting HUMINT [human intelligence] or encouraging discussion on specific issues; sending spoof emails and text messages as well as providing spoof online resources; and setting up spoof trade sites'.[469] Activists who may appear to be making strange or criminal posts or videos online could be victims of, or operatives working for, JTRIG.

The report advocates applying social, cognitive and neurosciences to online manipulation methods: 'social cognition, attitudes, persuasive communications, conformity, obedience, interpersonal relationships, trust and distrust, and psychological profiling'. Work should draw on research from 'advertising and marketing, and from criminology (i.e., crime prevention)'. The MoD's Defence Science and Technology Laboratory (DSTL) is advised to develop a programme which 'measures the generalisability of specific social influence techniques across cultural groups representative of the types of targets of interest to defence and security organisations so that techniques can be applied appropriately'. DSTL, according to the report, should create a programme to assess, 'the feasibility of compiling psychological profiles based on information available about the individual on the internet so that those conducting online HUMINT [Human Intelligence] operations can compile and exploit such profiles'. Interestingly, the report categorizes 'online HUMINT and effects' as 'doing things in cyberspace to make something happen'.[470]

JTRIG goes so far as to advocate creating fake online digital publications. (Keep this in mind because we discuss the ISIS publication *Dabiq* below. There is no evidence that the UK MoD specifically fabricated Issue 15 of *Dabiq*, but the MoD documents show that such general intentions exist.) JTRIG advocates '[p]roviding spoof online resources such as magazines and books that provide inaccurate information (to disrupt, delay, deceive, discredit, promote distrust, dissuade, deter or denigrate/degrade)'. This would make framing people easy. Extremist articles appearing to be written by individuals who are later blamed by the media for alleged assassinations, for instance, could be used to indict innocent victims and frame them for events perpetrated by the deep state: 'Staff suggested that the success of an operation may be threatened by factors such as the: ... Lack of photographs/visual images of online aliases', which implies their plan to produce fake photos and video.[471]

The ISIS forgery: The Islamic State of Iraq and Syria (ISIS) and its numerous monikers is not a monolithic organization. In addition, states on all sides have used it for their own short-term strategic advantages. These factors, coupled with the lack of credible on-the-ground reporting, make finding the truth almost impossible. But evidence of duplicity exists.

The ex-Israeli military officer Rita Katz allegedly has a history of fabricating information, which she denies. For example, Katz claims to have written a book (as Anonymous) called *Terrorist Hunter*, which purported to be an undercover exposé of *jihadis* preaching hate in US mosques. Many of the quotes actually came from preachers preaching in their own countries and can be found easily online.[472] Katz later founded the US-based private organization with links to the Pentagon, Search for International Terrorist Entities (SITE), which has an impressive ability to find terrorist videos and statements supposedly posted on the dark web. Even Katz with her dubious record confirmed that the cyber-attacks against ISIS were being conducted by the US. She writes: 'As governments and vigilantes around the world continue targeting IS online, apps circulated outside of Google Play or iOS stores provide new opportunities to plant disguised malware into the mix, and thus infiltrate the community. And indeed, as seen in [the June 1 (2016)] warning by IS of fake apps, such entities appear to be doing just that'.[473]

In July 2014, the Islamic State of Iraq and the Levant started publishing a propaganda magazine call *Dabiq*. In April 2016, the *New York Times* reported that the US Cyber Command was disrupting ISIS and ISIL operations: 'The goal of the new campaign is to disrupt the ability of the Islamic State to spread its message, attract new adherents, circulate orders from commanders and carry out day-to-day functions, like paying its fighters'.[474] Two months after the Pentagon announced its cyber war on ISIS, ISIS issued a statement that Issue 15 of *Dabiq* is a forgery and is *not* authored by them:

Brothers and sisters, We noticed that dubious attempts were made to spread a fake Dabiq magazine issue (claimed to be 'Issue 15', with two varying covers) ... We would like to clarify that Al-Hayat Media Center has not yet released any new Dabiq issues. We advise you not to download this fake magazine for your own safety.[475]

Iraq car bomb: the deaths that never were

An area of Baghdad called Al-Hurriyah (The Freedom) is the focus of this subchapter. There was a real car bombing there in October 2016, but the victims were fake. This is proven beyond doubt in CCTV video broadcast on LiveLeak[476] and confirmed and analyzed by Bellingcat,[477] the darling private organization of the British intelligence and mainstream western media.[478]

Al-Hurriyah: Like the British before them, the US played a deadly game of divide and rule in Iraq. The country is Shia majority, with a sizeable Sunni minority. Among ordinary Iraqis, religious affiliation didn't matter. There were mixed marriages and mixed neighbourhoods.[479] The US-British-supported regime of Saddam Hussein (1979–2003) played its own divide-and-rule game by absorbing a quarter of a million Sunni into his Baath Party's military-police apparatus.[480] (Using minorities to oppress majorities is also an old technique: In India, the British sided with the Muslim minority against the Hindu majority in the early years of colonial rule. In Sri Lanka, the British used the minority Tamils to oppress the majority Sinhalese. And so on.)

After the occupation, when Saddam was no longer the West's favourite dictator, the US and Britain 'de-Baathified' Iraq, laying off hundreds of thousands of Sunni. Meanwhile, US-led Shia death-squads were paid to murder alleged Saddam loyalists (the so-called Salvador Option).[481] As foreign 'al-Qaeda' fighters poured into Iraq (Sunni Salafist/Wahhabis), Shia areas were attacked and Sunnis in general blamed. Eventually, some Sunnis sided with the Shia and the occupiers and fought against 'al-Qaeda in Iraq' (Sunni Awakening).[482] Meanwhile, the US-British Shia-majority puppet government was killing fellow Shia of the Mahdi Army, an anti-occupation force led by Muqtada al-Sadr. By 2010, the Mahdi Army was back in Baghdad's Shia-majority Al-Hurriyah district.[483] By this time, the rival Islamic State was gaining ground, supposedly under the radar of most Western media. The Islamic State has its roots in 'al-Qaeda' and is comprised almost exclusively of Sunni extremists, the Salafi/ Wahhabi types.

In brief, multiple actors, including US special forces, had an interest in Iraqi districts, including Al-Hurriyah. The above are just some of the higher-profile actors. But who would have the resources and the motive to detonate a car bomb and pay actors to pretend to be killed and/or injured, when a real terrorist organization or army could (and do) do it for real and actually murder people?

Context: The fake deaths occurred during the 40-day period of Shia mourning for the grandson of the Prophet Mohammed. It became an especially dangerous time for Shia since the Anglo-American invasion because Sunni opposition groups have the opportunity to target large numbers of mourners. In addition, the fake deaths took place during the US-British-Iraqi government's mass destruction of Mosul (Kurdistan, Northern Iraq), supposedly in their efforts to 'liberate' it from ISIS.[484] Finally, the Iraqi government told international media that a wave of bombs had exploded across Iraq on 30 October, presumably in revenge for or as a tactic against the Mosul offensive. It is not known how many other of these bombings are fake. But the one in Al-Hurriyah was, for sure.

The explosion: On 30 October 2016, a CCTV camera captured video of a man (the bomber) doing something to a parked car in an empty street of Al-Hurriyah in daylight hours. To date, no one knows who the CCTV belongs to or who uploaded the footage to the internet. It is important to remember that the CCTV footage was filmed off a computer screen with a handheld camera by an unknown person, worsening the quality. No one knows why the CCTV footage is incomplete (it runs for just over two minutes, as opposed to the hours and hours which can be captured). Also, the trees in the video are red, indicating that a colour channel swap has occurred for an unknown reason. (Digital colour is based on an

RGB system; red, green, blue.) The camera's timestamp is wrong. It reads '03.40'. But sunrise in Baghdad in October begins at 0600.[485] Based on media reports that follow, we can assume that the time was 3.40pm, or 15.40.

Returning to the content: The car does not appear to have any passengers inside and is parked next to a scorched wall. The wall appears to be a reinforced blast wall, as it appears to sustain no damage and is grey, unlike the beige-colour surrounding walls. This would suggest that the bomb was strategically placed near a blast wall so as not to cause damage to surrounding property. The bomber gets into a white truck. There is a second man in the truck who appears to swap seats. The truck drives away out of sight.

Approximately 10 seconds later, the car explodes on the empty street, scattering metal debris everywhere. Approximately 10 seconds after the explosion, 16 people (including, it would appear, at least one child) run to the scene. Many of them wear red (possibly green due to the colour channel swap). At least seven non-red-wearers lie down, pretending to be dead or wounded. One individual in white waves a white van onto the scene. As a man in red gets out of the van, another enters the frame, pretending to treat a man pretending to be wounded. None appear to be from the Red Cross or Iraqi Red Crescent, as those organizations wear unique jackets, not random red shirts; added to which the actors in the video don't have those organizations' logos emblazoned on their clothes. The mock-dead and mock-injured are stretchered into the van by the mock-onlookers.

The full CCTV footage is not available, so from the limited content from the leaked video we can ascertain that the simulation was well-coordinated: We can assume there was no petrol in the car, otherwise the bomb explosion would have risked exploding the petrol tank at a later time, killing and injuring for real the crisis actors. This means that the car was towed there. We can also assume that the car had had the glass removed, otherwise the actors might have injured themselves by lying on glass fragments. (The low-resolution makes it hard to tell for sure.)

The aftermath: Another shaky, apparently amateur video emerged shortly after the event. It was taken at the scene, presumably by a curious local who approached the car, in the immediate aftermath. The actors playing the role of dead and injured had already been taken into the white van, mentioned above. It is not clear where are the other actors, who pretended to help. The video depicts crowds of Iraqis (mostly men) standing around talking, as well as motorbikes (common there) weaving in and out of onlookers who do not seem to realize that, although it was a real explosion, it was staged and that the 'victims' were actors. The smoky ruins of the car can be seen, which is still parked by the wall next to which it exploded. There is a red fire engine and firefighters are present, trying to put out the smoke. Interestingly, there are blood stains and pieces of torn clothing (including what appear to be sandals) on the ground, indicating that whoever faked the event also placed fake blood and shredded clothing to heighten the realism.

Next, we see two Iraqi police officers dressed in black talking on a communications system. A line of school children with their backpacks walk by, accompanied by their mothers. (Children go to Sunday schools in Iraq.) The video shows a white truck parked several dozen metres from the scene, in the same direction in which the bomber's white truck moved. Is it the same truck? The video shows a little girl in uniform looking terrified, quite a distance from the explosion, now on the main street. The cameraman seems to know the girl.

The video was posted on Twitter by the Iraq Network Press. The tweet (Google translation) says: 'A new clip of an eyewitness camera confirming the video of the surveillance camera, which documented the car bomb explosion in Al-Hurriya district on 30/10/2016'.[486]

ISIS claim: The same day, via its alleged Amāq News Agency, someone or some organization purporting to be the Islamic State claimed responsibility for the bombing. As noted above, unknown intelligence agencies are falsely attributing statements and sources to the Islamic State.

The media: According to Bellingcat, the first report of the Hurriyah bombing came from a small agency called Adhamiyah News via Twitter. The tweet reads (Google translation): 'Baghdad operations ... The explosion [in Freedom/Al-Hurriyah] was caused by a car bomb explosion parked near a shop'. Bellingcat traces the second report to the small, Egypt-based Reyhan News.[487]

According to the wire feed, the Associated Press reported at 1.30pm (Baghdad time) that Shia militias were joined by thousands of fighters in their war against ISIS in Mosul. At 1.45pm, AP reported: Turkey's PM Erdoğan warned that Turkey could counterattack if Shia forces hurt Turkey's interests in the Iraqi-Turkmen town of Tel Afar, near the border. At 2.15pm, AP's Qassim Abul-Zahra in Ibril, Iraq, reported that an Iraqi army helicopter crashed in the central province, Salahuddin. Iraqi officials 'spoke on the condition of anonymity because they weren't authorized to brief reporters'. The car bombing in Hurriyah and fake deaths occurred at 3.40pm. At 3.56pm, AP's Brian Rohan in Baghdad cited Iraqi officials as saying that 'a wave of bombings in predominantly Shiite [a.k.a. Shia] neighborhoods have killed at least seven people in the capital'. The unnamed officials attributed the bombings to improvised explosive devices at markets in Shaab, Topchi and Zataria. A fourth bomb reportedly struck a bus in Sadr City. Notice the same language as Abdul-Zahra's report: 'The officials – police and hospital authorities – spoke on condition of anonymity because they weren't authorized to brief reporters'. This is likely an editorial guideline or insert.[488]

At 5.18pm, Rohan reported on the Hurriyah bombing, that it 'hit a popular fruit and vegetable market' and killed 10. Again, Rohan writes: 'The officials spoke on condition of anonymity because they weren't authorized to brief reporters'.[489]

Why didn't these reporters actually go to the scene and investigate? Who were the officials that supposedly told them about the bombing? Why is the same editorial insert or guideline phrase inserted into different reports? Could it be that the officials spoke on condition of anonymity because they were Iraqi secret service agents spreading disinformation? Could it be that agents within the Associated Press knew the truth and were working with whoever set off the bomb to spread disinformation? One AP photographer,

Karim Kadin, arrived early the next morning and took photos of onlookers and the debris (the car had been removed and as noted the scorch marks on the wall were already there). It is not clear whether or not Kadin interviewed locals or witnesses, who would have either seen only the explosion from a distance and believed the deaths to be real or would have seen the actors and exposed the hoax.

A few hours after the explosion, two Reuters correspondents, one a senior correspondent for the agency in Baghdad (Ahmed Rasheed) said that '[a] car bomb parked in a shopping street of a Shi'ite district of Baghdad killed at least eight people and wounded more than 30 others'. They claimed their sources were 'police and medical staff'. It later says the district was Hurriyah specifically and adds: 'It wasn't clear if there was a suicide driver in the car'. Although the two individuals did the reporting, the story was written by Thomson Reuters' Iraq Bureau chief, Maher Chmaytelli. It was edited by Reuter's chief sub-editor at the time, Susan Fenton.[490]

From these wire reports, the story spread across the credulous mainstream print and online media.

The big reveal? Two years after the bombing was leaked online, two mainstream publications (the *Daily Mail* and the *New York Times*) reported on what they claim is the truth of the situation and the Iraqi intelligence units responsible. The NYT article examined below doesn't mention the Hurriyah bombing specifically, but does contextualize other fake bombings in Iraq.

In 2018 (26 August), reporters Larisa Brown, Ammar Shamary (additional reporting) and the unnamed 'security editor' of the *Daily Mail* claimed that the Hurriyah bombing was the work of Iraq's Captain Harith al-Sudani. Sudani was reportedly a spy working for Iraq's Falcon Intelligence Cell (Al Suquor). The Cell 'works with British Special Forces as it continues to hunt down jihadis' (ibid.). Reportedly, Sudani was a relatively secular Shia who had to learn about the more extreme forms of Sunni Islam practiced by ISIS members. Sudani operated as 'Abu Suhaib' and reportedly infiltrated the ISIS cells responsible for a series of car bombings. Sudani would reportedly switch the real bombs for less powerful ones and explode them in unpopulated areas. ISIS would then take responsibility for the attacks via their media outlet, even though, unbeknownst to ISIS, no one was really hurt. US organizations like SITE would report the bombings as real.

Sudani was reportedly killed in 2017, so the 'truth' about the Hurriyah car bombing could come out. Only the Hurriyah bombing has been reported on because that is the only bombing proven to be fake, even though the Falcons have faked other bombings (see below). Why don't the intelligence services provide a list of all the bombings they've faked? Why go to the trouble of actually blowing up a car or truck when the Iraqi forces could simply *report* a bombing on social media to make ISIS believe the latter succeeded? The official story says Sudani worked alone as a mole in the cells, but this does not explain the role of the crisis actors. Also, how and why did ISIS instruct Sudani to detonate the car bomb near a blast wall, as can be seen on the leaked video?

The *New York Times* (Margaret Coker, 12 August 2018) reports: 'the Falcons would stage fake explosions and issue fake news releases, sometimes claiming large casualties – part of the effort to keep Captain Sudani's cover intact'. This raises serious questions about death-tolls in Iraq attributed to ISIS and 'al-Qaeda'.

A masterclass: The fakery raises serious questions about a) how many other bombing victims are fake, both in Iraq and around the world, and b) the practices of the media. It is a masterclass in how fake news spreads, but also in how to spot possible fake events.

The wire services either invented, colluded with or were given information by sources who, if they were real people, were lying. This returns to the theme in the opening paragraph of the chapter: the gullibility on the part of the media when it comes to believing 'official' sources. Just because alleged police and alleged medics said the bombing victims were real, why did the media believe them? Why didn't the media check out the story as, for instance, Middle East correspondent Robert Fisk would do, by interviewing the families, wanting to see the bodies, etc.? Why did the wires fail to dispatch reporters to the scene right away? The most puzzling and disturbing aspect of the entire event is that even though it has been exposed as a hoax *prima facie* by the video and by organizations respected by Western media (Bellingcat, specifically), why do said news agencies not only refuse to retract or amend their stories, but also refuse to answer questions?

When anonymous officials quoted in credible journals are speaking against their or their government's own interests, such as admitting to terrorism, it is logical to assume that they are telling the truth; i.e., there must be a good reason for incriminating themselves or their employers. However, when they repeat the standard narrative, there is a logical reason to doubt; just because something is being told under the cloak of anonymity, it doesn't mean it is true: the sources could be pretending not to be allowed to give such information publicly in order to bolster the claim's credibility (reverse psychology).

The Babchenko Hoax: On 29 May 2018, a journalist named Arkaday Babchenko was reported dead. Not having learned their lessons from the Hurriyah hoax in Iraq in 2016, media reported that Babchenko, '[a] dissident Russian journalist' was 'shot at his apartment in Kiev', Ukraine, 'in a high-profile murder that police said may have been tied to his reporting' (*Guardian*).[491] Again, the erroneous reliance on 'official' sources instead of on-the-ground fact-checking (e.g., asking to see the body, getting a death certificate, etc.) caused great embarrassment to journalists.

The story was compounded by the release of a police photo, supposedly showing a dead and bloody Babchenko on the floor of his apartment, plus the supposed testimony of his wife, who 'found [him] bleeding'. The police even put out a sketch of a suspect, a man with a beard wearing a baseball cap. Nobody heard gunshots but neighbours said they saw an ambulance drive away (BBC). The implication drawn by media was that Babchenko had been murdered by agents of the Russian state at the behest of the demon, Vladimir Putin.[492]

The *Guardian* (not the only newspaper to get it wrong) issued a correction the next day: The Ukrainian state had faked Babchenko's death, supposedly as part of a sting operation. He 'emerged very much alive ... and said he staged his own death'. The BBC cited Babchenko as revealing that 'pig's blood and a make-up artist were used to pull off the stunt'. The hoax was supposedly perpetrated to catch a facilitator (a high-profile arms dealer) who was acting to find a hitman to take out Babchenko.[493] Others have reported that the facilitator was the actual, intended hitman.

However, the New York Times (NYT) later reported on the 'absence of solid facts and real evidence about any plot to kill [Babchenko]'. In earlier chapters, we noted the 'Christian' far-right's connections with Italy's Gladio. Oleksiy Tsimbalyuk is anti-Russian former deacon of the Ukrainian Orthodox Church and an associate of the Right Sector (a neo-Nazi militia based in Ukraine). He claims that he was hired to murder Babchenko, presumably to frame Russia. But this doesn't fit the sting operation narrative. At first, the Ukrainian security services denied Tsimbalyuk's involvement, but later confirmed it. The NYT also quotes a statement from the London-based Ukrainian Embassy, that Russia's alleged 'hybrid war' against Ukraine 'demands unorthodox approaches', like faking a state-killing.[494] Again, this confirms the UK MoD's prediction, that simulation will aid policymaking and blur the lines of illusion and reality.

The curious coincidence of drills

In addition to outright fakery, there are live-action drills and exercises. Drills and exercises are a common and (from a practical perspective) necessary part of policing, the military and the emergency services. But since 9/11 in 2001 (and even prior), several major terrorist attacks and shootings in the US and Europe (including the UK) have coincided with drills and exercises. Given the frequency of drills and exercises, it is not surprising that some would coincidentally occur at the same time as real-life terrorism.

However, the number of simultaneous real-world terror attacks and live-action drills/exercises, with some occurring on the same day, at the same time and same place as real-life terror attacks, suggests the possibility that some drills/exercises could be used as cover by deep state operatives in case their involvement in false-flag terrorism is exposed. The cases below may not necessarily be cover for deep state false-flags, but they reflect the Ministry of Defence prediction quoted above, concerning the increasingly authentic simulations which make it hard to distinguish them from reality.

The Russian apartments: Between 4–16 of September 1999, 293 Russians were murdered in a spate of apartment block RDX bombings in Buynaksk, Moscow and Volgodonsk. Russia blamed Chechen separatists and subsequently launched the Second Chechen War. Duma (parliament) motions to investigate the bombings were voted down. Two key members of the non-governmental Kovalev Commission, Sergei Yushenkov and Yuri Shchekochikhin (who filed the motions), ended up dead.[495] The Commission's lawyer, Mikhail Trepashkin, was imprisoned for betraying state secrets. FSB agent Alexander Litvinenko claimed that his own security service was behind the bombings. He was poisoned to death in London.[496]

Another bomb was discovered in Ryazan, which led the police to evacuate the buildings and call for the bomb disposal unit. The head of the FSB, Nikolai Patrushev, claimed the Ryazan bomb was a dummy, planted as part of a counterterrorism exercise.[497]

September 11, 2001: Several military exercises were being conducted on 9/11. Here are some of the most well-known: The National Reconnaissance Office was running an exercise simulating a small corporate jet crashing into a building. The Associated Press reports: 'In what the government describes as a bizarre coincidence, one U.S. intelligence agency was planning an exercise last Sept. 11 in which an errant aircraft would crash into one of its buildings'. It also notes that 'the cause wasn't terrorism – it was to be a simulated accident'.[498] The phrase bizarre or strange coincidence crops up a lot in US-European terrorism cases. Continuing with the drills: The North American Aerospace Defense Command (NORAD) was running Operation Northern Vigilance, which began on 9 September and ran for several days, as in the previous year.[499] NORAD was also running Vigilant Guardian, which involved several scenarios.[500] On the ground, the Federal Emergency Management

Agency was positioned in New York on the night of 10 September in preparation for Operation Tripod,[501] a huge counter-bioterrorism drill scheduled in New York for 12 September.[502] Although evidence in some cases was given, little of this information made it into the Bush administration's *9/11 Commission Report* (2004), which was 'set up to fail' in the words of the heads of the Commission, Thomas Kean and Lee Hamilton.[503]

11-M: On 10 March 2004, NATO concluded its counterterrorism training exercises CMX-04 in the capital cities of Europe, including Madrid.[504] The next day at 07.40 (approx.), 10 bombs exploded on four Madrid trains, murdering 191 people. Spaniards call it 11-M. Twenty-one people were convicted. PM José María Aznar of the right-wing People's Party personally contacted media outlets to pin the blame on ETA, the Basque separatists, rushing a draft resolution through the UN Security Council. Interior Minister Angel Acebes referred to press inquiries that perhaps 'al-Qaeda' was to blame, as 'a miserable attempt to disrupt information and confuse people'.[505]

El Mundo reported that at least two of the alleged bombers were informants working for the Spanish services: the Cuerpo Nacional de Policía, Guardia Civil, Centro Nacional de Inteligencia and the police.[506] Two of the accused had prior convictions for trafficking the explosive Goma 2 ECO.[507] The cell phones used to remotely detonate the bombs were taken from a store owned by a former policeman. The explosive Goma 2 ECO was supposedly used, which has not contained nitroglycerine since 1992. However, Juan Jesus Sánchez Manzano, head of TEDAX, the bomb disposal unit, informed the parliamentary commission: 'We managed to find traces of nitroglycerin, and nitroglycerin it is the component of all the dynamites'.[508] He later retracted the statement. Following a court order, more samples were taken which confirmed the presence of both nitroglycerine and dinitrotoluene (DNT). Other tests found both DNT and dibutyl phthalate (DBP), which is found in Goma 2 ECO.[509] The government destroyed the train carriages, and thus evidence, shortly after the explosions, as well as washing the samples, which might have cleansed them of nitroglycerine.[510] José

Luis Rodríguez Zapatero, future PM and leader of the Spanish Socialist Workers' Party, accused the government of destroying computer records linked to the case.[511]

Years later, the People's Party were out of government and campaigning for re-election in 2007–08. In late-2007, the trial of 28 Muslims was concluded, with 21 facing charges. Acebes accused the incumbent Spanish Socialist Party of being hasty with the convictions in order to win the next election and of (*Guardian* paraphrase), 'us[ing] a terrorist attack for electoral gains'. Terrorism specialist Scott Atran who attended the trial was equally sceptical: 'There isn't the slightest bit of evidence of any relationship with al-Qaida. We've been looking at it closely for years and we've been briefed by everybody under the sun … and nothing connects them' (ellipsis in original).[512]

7/7: Beginning at approximately 08.50 on 7 July 2005, 52 people were murdered when alleged suicide bombers began blowing up three tube trains and, later, a bus in London. The British government's Intelligence and Security Committee report, *Could 7/7 Have Been Prevented?*, reveals:

> Since 2003, the [Metropolitan Police] have run an annual exercise known as Operation HANOVER which develops different scenarios for attacks on London and rehearses how the Metropolitan Police Service would respond. By coincidence, their 2005 exercise, run by the Security Co-ordinator's office in the Anti-Terrorist Branch, took place just a few days before the attacks – on 1–2 July. The office-based scenario for this exercise was simultaneous bomb attacks on three London Underground trains at Embankment, Waterloo and St James's Park stations. Once again, the scenario is quite similar to what actually took place, and the fact that it took place so close to the actual attacks is an interesting coincidence.[513]

Even more interesting is the exercise that took place on the same morning and involved the same stations/lines being bombed. It was led by a former Metropolitan Police Anti-Terrorism Branch officer.

In 2004, the BBC produced a documentary simulating terror attacks on three of London's 270 London Underground lines/ stations, Hyde Park, Oxford Circus and Vauxhall Station, and on a road tanker containing chlorine. The producers invited crisis management experts to give a real-time response to the simulation.[514] One of the experts was a retired police officer and magistrate with specialist counterterrorism training[515] and intimate knowledge of the Underground,[516] Peter Power.

The BBC names Power as heading BET Security (1992–94), but that company's annual accounts don't include him on the list of directors.[517] (Was it a mistake or was he working for them anonymously?) The BBC also names him as head of Visor Consulting (sic); he actually heads Visor *Consultants*. Visor, according to its website, was founded in 1995.[518] Strangely, Companies House (the government's registry of businesses) lists Visor Consultants as incorporated as late as 2008.[519] (Was the company registered under a different name. If so, why isn't this mentioned in the annual filings? There is no listing for Visor *Consulting*.) Visor's team included individuals who worked for the Home Office (Admiral Bawtree), the Metropolitan Police (Power, Tom Pine and Dr Tony Burns-Howell) and the BBC (Fiona Cline, who had worked personally with PM Tony Blair).[520]

At the same time, two individuals, Rashid Rauf[521] and Haroon Aswat, were plotting bombings of the Underground from bases in Pakistan. Rauf's organization, Jaish e-Mohammed, was protected by Pakistani intelligence, presumably as a proxy against India.[522] Aswat, according to former US prosecutor John Loftus, was an MI6 informant.[523] Rauf met the British men Mohammad Siddique Khan and Shehzad Tanweer,[524] who were later blamed by media and politicians, but crucially not the inquest,[525] for the 7/7 bombings. In the 1990s, Khan worked for the UK Department of Trade and Industry and had worked with local police in Yorkshire to settle gang disputes.[526]

Remarkably, Rauf et al. also chose to attack three London Underground trains (the Circle lines near Aldgate/Liverpool Street, Edgware Rd/King's Cross and Piccadilly/Russell Sq.). Supposedly, a fourth suicide bomb was to be detonated on a fourth train, but the alleged bomber missed the train and blew up a bus instead, also in line with the BBC documentary (albeit the bus replaces the chlorine tanker).

Even more remarkable, Reed Elsevier (a firm whose subsidiary organizes arms fairs) hired Visor Consultants in 2005 to plan with them and conduct a small, office-based tabletop crisis management exercise.[527] Power told the BBC that the stations he and Reed Elsevier picked were Liverpool Street (on the Aldgate line), King's Cross (Edgware line) and Russell Sq. (Piccadilly line). The exercise was 'based on simultaneous bombs going off precisely at the railway stations that happened' (Power),[528] i.e., for real, on 7 July 2005. Even more remarkable, the exercise occurred on the morning of 7 July 2005 at the same time as the bombs were actually going off.

Power strongly denies any involvement in the real-life attacks and there is no suggestion here that he or anyone at Visor Consultants had any foreknowledge or involvement or acted illegally or immorally. The Intelligence and Security Committee's report notes that MI5, the Police and Transport for London deny any knowledge of or involvement in Power's exercise. It says of Power's exercise:

> that the exercise was taking place at roughly the same time that morning is indeed an astonishing coincidence. Unfortunately, his remarks were interpreted by some as direct evidence of a conspiracy. He himself has denied this, and we have not uncovered any evidence that this is anything other than a coincidence.[529]

Boston bombing: Every year since 2005, Sgt. Chris Connolly of the Boston police bomb squad inspected Boylston Street and other locations for bombs to protect the Marathon. There was a security presence at the Boston Marathon in case of a terrorist attack or other disaster. They had officers and dogs along the route, especially near the finish line.[530] Beginning in 2011, the Department of Homeland Security began the Urban Area Security Initiative. Part of the Initiative was Operation Urban Shield, an annual, large-scale terrorism-emergency response exercise.[531]

Brothers Tamerlan (deceased) and Dzhokhar are accused of perpetrating the Boston Marathon bombing (2013). The Tsarnaevs' father was born in Chechnya and forcibly removed by the atheist, anti-Muslim Soviet regime in the 1980s. The family lived in the Kalmyk Autonomous Soviet Socialist Republic and Kyrgyzstan, respectively. In 2002, the family moved to the US. The FBI had Tamerlan under investigation. In 2011, at the request of the Russian FSB, he was visited by four men claiming to be FBI agents. They showed him no ID and were 'tan' but had no 'accents'. The FBI report also says:

> TAMERLAN wants to box for the US Olympic team but does not have his citizenship yet. TAMERLAN has not thought about joining the military because he wants to become a professional boxer. TAMERLAN doesn't like to fight for the sake of violence. TAMERLAN has fought to protect others. TAMERLAN was in several fights as a child in school in Kyrgystan. TAMERLAN stood up for kids that were being bullied by others ... TAMERLAN has respect for all religions and feels that any religion makes your life better. TAMERLAN hopes to move his family to Revere, Massachusetts in the coming year ... TAMERLAN goes to mosque in Cambridge once a week for Friday prayers. TAMERLAN doesn't have any Muslim friends ... TAMERLAN doesn't search for anything related to extremist Islamic material ... TAMERLAN was open to all contact with the FBI and report any additional contact with the four unidentified individuals (UI) who claimed to be FBI.[532]

Within a year, Tamerlan had allegedly been radicalized and had allegedly fought with Chechen *mujahideen* against Russia, paying thousands of euros to return to America after *jihad*. How did a pleasant, non-extremist with ambitions of boxing for the US in championships allegedly end up being a terrorist in Russia and how come he was able to travel on international airlines without being stopped? Was he a US proxy? Was he in Russia at all? Investigative reporter Michele McPhee says: 'counterterrorism experts and law enforcement officials ... point [...] to Tamerlan having been a federal informant who went rogue'.[533] The theory that he 'went rogue' is just as valid or invalid as the one that says he was working for the FBI in order to fast-track his citizenship and was duped into taking part in what he thought was a counterterrorism drill but was actually a set up to make Americans frightened of people with Russian-sounding names. The evidence is only circumstantial.

Returning to the annual training exercises in Boston: James Baker, head of security consultancy firm the Cytel Group, which ran Urban Shield, 'helped Boston run two massive, 24-hour worst-case scenario simulations that bore no small resemblance to the situation unfolding this afternoon in Watertown', says the training and simulation company, Strategic Operations, referring to the post-bombing shoot-out. Urban Shield 2012 included 600 participants spread across 50 departments and agencies. 'The drills are intended to be strikingly lifelike. Urban Shield has worked with Strategic Operations, a Hollywood effects company that also helps prepare army medics for the battlefield.' (Their disaster scenario staff, Baker says, include an amputee.)[534]

Officials told the *Boston Herald* that in March 2012 Boston's 'top emergency agency' conducted a drill anticipating an attack envisaging bombs at the finish line and at the VIP grandstand on Boylston Street.[535] According to an NBC report, Ali Stevenson a coach at the University of Mobile's Cross Country, said that shortly after the actual bombing: 'They kept making announcements on the loud speaker that it was just a drill and there was nothing to worry about... It seemed like there was some sort of threat, but they kept telling us it was just a drill'.[536] Yet, Operation Urban Shield 2013 was not due to take place until June.

Three died in the alleged shrapnel/pressure-cooker bomb blasts and hundreds were injured.

Bataclan: Patrick Pelloux has experience in responding to and pushing for changes in the management of crises. Pelloux is head of the Association of Emergency Physicians of France. He said that he and others helped create the union in the late-1990s after a spate of violence against hospital workers, including a shooting at the

Kremlin-Bicêtre University Hospital.[537] He was also a contributor to *Charlie Hebdo*. In 2003, 15,000 French people, most of them elderly, died in a heatwave. '[T]he government dismissed a claim by [Pelloux] that 50 people had died in the capital' due to the heatwave (*Independent*).[538] Pelloux became a media figure after exposing government failures in the handling of the mass deaths. He knew and befriended future President François Hollande, then-first secretary of the Socialist Party.[539] Pelloux says: 'In 2004, we were received by Nicolas Sarkozy, Minister of the Interior at the time' and future President, 'following the violent escape of a prisoner in the Nice emergency' (sic).[540]

Pelloux is active in healthcare reform. In 2004, he was involved in the one-day mass strike of health sector workers. Pelloux arranged for Irish singer Paddy Sherlock to play in A&E wards, appearing on stage with the singer in return. Sherlock was also friends with the murdered editor of *Hebdo*, Stéphane Charbonnier.[541] In 2013, Pelloux was interviewed by the journal *Libération* about crises in healthcare, including the hostage-taking of medical staff. He said that security changes needed to be made:

> It has long been asked to have an emergency alert system in the emergency services at the police, an alarm system similar to that of banks or jewelers. If we can protect paintings and jewels in this way, we should be able to do the same for emergency personnel ... All that is required is a rapprochement between the emergency services and the police, so that the interventions are faster and more responsive, as well as means to work calmly.[542]

Pelloux was the first on the scene of the *Hebdo* attacks in January 2015. 'Since then he has been training doctors, nurses and paramedics in the skills of battlefield medics — including how to deal with bullets, shrapnel wounds and major bleeds', says Sky News.[543] He later received 1.4 million euros in compensation, allegedly due to his connections with Hollande. The journal *Le Point* reported that Pelloux received more compensation than surviving *Hebdo* staff. Pelloux denies any wrongdoing and announced his intention to sue for libel. There is no suggestion that Pelloux had any involvement in the attacks.[544]

On 13 November 2015, terrorists reportedly linked to Islamic State murdered 130 in a spate of shootings and explosions in Paris, mainly in the Bataclan Theatre. Pelloux revealed live on French radio (France Info): 'As luck would have it, in the morning at the Paris SAMU (EMT), a multi-site attack exercise had been planned, so we were prepared ... [T]here was a mobilization of police forces, firemen, EMTs, associations who came to [participate]. We tried to save as many lives as possible'.[545] *Stat* is a health news website owned by Boston Globe Media. It says: 'In the morning of Friday, Nov. 13 [2015], firefighters and emergency medical workers in Paris simulated how they might respond to a mass shooting event. They had no idea that they would be putting their skills into practice that same night'. It concludes: 'when the attacks began, some doctors thought it was another drill'.[546]

Sky News reported: 'By a chilling coincidence, a major training exercise had taken place on the morning of the recent attacks involving medics, the police and fire crews'. It quotes Pelloux: 'We were practising military medicine. Actually what we did on Friday morning is what we did on Friday night and I think it allowed us to save 60 to 100 lives'.[547]

Saumur: The penultimate example here is not apparently related to simultaneous or near-simultaneous terror attacks and drills, but given the context of Gladio outlined earlier the event raises some questions. In September 2016, a mowing contractor on a job near the church of Saint-Hilaire-des-Grottes, France, in an abandoned cave found what he thought was an ISIS hideout. Having seen three men leave in a white van, the contractor saw that the cave contained ISIS flags, videos and Arabic newspapers. Local police were informed. The military claimed that it was a part of a drill conducted by the Joint Nuclear, Radiological, Biological and Chemical Defence Centre, which had failed to warn local police.[548]

The Khater Coincidence: On 14 August 2018, Salih Khater, an alleged British citizen, a Sudanese refugee living in the UK, alleg-

162 MANUFACTURING TERRORISM

edly drove a Ford Fiesta into cyclists on Abingdon Street, Westminster, London. This was treated as an act of terrorism. Khater's alleged CV claims that he worked as a security guard in Nottingham. His license to work as a guard was supplied by the Security Industry Authority (SIA).[549] SIA was created in 2003 under the Private Security Industry Act (2001) as a non-departmental body under the authority of the Home Secretary (Theresa May, at the time of Khater's supposedly being granted citizenship). By an extraordinary coincidence, the alleged terror attack occurred on the same day as a training event 560+ miles away in Inverness, Scotland, conducted by SIA.[550] Were the events linked in some way?

Conclusion

This book has attempted to find some clarity and nuance in the extremely serious and often well-documented mass of information concerning how governments and deep state actors manufacture terrorism. Employing a set of fairly strict criteria, the book has tried to be honest enough to point out where evidence is lacking and where further research is needed. It has called for a tailored approach to understanding terrorism, not to dismiss every atrocity as either the work of extremists or, conversely, the deep state.

With few exceptions, mainstream media and academia use the lazy and factually irrelevant smear 'conspiracy theory' to 'pathologize dissent' (Michael J. Wood) and slander earnest researchers as kooks.

The mainstream is as bad as much, but not all, of the online and radio conspiracy industry. This network regularly claims with either no evidence or with data which it believes constitutes evidence, that every terror attack or mass shooting is either a false-flag or a hoax involving crisis actors. Just to complicate things further, self-styled debunkers like Metabunk.org and YouTube personalities like Myles Power pose as scientific-orientated researchers in order to put others at a psychological disadvantage by implying that, by virtue of their interests in science, they are intellectually superior.

Life is complicated enough to allow for a multitude of causalities. A single terrorist event can include multiple factors. There may be real networks of terrorists with real grievances against the West who attack western interests. At the same time, their leaders might be working as proxies for certain circles within Western agencies. It is also important to remember that information units within agencies can be at odds with the more politically-motivated operations units. The terrorists themselves might be using those agencies for their own interests and the agencies might in turn be using them. The terrorists might be allowed to operate by elements within certain agencies. At the same time, those agency-linked terrorists might recruit patsies who are manipulated by handlers whose goal is to boost the status of their agency and its funding. Terror attacks might involve multiple shooters (as witnesses frequently claim) who could well be special forces operatives, yet for convenience the event is blamed on patsies who could in turn have real grievances against the West or, conversely, believe they are working as part of a drill.

As this book has attempted to demonstrate, one or more of these scenarios is possible. Complicating things further is the fact that they can work simultaneously. Until mainstream researchers are willing to accept that the deep state does not exist to protect them from terrorists, but rather, to *selectively* protect them from certain terrorists, and until alternative researchers are willing to evaluate each case and abandon theories when the evidence doesn't fit, no progress will be made into deep state involvement in terrorism and, elites will continue with their dangerous, self-interested agendas.

Notes

1. Robert A. Pape (2006), *Dying to Win: The Strategic Logic of Suicide Terrorism*, London: Random House.
2. Ministry of Defence (UK) (2003), *Operations in Iraq: First Reflections*, pp. 24, 48, https://www.globalsecurity.org/military/library/report/2003/iraq2003operations_ukmod_july03.pdf. The report says the bombs were 'inert' and intended to leave structures intact. But this makes no sense. Structures or not, human flesh and bones, and thus the bodies of bystanders, cannot withstand massive blasts, as we shall see in Chapter 6.
3. US State Department and Lawrence Livermore Laboratory data cited in Seth Borenstein and Julie Reed Bell (2010), '2010 Extreme Weather', Associated Press, http://www.huffingtonpost.com/2010/12/20/2010-extreme-weather-dead_n_798956.html.
4. Les Roberts, Riyadh Lafta, Richard Garfield, Jamal Khudhairi and Gilbert Burnham (2004), 'Mortality before and after the 2003 invasion of Iraq: cluster sample survey', *The Lancet*, 364(9448): 1857–64.
5. Harlan Ullman and James Wade (1996), *Shock and Awe: Achieving Rapid Dominance*, Washington DC: National Defense University. The authors write, for instance: 'The intent here is to impose a regime of Shock and Awe through delivery of instant, nearly incomprehensible levels of massive destruction directed at influencing society writ large, meaning its leadership and public, rather than targeting directly against military or strategic objectives' (p. 23).
6. Eric Lichtblau (2016), 'F.B.I. steps up use of stings in ISIS cases', NYT, https://www.nytimes.com/2016/06/08/us/fbi-isis-terrorism-stings.html?_r=0.
7. Quoted in Heather Maher (2013), 'How the FBI helps terrorists succeed', *The Atlantic*, www.theatlantic.com/international/archive/2013/02/how-the-fbi-helps-terrorists-succeed/273537/.
8. *Mother Jones* (2011), 'Terror trials by the numbers', September–October, https://www.motherjones.com/politics/2011/08/terror-trials-numbers/.
9. Tom Whitehead (2013), 'Woolwich attack: Al Muhajiroun linked to one in five terrorist convictions', *Telegraph*, https://www.telegraph.co.uk/news/uknews/terrorism-in-the-uk/10079827/Woolwich-attack-Al-Muhajiroun-linked-to-one-in-five-terrorist-convictions.html.
10. Martin Evans, Nicola Harley, Ben Farmer and Ben Riley-Smith (2016), 'Radical preacher Anjem Choudary behind bars as police reveal his links to

500 Isil jihadists', *Telegraph*, https://www.telegraph.co.uk/news/2016/08/16/radical-preacher-anjem-choudary-behind-bars-after-drumming-up-su/.

11. Martin Evans and Ben Farmer (2016), 'MI5 stopped Scotland Yard taking Choudary down, sources claim', *Telegraph*, https://www.telegraph.co.uk/news/2016/08/21/mi5-stopped-scotland-yard-taking-choudary-down-sources-claim/.

12. Federation of American Scientists (2002), 'DOD examines "preemptive" intelligence operations', *Secrecy News*, Issue 107, https://fas.org/sgp/news/secrecy/2002/10/102802.html.

13. Defense Science Board (2002), *DSB Summer Study on Special Operations and Joint Forces in Support of Countering Terrorism*, p. 21, https://fas.org/irp/agency/dod/dsbbrief.ppt.

14. Jeremy H. Keenan (2017), 'Review: T. J. Coles, Britain's Secret Wars ...', *State Crime* 6(2): 286–94. See also Jeremy H. Keenan (2009), *The Dark Sahara: America's War on Terror in Africa*, London: Pluto Press.

15. Timewatch (1992), *Gladio*, BBC and Daniele Ganser (2005), *NATO's Secret Armies*, New York: Frank Cass.

16. See my *Britain's Secret Wars: How and Why the United Kingdom Sponsors Conflict Around the World* (2016), West Hoathly: Clairview Books.

17. Glenn Garvin (2018), 'Is the Deep State real – and is it really at war with Donald Trump?', *Miami Herald*, http://www.miamiherald.com/news/politics-government/article198038824.html. Greg Grandin (2017), 'What is the deep state?', *The Nation*, https://www.thenation.com/article/what-is-the-deep-state/+. Tom Porter (2017), 'Deep state: How a conspiracy theory went from political fringe to mainstream', *Newsweek*, www.newsweek.com/deep-state-conspiracy-theory-trump-645376+. See also Cynthia McKinney (2017), '"Je ne sais pas qui je suis": Making sense of tragedies like the *Charlie Hebdo* incident when the government narrative doesn't make sense' in T.J. Coles (ed.), *Voices for Peace: War, Resistance and America's Quest for Full Spectrum Dominance*, West Hoathly: Clairview Books, pp. 104–25.

18. McKinney op. cit., pp. 113–14.

19. Robin Ramsay (2015), 'Review: The American deep state', *Lobster Issue* 69, https://www.lobster-magazine.co.uk/free/lobster69/lob69-american-deep-state.pdf.

20. Former CIA analyst, Ray McGovern, for instance, asks: 'How do I explain what happened to ... my former analyst colleagues – not to mention folks I knew and, some of them I trusted, from the operations side? After the trauma of 9/11, something happened to [them]'. James Carden (2018), 'Ray McGovern on Gina Haspel, Torture, and His Recent Arrest', *The Nation*,

https://www.thenation.com/article/ray-mcgovern-on-gina-haspel-torture-and-his-recent-arrest/.

21. Niels H. Harrit et al. (2009), 'Active thermitic material discovered in dust from the 9/11 World Trade Center catastrophe', *The Open Chemical Physics Journal*, 2: 7–31. Kevin Ryan et al. (2009), 'Environmental anomalies at the World Trade Center: evidence for energetic materials', *The Environmentalist*, 29: 56–63.

22. Judy Wood (2010), *Where did the towers go? Evidence of directed free-energy technology on 9/11*, South Carolina: The New Investigation.

23. Dimitri Khalezov (2013), 'WTC nuclear demolition – damage inflicted to "bathtub" and to PATH', *Veterans Today*, https://www.veteranstoday.com/2013/09/02/nuclear-demolition-of-the-world-trade-center-damage-to-bath-tub/.

24. Robert A. Pape (2003), 'The strategic logic of suicide terrorism', *The American Political Science Review*, 97(3): 343–61.

25. Global Terrorism Database (live document), University of Maryland, https://www.start.umd.edu/gtd/.

26. On Israel and al-Nusra, which is not covered in this book, see United Nations Security Council (2013), *Report of the Secretary-General on the United Nations Disengagement Observer Force for the period from 12 September to 3 December 2013*, S/2013/716 http://www.securitycouncilreport.org/atf/cf/%7B65BFCF9B-6D27-4E9C-8CD3-CF6E4FF96FF9%7D/s_2013_716.pdf.

27. Richard Spencer (2014), 'Britain drew up plans to build 100,000-strong Syrian rebel army', *Telegraph*, https://www.telegraph.co.uk/news/world-news/middleeast/syria/10947773/Britain-drew-up-plans-to-build-100000-strong-Syrian-rebel-army.html.

28. FBI (2011), FD-302 (Rev. 10-695), 04/23/2011, https://vault.fbi.gov/tamerlan-tsarnaev/Tamerlan%20Tsarnaev%20Part%2001%20of%2001/view.

29. Lizzie Dearden (2017), 'Second German soldier arrested over "false flag" plot to assassinate left-wing politicians in terror attack', *Independent*, https://www.independent.co.uk/news/world/europe/german-soldiers-false-flag-arrests-refugees-assassinate-plot-far-right-left-wing-politicians-terror-a7726676.html.

30. ACLU (2005), 'Myths and realities about the Patriot Act', https://www.aclu.org/other/myths-and-realities-about-patriot-act.

31. Michael Saward (2016), 'The State and Civil Liberties in the Post-9/11 World', Open University, http://oro.open.ac.uk/16198/1/StateAndCivil.pdf.

32. Philip Johnston (2005), 'The police must end their abuse of anti-terror legislation', *Telegraph*, https://www.telegraph.co.uk/comment/

personal-view/3620110/The-police-must-end-their-abuse-of-anti-terror-legislation.html.

33. Johnston, op. cit.

34. Serious Organised Crime and Police Act (2005), http://www.legislation.gov.uk/ukpga/2005/15/pdfs/ukpga_20050015_en.pdf.

35. Lizzie Dearden (2017), 'Terror laws should be scrapped, says Government's independent reviewer of terrorism legislation', *Independent*, www.independent.co.uk/news/uk/home-news/terror-laws-uk-offences-abolish-max-hill-interview-independent-reviewer-legislation-isis-attack-a7883836.html.

36. Ricardo Alberto Arias (2007), *Letter dated 19 March 2007 from the Chairman of the Security Council Committee established pursuant to resolution 1373 (2001) concerning counter-terrorism addressed to the President of the Security Council*, United Nations Security Council Counterterrorism Committee, S/2007/164, http://www.refworld.org/pdfid/46de9f8c16.pdf.

37. Amnesty International (2018), 'Spain: Counter-terror law used to crush satire and creative expression online', https://www.amnesty.org/en/latest/news/2018/03/spain-counter-terror-law-used-to-crush-satire-and-creative-expression-online/.

38. Sam Jones (2018), 'Spanish anti-terror law has "chilling effect" on satire, says Amnesty International', *Guardian*, https://www.theguardian.com/world/2018/mar/13/spanish-anti-terror-law-has-chilling-effect-on-satire-says-amnesty-international.

39. Amnesty op. cit.

40. Alexander King and Bertrand Schneider (1991), *The First Global Revolution: A Report by the Council of the Club of Rome*, London: Orient Longman, front matter, 66–75.

41. Ibid.

42. Ibid.

43. M.J. Akbar quoted in Samuel P. Huntington (2002), *The Clash of Civilizations and the Remaking of World Order*, London: The Free Press, p. 213.

44. Huntington, op. cit., pp. 20–21.

45. Huntington, op. cit., pp. 129–30.

46. Ibid.

47. Joint Chiefs of Staff (1997), 'Vision for 2020', www.pipr.co.uk/archive.

48. Steven Metz and James Kievit (1994), 'The Revolution in Military Affairs and Conflict Short of War', US Army War College, http://ssi.armywarcollege.edu/pdffiles/pub241.pdf.

49. Ibid.

50. Harlan Ullman and James Wade (1996), *Shock and Awe: Achieving Rapid Dominance*, Fort Lesley J. McNair, DC: National Defense University and

Institute for National Strategic Studies,
http://www.dodccrp.org/files/Ullman_Shock.pdf.

51. Ibid.
52. Ibid.
53. Ibid. On Iraq, the death toll and how British media minimized it, see David Cromwell and David Edwards (2008), *Newspeak in the 21st Century*, London: Pluto Press.
54. Thomas Donnelly (2000), *Rebuilding America's Defenses: Strategy, Forces and Resources For a New Century*, Washington, DC: PNAC, www.informationclearinghouse.info/pdf/RebuildingAmericasDefenses.pdf.
55. Ibid.
56. Ibid.
57. Ibid.
58. Gary Hart (2001), US Commission on National Security in the 21st Century, https://www.youtube.com/watch?v=X-ezBk1ZFU0.
59. Quoted in P.W. Singer (2009), *Wired for War*, London: Penguin, p. 39.
60. *Haaretz* and Reuters (2008), 'Report: Netanyahu Says 9/11 Terror Attacks Good for Israel', http://www.haaretz.com/news/report-netanyahu-says-9-11-terror-attacks-good-for-israel-1.244044.
61. William Schneider (2004), *Report of the Defense Science Board Task Force on Strategic Communication*, Office of the Under Secretary of Defense For Acquisition, Technology, and Logistics, Washington, DC: Government Printing Office, https://fas.org/irp/agency/dod/dsb/commun.pdf.
62. Ministry of Defence (2010 4th), 'Strategic Trends Programme: Global Strategic Trends Out to 2040', Swindon: The DCDC, www.gov.uk/government/uploads/system/uploads/attachment_data/file/33717/GST4_v9_Feb10.pdf
63. Alex Evans and David Steven (2010), 'Organizing for Influence UK Foreign Policy in an Age of Uncertainty', Chatham House, https://www.chathamhouse.org/sites/files/chathamhouse/public/Research/Europe/r0610_stevens_evans.pdf. Alex Evans and David Steven (2010), 'UK and the World Governing in an Age of Uncertainty' (transcript), Chatham House, https://www.chathamhouse.org/sites/files/chathamhouse/public/Meetings/Meeting%20Transcripts/09062010alexevansetal.pdf.
64. Mike Rennie and Stephen Deakin (2011), 'Military Strategy, Ethics and Influence: a Response to Mackay and Tatham', Royal Military Academy Sandhurst Occasional Paper No. 7, https://www.army.mod.uk/documents/general/rmas_occ_paper_07.pdf.
65. For extensive details and sources, see my *Britain's Secret Wars*, op. cit., pp. 130–44.
66. Campbell McCafferty (2011), 'Piracy off the coast of Somalia', Foreign Affairs

Committee, https://www.publications.parliament.uk/pa/cm201012/cmselect/cmfaff/c1318-ii/c131801.htm.

67. Nick Dorman (2011), '2012 Terror Threat – Al Quada [sic] Offshoot Targeted In Somalia', *People*, www.people.co.uk/news/uk-world-news/2011/11/06/2012-terror-threat-al-quada-offshoot-targeted-in-somalia-102039-23540980/. (Dead link.)

68. Ted Dagne (2007), 'Somalia: Current Conditions and Prospects for a Lasting Peace', Congressional Research Service Order, Code RL33911, https://fas.org/sgp/crs/row/RL33911.pdf.

69. Ministry of Defence (2010), *Strategic Trends Programme: Future Character of Conflict*, http://www.atlanticuas.ca/sites/default/files/reference/DCDC_Future_Character_of_Conflict_11-05-10.pdf.

70. Ibid.

71. Adrian Levy and Cathy Scott-Clark (2013), 'CIA bin Laden hunter David Headley plotted Mumbai massacre', *The Times*, https://www.thetimes.co.uk/article/cia-bin-laden-hunter-david-headley-plotted-mumbai-massacre-bc0tpw20tpf+&cd=2&hl=en&ct=clnk&gl=uk.

72. BBC News Online (2001), 'Text: Bush address to Congress', http://news.bbc.co.uk/1/hi/world/americas/1555641.stm.

73. William Schneider (2004), *Report of the Defense Science Board Task Force on Strategic Communication*, Office of the Under Secretary of Defense For Acquisition, Technology, and Logistics, Washington: DC, https://fas.org/irp/agency/dod/dsb/commun.pdf.

74. Jon Schwarz (2017), 'British intelligence warned Tony Blair of Manchester-like terrorism if the West invaded Iraq', *The Intercept*, https://theintercept.com/2017/05/23/british-intelligence-warned-tony-blair-of-manchester-like-terrorism-if-the-west-invaded-iraq/.

75. Ministry of Defence (2007 3rd), *The DCDC Global Strategic Trends Programme: 2007–2036*, Swindon: The DCDC, http://www.cuttingthroughthematrix.com/articles/strat_trends_23jan07.pdf.

76. See my 'Remembering Iraq: The Sanctions Genocide' (2013), http://axisoflogic.com/artman/publish/printer_65877.shtml.

77. Quoted in Riaza Hassan (2011), *Life as a Weapon: The Global Rise of Suicide Bombings*, London: Routledge, eBook.

78. Robert Fisk (2008), 'The cult of the suicide bomber', *Independent*, http://www.independent.co.uk/voices/commentators/fisk/robert-fisk-the-cult-of-the-suicide-bomber-795649.html and Associated Press (2005), 'Most suicide bombers in Iraq are foreigners', http://www.nbcnews.com/id/8420885/ns/world_news-mideast_n_africa/t/most-suicide-bombers-iraq-are-foreigners/#.WTckeevyvIU.

79. JIC (2003), 'International Terrorism: War with Iraq', Iraq Inquiry, http://www.iraqinquiry.org.uk/media/230918/2003-02-10-jic-assessment-international-terrorism-war-with-iraq.pdf.

80. Quoted in Richard Norton-Taylor (2009), 'Cabinet told of Iraq war risk to UK, says ex-MI5 chief', Guardian, https://www.theguardian.com/politics/2009/jul/11/mi5-warning-iraq-war-terrorism. Chilcot (2016), 'The Report of the Iraq Inquiry Executive Summary', HC 264, http://www.iraqinquiry.org.uk/media/247921/the-report-of-the-iraq-inquiry_executive summary.pdf. Sam Marsden (2010), 'Iraq invasion "increased terror activity against UK"', Press Association, http://www.independent.co.uk/news/uk/politics/iraq-invasion-increased-terror-activity-against-uk-2030681.html and Decca Aitkenhead (2008), 'Free agent', Guardian, https://www.theguardian.com/commentisfree/2008/oct/18/iraq-britainand911.

81. National Intelligence Estimate (NIE), Trends in Global Terrorism: Implications for the United States NIE 2006-02R, http://www.governmentattic.org/5docs/NIE-2006-02R.pdf.

82. Ibid.

83. See my (2014), 'AFRICOM, NATO and the EU', Lobster, Issue 67, Summer, http://www.lobster-magazine.co.uk/free/lobster67/lob67-africom-nato-eu.pdf.

84. Sandia National Laboratories (no date), 'Osama bin Laden: A Case Study', National Security Agency, http://nsarchive.gwu.edu/NSAEBB/NSAEBB253/sandia.pdf.

85. Ibid.

86. MoD Strategic Trends 2040, op. cit.

87. Cameron Scott (2007), 'Assessing ISAF', BASIC, http://www.basicint.org/publications/cameron-scott/2007/assessing-isaf-baseline-study-natos-role-afghanistan. House of Commons Defence Committee (2007), 'UK Operations in Afghanistan', 13th Report of Session 2006–07, HC 408, London: The Stationery Office.

88. Luke N. Condra et al. (2010), 'The effect of civilian casualties in Afghanistan and Iraq', National Bureau of Economic, Research Working Paper 16152, www.nber.org/papers/w16152.

89. Ben Farmer (2009), 'Afghan war "could be lost if civilian death toll continues"', Telegraph, https://www.telegraph.co.uk/news/worldnews/asia/afghanistan/5437365/Afghan-war-could-be-lost-if-civilian-death-toll-continues.html.

90. Anonymous (2006), '"Rendition" hypocrisy', FT, https://web.archive.org/web/20060615192613/http://news.ft.com/cms/s/cea39a9e-f68b-11da-b09f-0000779e2340.html.

91. BBC News Online (2016), 'Barack Obama: "Guantanamo key magnet for jihadi recruitment"', http://www.bbc.co.uk/news/av/world-us-canada-35137623/barack-obama-guantanamo-key-magnet-for-jihadi-recruitment.

92. HRW (2014), *Facts and Figures: Military Commissions vs. Federal Courts*, http://www.hrw.org/features/guantanamo-facts-figures and Human Rights (UC Davis) (2013), 'Guantanamo's Children: The Wikileaked Testimonies', http://humanrights.ucdavis.edu/reports/guantanamos-children-the-wikileaked-testimonies/guantanamos-children-the-wikileaked-testimonies.

93. Jack Serle (2015), 'Almost 2,500 now killed by covert US drone strikes since Obama inauguration six years ago', Bureau of Investigative Journalism, https://www.thebureauinvestigates.com/stories/2015-02-02/almost-2-500-now-killed-by-covert-us-drone-strikes-since-obama-inauguration-six-years-ago-the-bureaus-report-for-january-2015 and David Kilcullen and Andrew McDonald (2009), 'Death from above, outrage down below', *NYT*, https://www.nytimes.com/2009/05/17/opinion/17exum.html.

94. Quoted in my 'A world of drones' (2011), Axis of Logic, http://axisoflogic.com/artman/publish/Article_63830.shtml.

95. *Telegraph* (2010), 'Times Square car bomber Faisal Shahzad pleads guilty "100 times"', https://www.telegraph.co.uk/news/worldnews/northamerica/usa/7845570/Times-Square-car-bomber-Faisal-Shahzad-pleads-guilty-100-times.html.

96. Emma Manna (2016), 'Exploring a link between drone strikes and retaliation', *Georgetown Public Policy Review*, http://gppreview.com/2016/07/08/exploring-link-drone-strikes-retaliation/.

97. Murtasa Hussain (2015), 'Retired General: Drones create more terrorists than they kill, Iraq war helped create ISIS', *The Intercept*, https://theintercept.com/2015/07/16/retired-general-drones-create-terrorists-kill-iraq-war-helped-create-isis/.

98. Jeffrey St. Clair and Alexander Cockburn (1998), 'How Jimmy Carter and I started the Mujahideen', *Counterpunch*, https://www.counterpunch.org/1998/01/15/how-jimmy-carter-and-i-started-the-mujahideen/.

99. Adam Jones (2010, 2nd), *Genocide: A Comprehensive Introduction*, London: Routledge, eBook.

100. On the Taliban, see Jason Burke (2003), *Al-Qaeda: The True Story of Radical Islam*, London: Penguin and Ahmed Rashid (2000), *Taliban: The Power of Militant Islam in Afghanistan and Beyond*, London: I.B. Tauris.

101. Robin Cook (2005), 'The struggle against terrorism cannot be won by military means', *Guardian*, https://www.theguardian.com/uk/2005/jul/08/july7.development.

102. Robert Dreyfuss (2006), *Devil's Game: How the United States Helped Unleash Fundamentalist Islam*, New York: Owl Books, pp. 35–46.

103. Dreyfuss op. cit., pp. 47–64.

104. Stephen Dorril writes: 'The CIA team training SAVAK remained in Iran until 1961, when it was replaced by a Mossad team. Under the direction of General Hussein Fardust, who helped train the "Special Bureau" was MI6, SAVAK developed its own training programme' (2002), *MI6: Inside the Covert World of Her Majesty's Secret Intelligence Service*, London: Simon & Schuster, p. 654.

105. Quoted in Dreyfuss, op. cit., pp. 261–62.

106. John K. Cooley (2002), *Unholy Wars*, Pluto Press, p. 78.

107. Steve Coll (2006), *Ghost Wars: The Secret History of the CIA, Afghanistan and Bin Laden*, London: Penguin, eBook.

108. Ibid.

109. Quoted in Dreyfuss, op. cit., p. 263.

110. Cooley, op. cit., p. 74.

111. Ibid., p. 201.

112. John Prados (2002), 'Notes on the CIA's Secret War in Afghanistan', *The Journal of American History*, 89(2): 466–71.

113. Cooley, op. cit.

114. Quoted Dreyfuss, op. cit., pp. 275–76.

115. Milton Bearden (2001), 'Afghanistan, Graveyard of Empires', *Foreign Affairs*, November–December, https://www.foreignaffairs.com/articles/afghanistan/2001-11-01/afghanistan-graveyard-empires.

116. Burke, op. cit., p. 78.

117. Coll, op. cit.

118. Jonathan Goodhand (2002), 'Aiding violence or building peace? The role of international aid in Afghanistan', *Third World Quarterly*, 25(3): 837–59.

119. Cooley, op. cit.

120. Ibid.

121. Dorril, op. cit., p. 752.

122. BBC News Online (2001), 'Scots link to US terror suspect [sic]', http://news.bbc.co.uk/1/hi/scotland/1546995.stm.

123. Cooley, op. cit., p. 78.

124. Mark Curtis (2010), *Secret Affairs: Britain's Collusion with Radical Islam*, London: Serpent's Tail, p. 147.

125. Cooley, op. cit.

126. Cooley, ibid., p. 75.

127. Ibid.

128. Ibid and Curtis, op. cit.

129. John Pilger (2003), *The New Rulers of the World*, London: Verso, p. 156.

130. Cooley, op. cit., p. 94.

131. Omar Nasiri (2007), *Inside the Jihad: My Life with Al Qaeda*, London: Hatchett.

132. Mahan Abedin (2004), 'Al-Muhajiroun in the UK: An Interview with Sheikh

Omar Bakri Mohammed', *Spotlight on Terror*, 2(5): https://jamestown.org/program/al-muhajiroun-in-the-uk-an-interview-with-sheikh-omar-bakri-mohammed/.

133. Ron Suskind (2009), *The Way of the World: A Story of Truth and Hope in the Age of Extremism*, London: Simon and Schuster, eBook.

134. Andrew Dismore (2001), 'Coalition against International Terrorism', Col 1086, https://publications.parliament.uk/pa/cm200102/cmhansrd/vo011016/debtext/11016-15.htm.

135. Hansard (2004), 'Abu Qatada', Col 1437, http://www.publications.parliament.uk/pa/ld200304/ldhansrd/vo040401/text/40401-02.

136. Bruce Crumley (2002), 'Sheltering a Puppet Master?', *TIME*, http://content.time.com/time/world/article/0,8599,300609,00.html.

137. Daniel McGrory and Richard Ford (2004), 'Al-Qaeda cleric exposed as an MI5 double agent', *Times* (London), http://www.thetimes.co.uk/tto/news/world/article1969239.ece.

138. Sue Reid (2012), 'Reda Hassaine: The brave agent who exposed Hamza only to be betrayed by MI5', *Mail on Sunday*, http://www.dailymail.co.uk/debate/article-2127942/Reda-Hassaine-The-brave-agent-exposed-Abu-Hamza-betrayed-MI5.html.

139. Sean O'Neill and Daniel McGrory (2010), *The Suicide Factory: Abu Hamza and the Finsbury Park Mosque*, London: HarperPerennial, eBook.

140. Curtis, *Secret Affairs*, op. cit., p. 212.

141. O'Neill and McGrory, op. cit.

142. Jamie Doward and Diane Taylor (2006), 'Hamza set up terror camps with British ex-soldiers', *The Observer*, http://www.theguardian.com/uk/2006/feb/12/terrorism.world.

143. Curtis, op. cit. Official quoted on p. 390n84.

144. See my *Britain's Secret Wars*, op. cit.

145. Ibid.

146. Peter Walker, Shiv Malik, Matthew Taylor, Sandra Laville, Vikram Dodd and Ben Quinn (2013), 'Suspect's journey from schoolboy football to phone-jacking and jihad', *Guardian*, https://www.theguardian.com/uk/2013/may/23/suspect-michael-adebolajo-woolwich-jihad.

147. Intelligence and Security Committee of Parliament (2014), *Report on the intelligence relating to the murder of Fusilier Lee Rigby*, HC 795, London: The Stationery Office, p. 13, https://b1cba9b3-a-5e6631fd-s-sites.googlegroups.com/a/independent.gov.uk/isc/files/20141125_ISC_Woolwich_Report%28website%29.pdf?attachauth=ANoY7cpm5ZngYy0nhXgq3Au7ETx6FXqZx02gbV0lHwC0H73Db__lB0fVDx0swCCAIJ4CSeIU_AfmghyAha0AZF_M3g7xkzO2g6UcLd1ND7m_ru68hr2MSO9ZRHkaG2xZgrLMd1_sM7oNF74SxS__

A2ADhK9OIO9CUoI7IDY0p0pF-KLEIJSF2_4Sj_
V5n7tIbwfl8EzqlLUM9JR7Xst__izZFbTsEQH8WrELkKqI_
BXlAE879v6BTVUdQBxynx6WlTgrnZdob6e8&attredirects=0.

148. Ibid., p. 25.

149. Tom Odulq (2013), 'UK soldier's suspected killer was arrested in Kenya',
Associated Press, https://www.timesofisrael.com/uk-soldiers-suspected-
killer-was-arrested-in-kenya/.

150. Intelligence and Security Committee, op. cit., pp. 30–39, 50.

151. BBC (2013), 'MI5 "tried to recruit" Michael Adebolajo, friend claims',
http://www.bbc.co.uk/news/av/uk-22664457/mi5-tried-to-recruit-michael-
adebolajo-friend-claims.

152. Intelligence and Security Committee, op. cit., p. 44.

153. It says: 'At 14:29 unarmed police arrived at the scene and set up a cordon,
remaining behind it until 14:34 when armed police arrived and approached
the attackers'. Intelligence and Security Committee, op. cit., p. 1.

154. Gordon Rayner and David Barrett (2015), 'Charlie Hebdo suspect "mentored" by Abu Hamza disciple', *Telegraph*, http://www.telegraph.co.uk/
news/worldnews/europe/france/11333776/Charlie-Hebdo-suspect-
mentored-by-Abu-Hamza-disciple.html.

155. O'Neill and McGrory, op. cit.

156. Bill Gardner (2015), 'Charlie Hebdo terror mentor's wife on benefits in
Leicester', *Telegraph*, http://www.telegraph.co.uk/news/uknews/terrorism-
in-the-uk/11337056/Charlie-Hebdo-terror-mentors-wife-on-benefits-in-
Leicester.html.

157. Sam Marsden (2015), 'The Finsbury Park connection', *Daily Mail*,
http://www.dailymail.co.uk/news/article-2902801/Charlie-Hebdo-One-
Paris-attack-suspects-mentored-terrorist-linked-notorious-Finsbury-Park-
mosque-London.html.

158. Gordon Rayner and David Barrett, op. cit.

159. Matthieu Suc (2015), 'Charlie Hebdo quand Cherif Kouachi recontrait des
dijihadistes sur un terrain de foot', *Le Monde*, http://www.lemonde.fr/police-
justice/article/2015/01/08/charlie-hebdo-quand-cherif-kouachi-
rencontrait-des-djihadistes-sur-un-terrain-de-foot_4552070_1653578.html.

160. BBC News Online (2015), 'Charlie Hebdo attacks: Suspects' profile',
http://www.bbc.co.uk/news/world-europe-30722038.

161. *Guardian* (2013), 'Cherif Kouachi during terror trial: "I've been set-up" –
video', http://www.theguardian.com/world/video/2015/jan/13/cherif-
kouachi-2008-terror-trial-paris-video.

162. Mapping Militant Organizations (no date), 'Ansar al-Shariah (Tunisia)',
Stanford University, http://web.stanford.edu/group/mappingmilitants/cgi-
bin/groups/view/547.

163. Camilla Turner (2015), 'Tunisia attack: gunman's links to Britain', *The Telegraph*, https://www.telegraph.co.uk/news/uknews/terrorism-in-the-uk/11707325/Tunisia-beach-massacre-gunmans-links-to-Britain.html.

164. Rana Jawad (2015), 'Tunisia dead rises to 27', http://www.bbc.co.uk/news/live/world-africa-33208573 and BBC News Online (2015), 'Tunisia attacks: As it happened', http://www.bbc.co.uk/news/live/world-africa-33208573.

165. Oliver Wheaton (2015), 'Tunisia terror attack: Gunmen "used inflatable boat" to reach the beach resort', *Metro*, http://metro.co.uk/2015/06/26/tunisia-terror-attack-gunmen-used-inflatable-boat-to-reach-the-beach-resort-5267939/.

166. BBC News Online (2015), 'Tunisia attacks: As it happened', http://www.bbc.co.uk/news/live/world-africa-33208573.

167. Chris Sheils (2015), 'Latest: Almost 3000 tourists leaving Sousse today', *Tunisia Live*, http://www.tunisia-live.net/2015/06/26/latest-sousse-terrorist-attack/.

168. Chris Stephen (2015), 'Tunisia attack', *Guardian*, http://www.theguardian.com/world/2015/jun/27/tunisia-attack-he-looked-right-at-me-i-thought-i-was-dead-says-tourist.

169. Sky News (2015), 'British and Irish Tourists Die in Beach Horror', Sky News Online, http://news.sky.com/story/1508894/british-and-irish-tourists-die-in-beach-horror.

170. SITE (2015), 'IS claims attack on Tunisian beach', Twitter, https://twitter.com/siteintelgroup. On Katz's background, see Benjamin Wallace-Wells (2006), 'Private Jihad', *New Yorker*, http://www.newyorker.com/magazine/2006/05/29/private-jihad.

171. Philosophy, Theology and Religion (no date), 'Wahhabiyyah', University of Cumbria, http://www.philtar.ac.uk/encyclopedia/islam/sunni/wahha.html.

172. Maud Saint-Lary (2012), 'From Wahhabism to Generic Reformism', *Cahiers d'Etudes Africaines*, 206(7): 449.

173. Jim Muir (2015), 'Relatives of Tunisia gunman "horrified" by beach massacre', BBC News Online, http://www.bbc.co.uk/news/world-africa-33298705.

174. Rukmini Callimachi and Eric Schmitt (2017), 'Manchester Bomber Met With ISIS Unit in Libya, Officials Say', *NYT*, https://www.nytimes.com/2017/06/03/world/middleeast/manchester-bombing-salman-abedi-islamic-state-libya.html.

175. Gilbert Reilhac (2015), 'Paris attacker was French army reject', Reuters, https://uk.reuters.com/article/us-france-shooting-attacker/paris-attacker-was-french-army-reject-idUKKBN0TU1SB20151211.

176. Jean-Charles Brisard and Kevin Jackson (2016), 'The French-Belgian Islamic State Attack Network', *CTC Sentinel*, 9(11): 8–15.

177. Timothy Holman (2015), 'The French Jihadist "Foreign Legion" in Syria and Iraq', *Terrorism Monitor*, 13(15): https://jamestown.org/program/the-french-jihadist-foreign-legion-in-syria-and-iraq/.

178. Tom Burgis (2015), 'Paris attacks: Samy Amimour, the "nice guy" who became a jihadi', *FT*, https://www.ft.com/content/472cec90-8eb7-11e5-8be4-3506bf20cc2b.

179. Alexandra Sims (2015), 'Paris terrorist Samy Amimour "trained at French police gun club" before Bataclan attack', *Independent*, https://www.independent.co.uk/news/world/europe/paris-terrorist-samy-amimour-trained-at-french-police-gun-club-before-bataclan-attack-a6756146.html.

180. Burgis, op. cit.

181. Angelique Chrisafis (2015), 'Life of Paris attacker Omar Ismail Mostefai: from petty crime to radicalisation', *Guardian*, https://www.theguardian.com/world/2015/nov/15/paris-attacker-omar-ismail-mostefai.

182. Martin Evans (2016), '"Man in the Hat" fundraiser claims he was MI5 informant', *Telegraph*, http://www.telegraph.co.uk/news/2016/12/12/man-hat-fundraiser-claims-mi5-informant/.

183. Sam Webb (2014), 'Al-Qaeda leader in Libya was detained by British police on suspicion of terror offences – but later released and fled the UK to train bombers', *Daily Mail*, http://www.dailymail.co.uk/news/article-2772495/Al-Qaeda-leader-Libya-detained-British-police-suspicion-terror-offences-later-released-fled-UK-train-bombers.html. See also Robert Mendrick, Tom Whitehead and Raf Sanchez (2014), 'Freed UK prisoner is al-Qaeda ring-leader', *Telegraph*, www.telegraph.co.uk/news/uknews/terrorism-in-the-uk/11125944/Freed-UK-prisoner-is-al-Qaeda-ringleader.html.

184. Cryptome.org (2000), 'The Qadahfi Assassination Plot', http://cryptome.org/qadahfi-plot.htm.

185. Martin Bright (2002), 'MI6 "halted bid to arrest bin Laden"', *Guardian*, www.theguardian.com/politics/2002/nov/10/uk.davidshayler. See also, Annie Machon (no date), '"Spies, Lies and Whistleblowers" – The Gaddafi Plot Chapters', http://anniemachon.ch/spies-lies-and-whistleblowers-the-gaddafi-plot-chapters.

186. Library of Congress (2012), 'Al-Qaeda in Libya: A Profile', http://fas.org/irp/world/para/aq-libya-loc.pdf.

187. Combating Terrorism Center (2011), 'Ali Mohamed: A biographical sketch', West Point Military Academy, https://ctc.usma.edu/app/uploads/2011/06/Ali-Mohammed.pdf.

188. Rukmini Callimachi and Eric Schmitt, op. cit.

189. Nazia Parveen (2017), 'Manchester bombing: police say Salman Abedi did

not act alone', *Guardian*, https://www.theguardian.com/uk-news/2017/jul/06/manchester-bombing-police-believe-salman-abedi-did-not-act-alone.

190. Ben Kentish (2017), 'FBI "warned MI5 in January that Salman Abedi was planning terror attack in UK"', *Independent*, http://www.independent.co.uk/news/uk/home-news/fbi-warned-mi5-january-manchester-attack-bomber-salman-abedi-manchester-arena-a7760756.html.

191. Samuel Osborne (2017), 'Salman Abedi: Manchester suicide bomber was known to MI5 but not under active investigation', *Independent*, http://www.independent.co.uk/news/uk/home-news/salman-abedi-manchester-suicide-bomber-known-to-mi5-not-under-active-investigation-latest-updates-a7761156.html.

192. Helen Pidd (2017), 'Police believe Manchester bomber Salman Abedi largely acted alone', *Guardian*, https://www.theguardian.com/uk-news/2017/may/31/police-believe-manchester-bomber-salman-abedi-acted-largely-alone.

193. Nafeez Ahmed (2017), 'ISIS recruiter who radicalised London Bridge attackers was protected by MI5', *Insurge Intelligence*, https://medium.com/insurge-intelligence/isis-recruiter-who-radicalised-london-bridge-attackers-was-protected-by-mi5-232998ab6421.

194. See my *Britain's Secret Wars*, op cit., p. 25.

195. Ahmed, op. cit.

196. Chalmers Johnson (2002), 'American Militarism and Blowback: The Costs of Letting the Pentagon Dominate Foreign Policy', *New Political Science*, 24(1): 21–38.

197. Subcommittee on Counterterrorism and Intelligence on Homeland Security (2011), 'Boko Haram: Emerging Threat to the U.S. Homeland', House of Representatives, 112th Congress, 1st Session, Washington, DC: Government Printing Office, p. 6, https://www.gpo.gov/fdsys/pkg/CPRT-112HPRT71725/pdf/CPRT-112HPRT71725.pdf.

198. Jason Burke (2010), 'Pakistan intelligence services "aided Mumbai terror attacks"', *Guardian*, https://www.theguardian.com/world/2010/oct/18/pakistan-isi-mumbai-terror-attacks.

199. Umair Jamal (2016), 'Is Pakistan Getting Ready to Abandon Lashkar-e-Taiba?', *The Diplomat*, https://thediplomat.com/2016/03/is-pakistan-getting-ready-to-abandon-lashkar-e-taiba/.

200. Where to begin on Palestine? See, for instance, former Israeli Foreign Minister, Shlomo Ben-Ami (2006), *Scars of War, Wounds of Peace: The Israeli-Arab Tragedy*, London: Phoenix, p. 192.

201. Richard Sale (2002), 'Analysis: Hamas history tied to Israel', UPI, https://www.upi.com/Business_News/Security-Industry/2002/06/18/Analysis-Hamas-history-tied-to-Israel/UPI-82721024445587/.

202. Full text of the National Conciliation Documents of the Prisoners, 28 June 2008, http://www.mideastweb.org/prisoners_letter.htm.

203. Press Association (2001), '40% of British Muslims support Bin Laden – survey', https://www.irishtimes.com/news/40-of-british-muslims-support-bin-laden-survey-1.402571.

204. Pew Research Center (2006), 'In Great Britain, Muslims Worry About Islamic Extremism', http://www.pewglobal.org/2006/08/10/in-great-britain-muslims-worry-about-islamic-extremism/.

205. Nicole Naurath (2011), 'Most Muslim Americans See No Justification for Violence', Gallup, http://news.gallup.com/poll/148763/muslim-americans-no-justification-violence.aspx.

206. William C. Mann (2012), 'Poll: Little Muslim support for bin Laden's group', Associated Press, https://web.archive.org/web/20120511170040/http://www.google.com/hostednews/ap/article/ALeqM5jeyhPPMreFe3Fmdj2xSrM9dxhjyQ?docId=bf30eebbae9e4741a3b04f56a6225022.

207. Pew Research Center (2013), 'Muslim Publics Share Concerns about Extremist Groups', http://www.pewglobal.org/2013/09/10/muslim-publics-share-concerns-about-extremist-groups/.

208. Jacob Poushter (2014), 'Support for al Qaeda was low before (and after) Osama bin Laden's death', Pew Research Center, http://www.pewresearch.org/fact-tank/2014/05/02/support-for-al-qaeda-was-low-before-and-after-osama-bin-ladens-death/.

209. David Miller (2001), 'Blair should read the polls', Guardian, https://www.theguardian.com/politics/2001/oct/03/afghanistan.britainand911.

210. Ipsos-MORI (2001), 'Support for War in Afghanistan – Trends 2001', https://www.ipsos.com/ipsos-mori/en-uk/support-war-afghanistan-trends-2001.

211. David W. Moore (2001), 'Eight of 10 Americans Support Ground War in Afghanistan', Gallup, http://news.gallup.com/poll/5029/eight-americans-support-ground-war-afghanistan.aspx.

212. Miller, 'Blair . . .', op. cit.

213. Quoted in Steven Kull, Clay Ramsay and Evan Lewis (2003–04), 'Misperceptions, the Media, and the Iraq War', Political Science Quarterly, 118(4): 569–98.

214. Kull et al., op. cit.

215. Ipsos-MORI (2007), 'War With Iraq – Trends (2002–2007)', https://ems.ipsos-mori.com/researchpublications/researcharchive/55/War-With-Iraq-Trends-20022007.aspx.

216. Ipsos-MORI (2003), 'Iraq, The Last Pre-War Polls', https://www.ipsos.com/ipsos-mori/en-uk/iraq-last-pre-war-polls.

217. Jeffrey M. Jones (2011), 'Americans Approve of Military Action Against Libya, 47% to 37%', Gallup, http://news.gallup.com/poll/146738/Americans-Approve-Military-Action-Against-Libya.aspx.

218. Lydia Saad (2011), 'Americans Resist a Major U.S. Role in Libya', Gallup, http://news.gallup.com/poll/146840/Americans-Resist-Major-Role-Libya.aspx.

219. Jeffrey M. Jones (2011), 'Americans Shift to More Negative View of Libya Military Action', Gallup, http://news.gallup.com/poll/148196/americans-shift-negative-view-libya-military-action.aspx.

220. Reuters/Ipsos-MORI (2011), 'Reuters/Ipsos MORI International poll on Libya', https://www.ipsos.com/ipsos-mori/en-uk/reutersipsos-mori-international-poll-libya.

221. Ipsos-MORI (2011), 'Intervention in Libya, and public opinion around our involvement', https://www.ipsos.com/ipsos-mori/en-uk/intervention-libya-and-public-opinion-around-our-involvement.

222. Anthony Wells (2011), 'Analysis: Opinions on Libya', YouGov, https://yougov.co.uk/news/2011/03/22/analysis-opinions-libya/.

223. Julie Ray (2011), 'Ahead of Protests, Many Libyans Discontent With Freedom, Jobs', Gallup, http://news.gallup.com/poll/146399/Ahead-Protests-Libyans-Discontent-Freedom-Jobs.aspx.

224. William Hague (2014), 'Statement on the Historical Role of UK Companies in Supplying Dual Use Chemicals to Syria', Foreign and Commonwealth Office, https://www.gov.uk/government/speeches/statement-on-the-historical-role-of-uk-companies-in-supplying-dual-use-chemicals-to-syria.

225. Reprieve (2015), 'UK pilots conducted strikes in Syria', https://reprieve.org.uk/press/uk-pilots-conducted-strikes-in-syria/.

226. YouGov (2013), 'Syria and the shadow of Iraq', https://yougov.co.uk/news/2013/08/28/syria-and-shadow-iraq/.

227. Andrew Dugan (2013), 'U.S. Support for Action in Syria Is Low vs. Past Conflicts', Gallup, http://news.gallup.com/poll/164282/support-syria-action-lower-past-conflicts.aspx.

228. Frank Newport (2013), 'Americans Disapprove of U.S. Decision to Arm Syrian Rebels', Gallup, http://news.gallup.com/poll/163112/americans-disapprove-decision-arm-syrian-rebels.aspx.

229. Bill Gardner (2014), 'Foley murder video "may have been staged"', *Telegraph*, https://www.telegraph.co.uk/journalists/bill-gardner/11054488/Foley-murder-video-may-have-been-staged.html.

230. Will Dahlgreen (2014), 'ISIS: How 57% came to favour air strikes', YouGov, https://yougov.co.uk/news/2014/09/26/isis-how-majority-came-favour-air-strikes/.

231. Jeffrey M. Jones and Frank Newport (2014), 'Slightly Fewer Back ISIS Mili-

tary Action vs. Past Actions', Gallup, http://news.gallup.com/poll/177263/slightly-fewer-back-isis-military-action-past-actions.aspx.

232. Will Dahlgreen (2015), 'Support for Syria air strikes falls again', YouGov, https://yougov.co.uk/news/2015/12/06/support-syria-air-strikes-falls-again/.

233. Puneet Khurana and J.S. Dala (2011), 'Bomb blast injuries', *Journal of the Punjab Academy of Forensic Medical Toxicology*, 11(1): 37–39.

234. Frederic G. Hirsch (1966), *Effects of overpressure on the ear – A review*, Albuquerque: Lovelace Foundation for Medical Education and Research, https://web.archive.org/web/20161020163254/http://www.dtic.mil/dtic/tr/fulltext/u2/653129.pdf.

235. Centers for Disease Control (no date), *Explosions and blast injuries: A primer for clinicians*, Washington, DC: Department of Health and Human Services, https://www.cdc.gov/masstrauma/preparedness/primer.pdf.

236. Ajay K. Singh et al., 'Radiologic features of Injuries from the Boston Marathon bombing at three hospitals', *American Journal of Roentgenology*, 203: 235–39.

237. David S. Kauvar, Michael A. Dubick, Lorne H. Blackbourne and Steve E. Wolf (2016), 'Quaternary blast injury: Burns' in Nabil M. Elsayed and James L. Atkins (eds.), *Explosion and Blast-Related Injuries: Effects of Explosion and Blast from Military Operations and Acts of Terrorism*, London: Springer, pp. 142–60.

238. Samira Alaani, Muhammed Tafash, Christopher Busby, Malak Hamdan and Eleonore Blaurock-Busch (2011), 'Uranium and other contaminants in hair from the parents of children with congenital anomalies in Fallujah, Iraq', *Conflict and Health*, 5(15): doi: 10.1186/1752-1505-5-15.

239. Alice Ross and James Ball (2015), 'GCHQ documents raise fresh questions over UK complicity in US drone strikes', *Guardian*, https://www.theguardian.com/uk-news/2015/jun/24/gchq-documents-raise-fresh-questions-over-uk-complicity-in-us-drone-strikes.

240. Nicholas Watt (2015), 'The "kill list": RAF drones have been hunting UK jihadis for months', *Guardian*, https://www.theguardian.com/uk-news/2015/sep/08/drones-uk-isis-members-jihadists-syria-kill-list-ministers.

241. On the blurred lines, see Human Rights Watch (2012), 'US: Transfer CIA Drone Strikes to Military', https://www.hrw.org/news/2012/04/20/us-transfer-cia-drone-strikes-military.

242. For example, two Parliamentary researchers write: 'In humanitarian law, a "civilian" is "any person not a combatant"; but the definition of combatant is narrow and does not cover rebel forces unless they: ● are under an effective command structure that enforces the international law of armed conflict; and ● distinguish themselves from the civilian population while they are attacking, or carry arms openly during each military engagement'. Ben Smith and Arabella Thorp (2011), 'Interpretation of Security Council Resolution

1973 on Libya', House of Commons Library, SN/IA/5916, p. 2, http://researchbriefings.files.parliament.uk/documents/SN05916/ SN05916.pdf.

243. Jack Serle and Jessica Purkiss (live document), 'Drone Wars: The Full Data', Bureau of Investigative Journalism, https://www.thebureauinvestigates.com/stories/2017-01-01/drone-wars-the-full-data.

244. Philip Alston (2010), 'Report of the Special Rapporteur on extrajudicial, summary or arbitrary executions', United Nations General Assembly Human Rights Commission, A/HRC/14/24/Add.6, http://www2.ohchr.org/ english/bodies/hrcouncil/docs/14session/A.HRC.14.24.Add6.pdf.

245. Serle and Purkiss, op. cit.

246. Spencer Ackerman (2014), '41 men targeted but 1,147 people killed: US drone strikes – the facts on the ground', *Guardian*, https://www.theguardian.com/us-news/2014/nov/24/-sp-us-drone-strikes-kill-1147.

247. Ghaith Abdul-Ahad (2009), 'Victims' families tell their stories following Nato airstrike in Afghanistan', *Guardian*, https://www.theguardian.com/world/ 2009/sep/11/afghanistan-airstrike-victims-stories.

248. Amnesty International (2013), *"Will I be next?" US Drone Strikes in Pakistan*, ASA 33/013/2013, New York: Amnesty International, p. 19, https://www.amnestyusa.org/files/asa330132013en.pdf.

249. Chavala Madlena, Hannah Patchett and Adel Shamsan (2015), 'We dream about drones, said 13-year-old Yemeni before his death in a CIA strike', *Guardian*, https://www.theguardian.com/world/2015/feb/10/drones-dream-yemeni-teenager-mohammed-tuaiman-death-cia-strike.

250. Molly Hennessy-Fisk and W.J. Hennigan (2017), 'More than 200 civilians killed in suspected U.S. airstrike in Iraq', *LA Times*, www.latimes.com/world/ middleeast/la-fg-mosul-civilians-airstrike-20170324-story.html.

251. *The Journal* (Ireland) (2017), 'McGuinness on his IRA past: "I fought against the British Army on the streets of Derry" ', http://www.thejournal.ie/martin-mcguinness-ira-past-2015-interview-3298901-Mar2017/.

252. *Belfast Telegraph* (2010), 'How the Bloody Sunday Victims died', https://www.belfasttelegraph.co.uk/news/bloody-sunday/how-the-bloody-sunday-victims-died-28541680.html.

253. Freya McClements (2017), 'My journey towards the IRA started on Bloody Sunday', *The Irish Times*, https://www.irishtimes.com/news/ireland/irish-news/my-journey-towards-the-ira-started-on-bloody-sunday-1.3247159.

254. Interviewed in *Behind the Mask* (?), https://www.youtube.com/watch?v=ZEv44pv4Ybw. The credits have been removed by the uploader. An identical version is posted as *Behind the Mask*

on YouTube, dated 1997. Yet, Internet Movie Database lists *Behind the Mask* as released in 1991. However, that appears to be a different film.

255. *Derry Journal* (2015), ' "I would have joined the IRA" – ex British soldier', https:%2F%2Fwww.derryjournal.com%2Fnews%2Fi-would-have-joined-the-ira-ex-british-soldier-1-6868480%20.

256. Paul Gill and John Horgan (2013), 'Who Were the Volunteers? The Shifting Sociological and Operational Profile of 1240 Provisional Irish Republican Army Members', *Terrorism and Political Violence*, 25: https://doi.org/10.1080/09546553.2012.664587.

257. Physicians for Social Responsibility, Physicians for Global Survival and IPPNW (Germany, 2015), *Body Count: Casualty Figures after 10 Years of the "War on Terror"*, http://www.psr.org/assets/pdfs/body-count.pdf.

258. Medact (2012), *Drones: the physical and psychological implications of a global theatre of war*, https://www.medact.org/wp-content/uploads/2012/10/report-drones-2012.pdf.

259. Osama bin Laden (1998), 'Jihad against Jews and crusaders', World Islamic Front Statement, https://fas.org/irp/world/para/docs/980223-fatwa.htm.

260. BBC (2005), 'Text: Zawahiri berates Queen', http://news.bbc.co.uk/1/hi/world/middle_east/4443364.stm.

261. Faisal Shahzad (2006), 'My beloved and peaceful ummah', email, https://www.nytimes.com/interactive/projects/documents/e-mail-from-faisal-shahzad.

262. James Dao (2010), 'A Muslim Son, a Murder Trial and Many Questions', *New York Times*, https://www.nytimes.com/2010/02/17/us/17convert.html.

263. Abdul Hakim Muhammad (2010), Letter to Judge Wright, Jr., http://graphics8.nytimes.com/packages/pdf/us/20100210-convert-letter.pdf.

264. BBC (2011), 'Profile Umar Farouk Abdulmutallab', http://www.bbc.co.uk/news/world-us-canada-11545509.

265. *Detroit Free Press* (2011), 'Transcript: Read Abdulmutallab's statement on guilty plea', https://web.archive.org/web/20111022131614/ http://www.freep.com/article/20111012/NEWS01/111012038/ Transcript-Read-Abdulmutallab-s-statement-guilty-plea.

266. Daniel Zwerdling (2009), 'Did A File Error Stall FBI Inquiry Into Hasan?', NPR, https://www.npr.org/templates/story/story.php?storyId=120765741.

267. FBI (2011), FD-302 (Rev. 10-6-95), 07/28/2011, http://bloximages.newyork1.vip.townnews.com/kdhnews.com/content/ tncms/assets/v3/editorial/4/e7/4e713a46-f8a6-11e2-9e39-0019bb30f31a/ 51f6fb3d1f7b1.pdf.pdf.

268. United States District Court Eastern District of New York (2010), *USA vs. Zazi*, Docket No. 09 CR 663 (S-1),
https://www.cbsnews.com/htdocs/pdf/USvZazi.pdf.

269. Orland Bosch interview (2011), 'I was the chief of that'. Uploaded by MambiWatch, https://www.youtube.com/watch?v=RwMIoFHxUeE.

270. Nora Gámez Torres and Alfonso Chardy (2015), 'Declassified document says Posada Carriles likely planned 1976 bombing of Cuban plane', *Miami Herald*, http://www.miamiherald.com/news/nation-world/world/americas/cuba/article23119197.html.

271. Patrick Cockburn (1996), 'Clinton backed Baghdad bombers', *Independent*,
https://www.independent.co.uk/news/world/clinton-backed-baghdad-bombers-1344138.html.

272. Patrick Cockburn (1998), 'Iraqi officers pay dear for West's coup fiasco', *Independent*, https://www.independent.co.uk/news/iraqi-officers-pay-dear-for-wests-coup-fiasco-1145298.html.

273. Seymour M. Hersh (2012), 'Our men in Iran?', *New Yorker*,
https://www.newyorker.com/news/news-desk/our-men-in-iran.

274. Ben Smith (2016), 'The People's Mujahiddeen of Iran (PMOI)', House of Commons Library, Briefing Paper CBP 5020, https://web.archive.org/web/20170214212144/http://researchbriefings.files.parliament.uk/documents/SN05020/SN05020.pdf.

275. Chris McGreal (2012), 'Q&A: what is the MEK and why did the US call it a terrorist organisation?', *Guardian*, https://www.theguardian.com/politics/2012/sep/21/qanda-mek-us-terrorist-organisation.

276. Muhammad Sahimi (2009), 'Who supports Jundallah?', PBS,
https://www.pbs.org/wgbh/pages/frontline/tehranbureau/2009/10/jundallah.html.

277. William Lowther and Colin Freeman (2007), 'US funds terror groups to sow chaos in Iran', *Telegraph*, https://www.telegraph.co.uk/news/worldnews/1543798/US-funds-terror-groups-to-sow-chaos-in-Iran.html#.

278. Brian Ross and Christopher Isham (2007), 'ABC News Exclusive: The Secret War Against Iran', ABC News, https://web.archive.org/web/20070406192341/http://blogs.abcnews.com/theblotter/2007/04/abc_news_exclus.html.

279. James Risen and Matt Apuzzo (2014), 'Getting close to terror, but not to stop it', *NYT*, https://www.nytimes.com/2014/11/09/world/despite-cia-fears-thomas-mchale-port-authority-officer-kept-sources-with-ties-to-iran-attacks.html.

280. Seymour M. Hersh (2007), 'Preparing the battlefield', *New Yorker*,
https://www.newyorker.com/magazine/2008/07/07/preparing-the-battlefield.

281. '[M]any FTFs [foreign terrorist fighters] serving as foot soldiers lack opportunity, are disadvantaged economically, lack education and have poor labour prospects, even when they come from Western societies'. Hamed el-Said and Richard Barrett (2017), *Enhancing the Understanding of the Foreign Terrorist Fighters Phenomenon in Syria*, Geneva: United Nations Office of Counter-Terrorism, p. 3.

282. Nowhere in the UN Charter (1945) is regime change authorized. Britain's Attorney General Lord Goldsmith secretly warned PM Tony Blair that regime change in Iraq is contrary to international law and PM David Cameron refused to release in full – note, in full – the advice of Attorney General Dominic Grieve when it came to the invasion of Libya in 2011, indicating its illegality.

283. The paraphrase of the unnamed official is from Pakistan's former Foreign Minister, Niaz Naik, who attended an international meeting concerning Afghanistan. US attendee Lee Coldren confirmed that '[US] might be considering some military action' in Afghanistan, prior to 9/11. While another US attendee, Tom Simons, says that a drunk official '[may have] evoked the gold carpets and the carpet bombs'. Each quoted in Jean-Charles Brisard and Guillaume Dasquié (2002), *Forbidden Truth: U.S.-Taliban Secret Oil Diplomacy and the Failed Hunt for Bin Laden*, Lucy Rounds (trans.), NY: Thunder's Mouth/Nation Books, p. 43. See also Sanjeev Miglani (2008), 'Pakistan's peace deals with militants: the march of folly?', Reuters, http://blogs.reuters.com/pakistan/2008/05/24/pakistans-peace-deals-with-militants-the-march-of-folly/.

284. W.J. Bender (2002), 'Strategic Implication for U.S. Policy in Iraq: What Now?', Strategy Research Project 20020604 207, Pennsylvania: US Army War College, Carlisle Barracks.

285. Ben Smith (2011), 'UK relations with Libya', House of Commons Library, Standard Note SN/IA/5886, p. 17.

286. Andrew Tabler (2007), 'The high road to Damascus: Engage Syria's private sector', The Stanley Foundation, https://www.stanleyfoundation.org/publications/pab/Tabler_PAB_807.pdf.

287. Craig Whitlock (2011), 'U.S. secretly backed Syrian opposition groups, cables released by WikiLeaks show', *Washington Post*, https://www.washingtonpost.com/world/us-secretly-backed-syrian-opposition-groups-cables-released-by-wikileaks-show/2011/04/14/AF1p9hwD_story.html?noredirect=on&utm_term=.bc6ad13abac5.

288. Ibid.

289. Ministry of Defence (UK, 2010), *Strategic Trends Programme: Future Character of Conflict*, Swindon: Development, Concepts and Doctrine Centre, p. 36.

290. MoD *Strategic Trends 2040*, op. cit.

291. Ça vous regarde (2013), *Syrie: Les preuves du massacre*, https://www.youtube.com/watch?v=lI0NBZa3InI.

292. Foreign and Commonwealth Office (UK), 'Foreign office minister meets Syrian National Council Members', https://www.gov.uk/government/news/ foreign-office-minister-meets-syrian-national-council-members.

293. Elite UK Forces (2012), 'British Special Forces training Syrian rebels?', http://www.eliteukforces.info/uk-military-news/0501012-british-special- forces-syria.php.

294. Christopher Philips (2016), *The Battle for Syria: International Rivalry in the New Middle East*, New Haven: Yale University Press, p. 43.

295. Arab Reform Institute (live document), 'Governance structure', https://www.arab-reform.net/en/content/governance-structure.

296. Rania El Gamal and Regan Doherty (2012), 'Syrian opposition unity plan runs into resistance', Reuters, https://uk.reuters.com/article/uk-syria-crisis- doha-opposition/syrian-opposition-unity-plan-runs-into-resistance- idUKBRE8A62IX20121107.

297. Seymour M. Hersh (2014), 'The red line and the rat line', *London Review of Books*, 36(8): 21–24, https://www.lrb.co.uk/v36/n08/seymour-m-hersh/ the-red-line-and-the-rat-line.

298. Julian Borger and Nick Hopkins (2013), 'West training Syrian rebels in Jordan', *Guardian*, https://www.theguardian.com/world/2013/mar/08/ west-training-syrian-rebels-jordan.

299. Kim Sengupta (2013), 'Revealed: What the West has given Syria's rebels', *Independent*, https://www.independent.co.uk/news/world/middle-east/ revealed-what-the-west-has-given-syrias-rebels-8756447.html.

300. BBC News Online (2013), 'Guide to the Syrian rebels', http://www.bbc.co.uk/news/world-middle-east-24403003.

301. House of Commons Defence Committee (2016), 'UK military operations in Syria and Iraq', Second report of session 2016–17, London: The Stationery Office, p. 31.

302. Defense Intelligence Agency (US) (2012), 14-L-0552/DIA/289, http://www.judicialwatch.org/wp-content/uploads/2015/05/Pg.-291-Pgs.- 287-293-JW-v-DOD-and-State-14-812-DOD-Release-2015-04-10-final- version11.pdf.

303. Patrick Cockburn (2014), 'MI6, the CIA and Turkey's rogue game in Syria', *Independent*, https://www.independent.co.uk/voices/comment/mi6-the-cia- and-turkeys-rogue-game-in-syria-9256551.html.

304. HRW (2015), *"He didn't have to die": Indiscriminate attacks by opposition groups in Syria*, NY: HRW, https://www.hrw.org/sites/default/files/reports/syria0315_ForUpload.pdf.

305. BBC News Online (2012), 'Syria conflict: Aleppo car bomb "kills 17"',
http://www.bbc.co.uk/news/world-middle-east-19539410.

306. Sara C. Nelson (2012), 'Andrei Arbashe, Christian Taxi-Driver "Beheaded By
Syrian Rebels & Fed To Dogs"', *Huffington Post*,
https://www.huffingtonpost.co.uk/2012/12/31/andrei-arbashe-christian-
taxi-driver-beheaded-syrian-rebels-dogs_n_2387421.html.

307. Associated Press (2016), '"A war crime": Beheading of a 12-year-old boy in
Syria triggers backlash against U.S.-supported rebels',
http://nationalpost.com/news/world/child-beheading-in-syria-triggers-
backlash-against-rebels.

308. Rod Nordland (2018), 'Videos of Syrian militia abusing Kurdish fighter's
corpse stir outrage', *NYT*, https://www.nytimes.com/2018/02/05/world/
middleeast/syria-video-kurds.html.

309. The Minister of State, Foreign and Commonwealth Office (Lord Ahmad of
Wimbledon), 'Syria', House of Lords Order of Business, 785(36), London:
The Stationery Office, p. 668.

310. House of Commons Foreign Affairs Committee (2016), *Libya: Examination of
intervention and collapse and the UK's future policy options*, Third Report of
Session 2016–17, HC 119, https://publications.parliament.uk/pa/
cm201617/cmselect/cmfaff/119/119.pdf.

311. Aaron Y. Zelin and Vice Admiral Michael T. Franken (Ret.) (summary by
Aviva Weinstein) (2018), 'Foreign Fighters in Libya: Consequences for Africa
and Europe', *Policywatch*, No. 2934, Washington, DC: WINES,
http://www.washingtoninstitute.org/policy-analysis/view/foreign-fighters-
in-libya-consequences-for-africa-and-europe.

312. Frank Gardner (2016), 'Islamic State foothold in Libya poses threat to
Europe', BBC News Online, http://www.bbc.co.uk/news/uk-35533787.

313. Nafeez Ahmed (2017), 'ISIS was state-sponsored by US allies, says former
government intelligence analyst', *Insurge Intelligence*, https://medium.com/
insurge-intelligence/isis-was-state-sponsored-by-us-allies-says-former-
government-intelligence-analyst-exclusive-51a9e999c437.

314. DIA, op. cit.

315. Parker, Walton and the defector quoted in Ruth Sherlock and Tom Whitehead (2014), 'Al-Qaeda training British and European "jihadists" in Syria to
set up terror cells at home', *Telegraph*, https://www.telegraph.co.uk/news/
worldnews/middleeast/syria/10582945/Al-Qaeda-training-British-and-
European-jihadists-in-Syria-to-set-up-terror-cells-at-home.html.

316. Abbas and Long quoted in Mark White (2017), 'More than 400 former jihadi
fighters back in Britain, say security sources', *Sky News*,
https://news.sky.com/story/battle-hardened-returning-jihadists-pose-uk-
terror-threat-10815737.

317. Gerry Wills (1975), 'Someone to watch over you: The Abuses of the Intelligence Agencies by The Center for National Security Studies...', *New York Review*, reprinted in CIA (1975), 'News, Views and Issues', Backgrounder No. 24, CIA-RDP77-00432R000100380003-3, p. 7, https://www.cia.gov/library/readingroom/docs/CIA-RDP77-00432R000100380003-3.pdf.

318. Office of Strategic Services (1944), *Special Operations Field Manual – Strategic Services (Provisional)*,Washington, DC: OSS, https://www.cia.gov/library/readingroom/docs/CIA-RDP89-01258R000100010010-5.pdf.

319. David S. Robarge (2003), 'All the Shah's Men: An American Coup and the Roots of Middle East Terror', *Intelligence in Recent Public Literature*, 48(2): https://www.cia.gov/library/center-for-the-study-of-intelligence/csi-publications/csi-studies/studies/vol48no2/article10.html.

320. Cpt. Wolfgang K. Kressin (1991), *Prime Minister Mossadegh and Ayatullah Kashani from Unity to Enmity: As Viewed from the American Embassy in Tehran*, Ohio: Wright-Patterson AFB and Austin: University of Texas at Austin, p. 56, http://www.dtic.mil/dtic/tr/fulltext/u2/a239339.pdf.

321. Staff Report of the Select Committee to Study Governmental Operations with Respect to Intelligence Activities (1975), *Covert Action in Chile 1963–1973*, United States Senate 94th Congress, 1st Session, Washington, DC: Government Printing Office, p. 6,
https://www.intelligence.senate.gov/sites/default/files/94chile.pdf.

322. John Ware (2002), *Panorama: A License to Murder, Part 1*, BBC (transcript), http://cain.ulst.ac.uk/issues/collusion/docs/panorama190602.htm.

323. Ibid.

324. Ibid.

325. Cooley, op. cit., p. 28.

326. Cooley, op. cit., p. 31.

327. Dreyfuss op. cit., Chapter 4.

328. Combating Terrorism Center (2011), 'Ali Mohamed: A biographical sketch', West Point Military Academy,
https://ctc.usma.edu/app/uploads/2011/06/Ali-Mohammed.pdf.

329. Ibid.

330. Malia Zimmerman (2015), 'Gangster-turned-radical imam may have radicalized dozens behind bars', Fox News, http://www.foxnews.com/us/2015/06/04/feds-say-gangster-turned-radical-imam-radicalized-dozens-behind-bars.html.

331. Chris Spargo (2015), 'US marine and FBI agent turned Muslim extremist', *Daily Mail*, http://www.dailymail.co.uk/news/article-3112544/US-Marine-FBI-agent-turned-Muslim-extremist-worked-World-Trade-Center-bomber-radicalizing-dozens-fellow-prisoners-bars.html.

332. Murtaza Hussain (2015), 'Florida imam who claimed to be covert govern-

ment operative is accused of terrorism', *The Intercept*, https://theintercept.com/2015/06/09/abu-taubah-case/

333. Lawrence Wright (2002), 'The counter-terrorist', *The New Yorker*, https://www.newyorker.com/magazine/2002/01/14/the-counter-terrorist.

334. Richard Bernstein and Ralph Blumenthal (1993), 'Bomb informer's tapes give rare glimpse of F.B.I. dealings', *NYT*, https://www.nytimes.com/1993/10/31/nyregion/bomb-informer-s-tapes-give-rare-glimpse-of-fbi-dealings.html.

335. Josh Meyer and Eric Lichtblau (2001), 'FBI let suspected terrorist get away', *LA Times*, http://articles.latimes.com/2001/oct/12/news/mn-56401.

336. Richard Behar (2001), 'The secret life of Mahmud the Red', *TIME*, https://web.archive.org/web/20140306141619/content.time.com/time/magazine/article/0,9171,162453,00.html.

337. Gebe Martinez and William C. Rempel (1993), 'Bombing suspects: Ties that bind a seemingly odd pair', *LA Times*, http://articles.latimes.com/1993-03-11/news/mn-1015_1_nidal-ayyad.

338. James C. McKinley (1995), 'Suspect is said to be longtime friend of bombing mastermind', *NYT*, https://www.nytimes.com/1995/08/04/nyregion/suspect-is-said-to-be-longtime-friend-of-bombing-mastermind.html.

339. Laurie Mylroie (1995–96), 'The World Trade Center bomb: Who is Ramzi Yousez? And why it matters', *National Interest*, https://fas.org/irp/world/iraq/956-tni.htm.

340. Athan G. Theoharis et al. (eds., 1999), *The FBI: A Comprehensive Reference Guide*, Phoenix: Oryx Press, p. 95.

341. Emad Salem (1993), Taped telephone conversion with John Anticev. Available at https://www.youtube.com/watch?v=3M8QtYTplyk.

342. Ralph Blumenthal (1993), 'Tapes depict proposal to thwart bomb used in Trade Center blast', *NYT*, https://www.nytimes.com/1993/10/28/nyregion/tapes-depict-proposal-to-thwart-bomb-used-in-trade-center-blast.html.

343. Death counts are always controversial and inexact. Data can be found from various sources, including: *Guardian* (2010), 'Deaths from the conflict in Ireland by year and status', https://docs.google.com/spreadsheets/d/1hRidYe3-avd7gvlZWVi1YZB7QY6dKhekPS1I1kbFTnY/edit#gid=0. Malcolm Sutton (2001), 'Statistical breakdown of deaths in the Troubles of Northern Ireland 1969 – 2001', Belfast Child, https://belfastchildis.com/lost-lives/the-troubles-1969–1998-statistical-breakdown-of-deaths-in-the-troubles/. A bibliography is available: Martin Melaugh (live document), 'Victims of the Northern Ireland Conflict', Conflict Archive on the Internet (University of Ulster), http://cain.ulst.ac.uk/issues/victims/index.html.

344. Brian Lavery (2002), 'I.R.A. apologizes for civilian deaths in its 30-year

campaign', *NYT*, https://www.nytimes.com/2002/07/17/world/ira-apologizes-for-civilian-deaths-in-its-30-year-campaign.html.

345. Liam Clarke (2011), 'Half of all top IRA men "worked for security services"', *Belfast Telegraph*, https://www.belfasttelegraph.co.uk/news/northern-ireland/half-of-all-top-ira-men-worked-for-security-services-28694353.html.

346. Interviewed in Panorama (2017), *The Spy in the IRA*, BBC.

347. Ibid.

348. RTE (2012), 'MI5's role in the Smithwick Tribunal', https://www.rte.ie/news/special-reports/2012/0727/330852-mi5s-role-in-smithwick-tribunal/.

349. BBC News Online (2015), 'UK agents "worked with NI paramilitary killers"', http://www.bbc.co.uk/news/uk-32887445.

350. RTE (2010), 'Nevin denied access to files on 1974 bombings', https://www.rte.ie/news/2010/0324/129111-nevin/.

351. Terry Kirby (1993), 'INLA informer admits receiving pounds 400,000', *Independent*, https://www.independent.co.uk/news/uk/inla-informer-admits-receiving-pounds-400000-1464932.html.

352. Susan McKay (2016), 'Kingsmill massacre anniversary: "We need to know the truth"', *The Irish Times*, www.irishtimes.com/news/ireland/irish-news/kingsmill-massacre-anniversary-we-need-to-know-the-truth-1.2486028.

353. Sean Rayment (2007), 'Top secret army cell breaks terrorists', *The Telegraph*, https://www.telegraph.co.uk/news/uknews/1541542/Top-secret-army-cell-breaks-terrorists.html.

354. Martin Ingram (2003), 'My part in the dirty war', *Guardian*, https://www.theguardian.com/politics/2003/apr/16/northernireland.northernireland.

355. Ed Moloney (2002), 'Panorama missed the real story of collusion in Ulster', *Telegraph*, https://www.telegraph.co.uk/comment/personal-view/3578340/Panorama-missed-the-real-story-of-collusion-in-Ulster.html.

356. Rosie Cowan (2003), 'He did the IRA's dirty work for 25 years – and was paid £80,000 a year by the government', *Guardian*, https://www.theguardian.com/uk/2003/may/12/northernireland.northernireland1.

357. Neil Mackay (2002), 'The army asked me to make bombs for the IRA, told me I had the Prime Minister's blessing ... then tried to kill me', *Sunday Herald* (Scotland). Archived at https://web.archive.org/web/20110612214025/www.whale.to/b/ni22.html.

358. Ibid.

359. Diarmaid Fleming (2014), 'Dublin-Monaghan: Ireland's unsolved bomb massacre 40 years on', BBC News Online, http://www.bbc.co.uk/news/world-europe-27399721.

360. Ian Cobain (2014), 'Disappeared but not forgotten: the grim secrets the IRA could not bury', *Guardian*, https://www.theguardian.com/uk-news/2014/may/10/disappeared-ira-troubles-northern-ireland.

361. Ian Cobain (2012), 'UK accused of helping to supply arms for Northern Ireland loyalist killings', *Guardian*, https://www.theguardian.com/uk/2012/oct/15/uk-arms-northern-ireland-loyalist-massacre.

362. *The Journal* (Ireland, 2015), 'Gardaí have finally started handing over their files on massacre of Protestants', www.thejournal.ie/kingsmill-massacre-gardai-ordered-to-hand-over-files-2176494-Jun2015/.

363. Connla Young (2017), 'Secret file proves existence of IRA informer', *Irish News*, https://www.irishnews.com/news/2017/05/02/news/document-proves-existence-of-ira-informer-1013750/.

364. *Irish News* (2017), 'Attacks involving secret agent Kevin Fulton "not properly investigated," court hears', https://www.irishnews.com/news/northernirelandnews/2017/04/06/news/attacks-involving-secret-agent-not-properly-investigated-court-hears-988913/.

365. Stephen Ward (1994), ' "Proud" IRA bombers jailed for 30 years: Police remain mystified why two Englishmen, who had no apparent connections with Ireland, became terrorists', *Independent*, https://www.independent.co.uk/news/uk/proud-ira-bombers-jailed-for-30-years-police-remain-mystified-why-two-englishmen-who-had-no-apparent-1435755.html.

366. Mackay, op. cit.

367. Allison Morris (2016), 'IRA commander at time of Shankill bombing was informer', *Irish News*, https://web.archive.org/web/20160206024613/http://www.irishnews.com/news/2016/01/25/news/the-ira-commander-at-time-of-shankill-bombing-was-a-police-informer-393891/.

368. Allisson Morris (2016), 'Top level agent gave information on Shankill attack', *Irish News*, https://web.archive.org/web/20160129143602/http://www.irishnews.com:80/news/2016/01/25/news/top-level-agent-gave-information-on-shankill-attack-393522/.

369. Mackay, op. cit.

370. Henry McDonald (2013), 'Intelligence on Omagh bomb "withheld from police" ', *Guardian*, https://www.theguardian.com/uk-news/2013/aug/08/omagh-bombing-intelligence-withheld-ira.

371. Neil Mackay and Louise Branson (2001), 'British double-agent was in IRA's Omagh bomb team', *Sunday Herald* (Scotland), https://web.archive.org/web/20011230123418/http://www.sundayherald.com/17827.

372. Ken Foy (2014), 'MI5 discover rogue garda leaking information to IRA', *Herald* (Ireland), published at: https://www.independent.ie/irish-news/mi5-discover-rogue-garda-leaking-information-to-ira-30546886.html.

373. Ron Suskind (2007), *The One Percent Doctrine: Deep Inside America's Pursuit of Its Enemies Since 9/11*, London: Pocket Books, p. 21.

374. Curtis, op. cit., p. 181.

375. Martin Meredith (2006), *The State of Africa: A History of Fifty Years of Independence*, London: The Free Press, pp. 590–93.

376. Osama bin Laden (1996), 'Declaration of war against the Americans occupying the two holy places'. Different versions and translations are available. See, for instance, the version at West Point's Combating Terrorism Center, https://ctc.usma.edu/app/uploads/2013/10/Declaration-of-Jihad-against-the-Americans-Occupying-the-Land-of-the-Two-Holiest-Sites-Translation.pdf.

377. Curtis, op. cit.

378. Officials interviewed in BBC (2010), *The Conspiracy Files: Osama bin Laden – Dead or Alive?*.

379. Osama bin Laden (1998), 'Jihad against Jews and Crusaders', World Islamic Front Statement, https://fas.org/irp/world/para/docs/980223-fatwa.htm.

380. Brisard and Dasquié, op. cit., pp. 101–02.

381. Curtis, op. cit., pp. 229–30.

382. BBC (2010), *The Conspiracy Files: Osama bin Laden – Dead or Alive?*

383. Ibid.

384. Combating Terrorism Center (2011), 'Ali Mohamed: A biographical sketch', West Point Military Academy, https://ctc.usma.edu/app/uploads/2011/06/Ali-Mohammed.pdf.

385. Anthea Temple (2002), 'The spy who loved me', *Guardian*, https://www.theguardian.com/politics/2002/oct/02/freedomofinformation.uk.

386. Curtis, op. cit., pp. 181–82.

387. Wright, op. cit.

388. Peter L. Bergen (2005), *Holy War, Inc.: Inside the Secret World of Osama bin Laden*, New York: Touchstone, pp. 208–09.

389. Curtis, op. cit.

390. Burke, op. cit., pp. 158–60.

391. CNN (2017), '1998 US Embassies in Africa Bombings Fast Facts', https://edition.cnn.com/2013/10/06/world/africa/africa-embassy-bombings-fast-facts/index.html.

392. Robert Windrem (2015), 'Slow-motion manhunt: US relentlessly pursues "98 embassy bombing suspects" ', NBC News, www.nbcnews.com/news/world/slow-motion-manhunt-us-relentlessly-pursues-98-embassy-bombing-suspects-flna8C11354614.

393. Interviewed in BBC (2010), *The Conspiracy Files: Osama bin Laden – Dead or Alive?*

394. Philip Bump (2013), 'What Is a "False Flag" Attack, and What Does Boston

Have to Do with This?', *The Atlantic*, www.theatlantic.com/national/archive/2013/04/what-is-false-flag-attack-boston-bombing/316235/.
See also Stephen Robinson (2016), *False Flags: Disguised German Raiders of World War II*, Wollombi: Exisle Publishing.

395. Joint Chiefs of Staff (1962), 'Justification for US military intervention in Cuba (TS)', https://nsarchive2.gwu.edu/news/20010430/northwoods.pdf.

396. Lieutenant Commander Peter Paterson (2008), 'The truth about Tonkin', *Naval History Magazine*, 22(1): https://www.usni.org/magazines/navalhistory/2008-02/truth-about-tonkin.

397. The late Labour Party MP, Michael Meacher, wrote: 'Fifteen of the 9/11 hijackers obtained their visas in Saudi Arabia. Michael Springman, the former head of the American visa bureau in Jeddah, has stated that since 1987 the CIA had been illicitly issuing visas to unqualified applicants from the Middle East and bringing them to the US for training in terrorism for the Afghan war in collaboration with Bin Laden (BBC, November 6 2001). It seems this operation continued after the Afghan war for other purposes. It is also reported that five of the hijackers received training at secure US military installations in the 1990s'. Michael Meacher (2003), 'This war on terrorism is bogus', *Guardian*,
https://www.theguardian.com/politics/2003/sep/06/september11.iraq.

398. OilEmpire.Us (no date), 'Remote controlled Boeings on 9/11?',
http://www.oilempire.us/remote.html.

399. Jim Fetzer (2015), 'Planes/No planes and "video fakery"', Blog,
http://jamesfetzer.blogspot.co.uk/2015/05/planesno-planes-and-video-fakery.html.

400. Bob Graham (2009), 'World War II's first victim', *Telegraph*,
https://www.telegraph.co.uk/history/world-war-two/6106566/World-War-IIs-first-victim.html.

401. William R. Trotter (2000), *A Frozen Hell: The Russo-Finnish Winter War of 1939–1940*, New York: Algonquin Books, p. 22.

402. Andrew Roberts (2010), 'MI6 attacked Jewish refugee ships after WWII', *Daily Beast*, https://www.thedailybeast.com/mi6-attacked-jewish-refugee-ships-after-wwii. Roberts, a proud imperialist, claims that the British government was under the control of nasty Arabs.

403. Mark Nicol (2012), 'The "murder and mayhem" squad', *Mail on Sunday*, http://www.dailymail.co.uk/news/article-2252237/The-murder-mayhem-squad-Shocking-new-revelations-undercover-soldier-carried-shoot-ask-questions-later-attacks-IRA-terrorists-British-Army.html.

404. Interviewed in Panorama (2013), *Britain's Secret Terror Force*, BBC, https://www.dailymotion.com/video/x2re8m0.

405. Adrian Rutherford (2013), 'British Army's secret "terror unit" Military

Reaction Force shot dead innocent civilians in Northern Ireland: claim',
Belfast Telegraph, https://www.belfasttelegraph.co.uk/news/northern-
ireland/british-armys-secret-terror-unit-military-reaction-force-shot-dead-
innocent-civilians-in-northern-ireland-claim-29772266.html.

406. *Belfast Daily* (2013), 'Revealed: BBC exposé on secret army "ghost squad"
which hunted down IRA members', www.belfastdaily.co.uk/2013/11/21/
revealed-bbc-expose-on-secret-army-ghost-squad-which-hunted-down-ira-
members/.

407. Truth and Reconciliation Commission (2001), AM3751/96, Amnesty Committee AC/2001/233,
http://www.justice.gov.za/trc/decisions%5C2001/ac21233.htm.

408. Ibid.

409. Keenan *Dark Sahara*, op. cit.

410. Habib Souaïdia (2012), *La sale guerre : Le témoignage d'un ancien officier des
forces spéciales de l'armée algérienne*, Paris: Editions La Découverte.

411. Amnesty International (2002), 'Algeria: Habib Souaidia's trial highlights
concerns over failure to conduct investigations',
https://www.amnesty.org.uk/press-releases/algeria-habib-souaidias-trial-
highlights-concerns-over-failure-conduct-investigations.

412. Yasmine Ryan (2010), 'Uncovering Algeria's civil war', *Al Jazeera*,
https://www.aljazeera.com/indepth/2010/11/
2010118122224407570.html.

413. FBI (no date), 'Amerithrax or Anthrax Investigation', History, https://
www.fbi.gov/history/famous-cases/amerithrax-or-anthrax-investigation.

414. Jennifer Welsh (2011), 'Anthrax in 2001 Letters Was Traced to Maryland by
Genetic Mutations', *Live Science*,
www.livescience.com/13229-anthrax-attacks-2001-genetics-110314.html.

415. Joe Johns and Andy Segal (2011), 'Strange sorority fixation was link that led
to anthrax suspect', CNN,
www.cnn.com/2011/10/01/us/anthrax-killer-case/index.html.

416. James Gordon Meek (2008), 'FBI was told to blame Anthrax scare on Al
Qaeda by White House officials', *New York Daily News*,
http://www.nydailynews.com/news/world/fbi-told-blame-anthrax-scare-al-
qaeda-white-house-officials-article-1.312733.

417. Scott Shane and Eric Lichtblau (2008), 'Scientist's suicide linked to anthrax
inquiry', *New York Times*,
https://www.nytimes.com/2008/08/02/washington/02anthrax.html.

418. Timewatch (1992), *Gladio*, BBC
https://www.youtube.com/watch?v=yXavNe81XdQ.

419. Quoted in Daniele Ganser (2005), *NATO's Secret Armies: Operation Gladio
and Western Terrorism in Europe*, New York: Frank Cass, p. 36.

420. David Pallister (1990), 'Gladio: How MI6 and SAS joined in', *Guardian*, http://www.cambridgeclarion.org/press_cuttings/gladio.mi6.sas_graun_5dec1990.html.

421. Richard Norton-Taylor and David Gow (1990), 'Secret Italian united "trained in Britain" ', *Guardian*, http://www.cambridgeclarion.org/press_cuttings/gladio.terrorism.inquiry_graun_17nov1990.html.

422. Hugh O'Shaughnessy (1992), 'GLADIO: Europe's best kept secret', *The Observer*, http://www.cambridgeclarion.org/press_cuttings/gladio_obs_7jun1992.html.

423. Select Committee to Study Governmental Operations (1976), *Foreign and Military Intelligence: Book I*, 94th Congress, 2nd Session Report, No. 94-755, Washington, DC: Government Printing Office, p. 22, https://www.intelligence.senate.gov/sites/default/files/94755_I.pdf.

424. Daniele Ganser, op. cit., p. 28.

425. Pallister, op. cit.

426. Quoted in Ganser, op cit., p. 105.

427. Clare Pedrick (1990), 'CIA organized secret army in Western Europe', *Washington Post*, https://www.washingtonpost.com/archive/politics/1990/11/14/cia-organized-secret-army-in-western-europe/e0305101-97b9-4494-bc18-d89f42497d85/?utm_term=.eb3f0d05278b.

428. Ganser, op. cit., p. 42.

429. Ganser, op. cit., pp. 144–47.

430. Pedrick, op. cit.

431. Ganser, op. cit., p. 216.

432. Michael Wala (2016), 'Stay-behind operations, former members of SS and Wehrmacht, and American intelligence services in early Cold War Germany', *Journal of Intelligence History*, 15(2): 71–79.

433. Chief of Station, Karlsruhe (1952), 'KIBITZ Progress Report', Central Intelligence Agency Library, MGK [?]-32195, https://www.cia.gov/library/readingroom/docs/KOPP%2C%20WALTER%20%20%20VOL.%201_0025.pdf.

434. Norton-Taylor and Gow, op. cit.

435. Jeffrey McKenzie Bale (1994), *The "Black" Terrorist International: Neo-Fascist Paramilitary Networks and the "Strategy of Tension" in Italy, 1968–1974* (Doctoral thesis), University of California at Berkeley, pp. 107, 114, https://www.economicsvoodoo.com/wp-content/uploads/DISSERTATION-The-Black-Terrorist-International-Neo-Fascist-Paramilitary-Networks-Strategy-of-Tension-in-Italy-1968-1974_Jeffrey-Bale.pdf.

436. John Hooper (2002), 'Neo-Nazi leader "was MI6 agent" ', *Guardian*, https://www.theguardian.com/world/2002/aug/13/johnhooper.

437. Bale op. cit., p. 97.

438. Jan Friedmann, Conny Neumann, Sven Röbel and Steffen Winter (2010), '1980 Oktoberfest: Bombing Did Neo-Nazi Murderer Really Act Alone?', *Spiegel Online*, https://web.archive.org/web/20170110021102/ http://www.spiegel.de:80/international/germany/1980-oktoberfest-bombing-did-neo-nazi-murderer-really-act-alone-a-717229.html and part 2 https://web.archive.org/web/20161117202504/http://www.spiegel.de:80/ international/germany/1980-oktoberfest-bombing-did-neo-nazi-murderer-really-act-alone-a-717229-2.html.

439. Blake, op. cit., p. 109.

440. Ganser, op. cit., p. 122.

441. Richard Norton-Taylor (1991), 'UK trained secret Swiss force', *Guardian*, http://www.cambridgeclarion.org/press_cuttings/swiss.subversion_graun_20sep1991.html.

442. O'Shaughnessy, op. cit.

443. Ed Vulliamy (1990), 'Secret agents, freemasons, fascists ... and a top-level campaign of political "destabilisation"', *Guardian*, http://www.cambridgeclarion.org/press_cuttings/vinciguerra.p2.etc_graun_5dec1990.html.

444. Ganser, op. cit., pp. 119–20.

445. Norton-Taylor and Gow, op. cit. See also O'Shaughnessy, op. cit.

446. Timewatch, op. cit.

447. Vulliamy, op. cit.

448. Vulliamy, op. cit.

449. O'Shaughnessy, op. cit.

450. Ed Vulliamy, op. cit.

451. O'Shaughnessy, op. cit.

452. CIA (1991), 'Take 1 of 2 – President Cossiga Rebuts PDS Accusations', UNCALS/PMU, Serial: WA0912173691, http://documents.theblackvault.com/documents/coldwarera/gladiocia.pdf.

453. Pedrick, op. cit.

454. House of Commons (1992), 'Operation Gladio', HC Deb, vol 209, c424W, https://api.parliament.uk/historic-hansard/written-answers/1992/jun/15/ operation-gladio.

455. European Parliament (1990), *Resolution on the Gladio Affair*, CELEX: 51990IP2021.

456. Katrin Voltmer (2009), 'The media, government accountability, and citizen engagement' in Pippa Norris (ed.), *Public Sentinel: New Media and the Governance Agenda*, New York: The World Bank Group, p. 141.

457. William M. Arkin (1999), 'When seeing and hearing isn't believing', *Washington Post*, http://www.washingtonpost.com/wp-srv/national/dotmil/ arkin020199.htm.

458. Ibid.

459. Ibid.

460. Ibid.

461. Jeff Stein (2010), 'CIA unit's wacky idea: Depict Saddam as gay', *Washington Post*, http://voices.washingtonpost.com/spy-talk/2010/05/cia_group_had_wacky_ideas_to_d.html.

462. Brian Whitaker (2002), 'Swiss scientists 95% sure that Bin Laden recording was fake', *Guardian*, https://www.theguardian.com/world/2002/nov/30/alqaida.terrorism.

463. Robert Windrem and Victor Limjoco (2007), 'Was bin Laden's latest video faked?', NBC News, http://www.nbcnews.com/id/21530470/ns/nbc_nightly_news_with_brian_williams/t/was-bin-ladens-last-video-faked/#.WPaH1GnyvIU.

464. These were a series of memos exposed by the *New York Times* and other mainstream news organizations suggesting supposedly lawful ways to circumvent torture restrictions during the so-called war on terror. See, among many others, David Cole (ed., 2009), *Torture Memos: Rationalizing the Unthinkable*, San Francisco: The New Press.

465. John Yoo (2005), 'Go on the offensive against terror', *LA Times*, https://articles.latimes.com/2005/jul/13/opinion/oe-yoo13+.

466. Ministry of Defence (UK, 2007), 'The DCDC Global Strategic Trends Programme: 2007–2036', Swindon: DCDC, p. 21, http://www.cuttingthroughthematrix.com/articles/strat_trends_23jan07.pdf.

467. Crofton Black and Abigail Fielding-Smith (2016), 'Fake News and False Flags', Bureau of Investigative Journalism, http://labs.thebureauinvestigates.com/fake-news-and-false-flags/.

468. Ibid.

469. Mandeep K. Dhami (2011), 'Behavioural Science Support for JTRIG's (Joint Threat Research and Intelligence Group's) Effects and Online HUMINT Operations', Human Systems Group, Information Management Department, Defence Science Technology Laboratory, http://www.statewatch.org/news/2015/jun/behavioural-science-support-for-jtrigs-effects.pdf and Glenn Greenwald (2014), 'How covert agents infiltrate the internet to manipulate, deceive, and destroy reputations', *The Intercept*, https://theintercept.com/2014/02/24/jtrig-manipulation/.

470. Ibid.

471. Ibid.

472. See my *The New Atheism Hoax*, Chapter 1 (forthcoming).

473. Rita Katz (2016), 'ISIS's mobile app developers are in crisis mode', *Vice*, https://motherboard.vice.com/en_us/article/qkj34q/isis-mobile-app-developers-are-in-crisis-mode.

474. David E. Sanger (2016), 'U.S. cyberattacks target ISIS is a new line of combat', *NYT*, https://www.nytimes.com/2016/04/25/us/politics/us-directs-cyberweapons-at-isis-for-first-time.html.

475. Quoted in Davide Mastracci (2016), 'Someone is spreading fake copies of the Islamic State's magazine', *Vice*, https://news.vice.com/article/someone-is-spreading-fake-copies-of-the-islamic-states-magazine.

476. Uploaded by user Nomore123 (2016), 'Iraqis made fake video for car suicide bombing (stage)' (sic), LiveLeak, https://www.liveleak.com/view?i=b3a_1478036670.

477. Christiaan Triebert (2016), 'The Remarkable Case of an Iraqi Car Bomb', Bellingcat, https://www.bellingcat.com/news/mena/2016/11/04/remarkable-case-iraqi-car-bomb/.

478. Supposedly set up by a single, non-professional photo and video analyst as a hobby, Bellingcat has grown to employ numerous ex-British intelligence agents who worked at various levels across various agencies, as well as many other, independent researchers. The organization mostly focuses on the alleged crimes of Britain's state enemies, notably Russia's actions in Syria and Ukraine. As far as western media go, they vouch for the site's credibility by frequently referencing it in online reports.

479. For a devastating analysis from an on-the-ground reporter, see Patrick Cockburn (2006), *The Occupation: War and Resistance in Iraq*, London: Verso.

480. For example: Harith Hasan Al-Qarawee (2014), 'Iraq's sectarian crisis: A legacy of exclusion', Carnegie Middle East Center, http://carnegie-mec.org/2014/04/23/iraq-s-sectarian-crisis-legacy-of-exclusion-pub-55372.

481. See, for instance, Jeremy Scahill (2008), *Blackwater: The Rise of the World's Most Powerful Mercenary Army*, London: Serpent's Tail, pp. 354–55.

482. Martha L. Cottam and Joe W. Huseby (2016), *Confronting al Qaeda: The Sunni Awakening and American Strategy in al Anbar*, London: Rowman and Littlefield.

483. Australian Government Refugee Review Tribunal (2010), 'Country Advice: Iraq', https://www.justice.gov/sites/default/files/eoir/legacy/2013/06/11/Mahdi%20Army-Sharia%20Law.pdf.

484. Reuters reports that the offensive began on 17 October. Reuters (2016), 'Iraqi forces resume offensive towards eastern Mosul', https://www.reuters.com/article/us-mideast-crisis-iraq-advance-idUSKBN12V0H5.

485. TimeAndDate.com (2018), 'Baghdad, Iraq – Sunrise, Sunset, and Daylength', https://www.timeanddate.com/sun/iraq/baghdad?month=10.

486. INP+ (2016), Twitter, https://twitter.com/INP_PLUS/status/793408734508834817.

487. ReYhan News (2016), Twitter, https://twitter.com/Reyhan_News/status/792727274193821697.

488. Associated Press (2016), 'The Latest: Parked car bomb kills 10 in Baghdad neighborhood', http://www.dailymail.co.uk/wires/ap/article-3886924/The-Latest-Erdogan-warns-Shiite-militias-Tel-Afar.html.

489. Ibid.

490. Reuters (2016), 'Car bomb kills at least eight in Baghdad market: police, medics', https://www.reuters.com/article/us-mideast-crisis-iraq-blast-idUSKBN12U0JY.

491. Andrew Roth (2018), 'Russian journalist and Kremlin critic Arkady Babchenko shot dead in Kiev', *Guardian*.

492. Roth, op. cit. and BBC (2018), 'Arkady Babchenko's hoaxed death in Ukraine used pig's blood'.

493. Ibid.

494. Neil MacFarquhar (2018), 'After the faked journalist killing in Ukraine, the murk deepens', *New York Times*.

495. David Filipov (2017), 'Here are 10 critics of Vladimir Putin who died violently or in suspicious ways', *Washington Post*, https://www.washingtonpost.com/news/worldviews/wp/2017/03/23/here-are-ten-critics-of-vladimir-putin-who-died-violently-or-in-suspicious-ways/?noredirect=on&utm_term=.91380d62dc3c.

496. Scott Anderson (2017), 'None dare call it conspiracy', *GQ*, https://www.gq.com/story/moscow-bombings-mikhail-trepashkin-and-putin.

497. BBC (1999), 'Ryazan "bomb" was security service exercise', http://news.bbc.co.uk/1/hi/world/europe/456848.stm.

498. John Lumpkin (2002), 'Agency planned exercise on Sept. 11 built around a plane crashing into a building', Associated Press, https://www.boston.com/news/packages/sept11/anniversary/wire_stories/0903_plane_exercise.htm.

499. NORAD (2001), 'NORAD maintains Northern Vigilance', Public Affairs, http://www.norad.mil/Newsroom/Article/578022/norad-maintains-northern-vigilance/.

500. Department of Defense (US, 2001), *Battle Staff Exercise: Vigilant Guardian 01–02*, Brief Morning, 11 September 2001, RDOD0301314[2?], https://www.archives.gov/files/declassification/iscap/pdf/2013-002-doc4.pdf.

501. Dan Rather interview with Tom Kenney of the FEMA Urban Search and Rescue Team (2001), 'Attack on America', CBS, https://www.youtube.com/watch?v=SmMRWL-jEVE.

502. New York City (2002), 'Tripod', Press Release, https://web.archive.org/web/20030626185936/http://nyc.gov/html/oem/html/other/sub_news_pages/tripod05_22_02.html.

503. Thomas H. Kean and Lee H. Hamilton (2006), *Without Precedent: The Inside Story of the 9/11 Commission*, New York: Knopf Doubleday.

504. NATO (2004), 'Press Statement NATO to conduct its annual crisis management exercise CMX 2004 from 4 to 10 march 2004', Press Release, (2004) 022, https://www.nato.int/docu/pr/2004/p04-022e.htm.

505. Keith B. Richburg (2004), 'Spain campaigned to pin blame on ETA', *Washington Post*, https://www.washingtonpost.com/archive/politics/2004/03/17/spain-campaigned-to-pin-blame-on-eta/5872ae4d-440a-4552-b931-c6d9844294f1/?utm_term=.f1c09e7e9993.

506. Stratfor (2004), 'Spain: Suspects informants?', https://worldview.stratfor.com/article/spain-suspects-informants.

507. ABC.es (2007), 'Trashorras and Toro, sentenced to more than 10 years in prison for drug trafficking and possession of explosives' (Google Translate), http://www.abc.es/hemeroteca/historico-31-01-2007/Nacional/trashorras-y-toro-condenados-a-mas-de-10-a%C3%B1os-de-carcel-por-trafico-de-drogas-y-tenencia-de-explosivos_1631217658721.html.

508. Congreso de los diputados (2004), Legislature, 8 Volume, 3 Session 7, p. 4, http://www.congreso.es/public_oficiales/L8/CONG/DS/CI/CI_003.PDF. (Google Translate).

509. Ministerio del interior (2007), Informe pericial, http://estaticos.elmundo.es/documentos/2007/05/16/01_antecedentes_metodologia_analisis.pdf.

510. *El Mundo* (2007), 'The manufacturer of Goma 2 EC ensures that this dynamite has no nitroglycerin since 1992', www.elmundo.es/elmundo/2007/06/01/espana/1180724976.html. (Google Translate).

511. Elizabeth Nash (2004), 'Anzar "purged all records in Madrid bombings cover-up"', *Independent*, www.independent.co.uk/news/world/europe/aznar-purged-all-records-in-madrid-bombings-cover-up-686574.html.

512. Paul Hamilos and Mark Tran (2007), '21 guilty, even cleared over Madrid train bombings', *Guardian*, https://www.theguardian.com/world/2007/oct/31/spain.marktran.

513. Intelligence and Security Committee (2009), *Could 7/7 Have Been Prevented?*, Cm 7617, London: The Stationary Office, p. 68.

514. Panorama (2004), *London Under Attack*, BBC, https://www.youtube.com/watch?v=x7uljg9dtoI.

515. Visor Consultants (2018), 'The Visor team', website, http://www.visorconsultants.com/businesscontinuityteam.htm.

516. Witness (2003), '1987: Disaster underground', BBC, https://web.archive.org/web/20031123143827/http://news.bbc.co.uk/onthisday/hi/witness/november/18/newsid_3267000/3267833.stm.

517. For example, BET Security (1993), *BET Security and Communications Limited*

Annual Report and Accounts for the Year Ended 27th March 1993, London: Companies House.

518. Visor Consultants (2001), 'An Introduction to Visor Consultants', website, https://web.archive.org/web/20010303140204/ http://www.visorconsultants.com:80/aboutvisor.html.

519. Companies House (2018), 'Visor Consultants (UK) Limited', Company Number 06497980, https://beta.companieshouse.gov.uk/company/ 06497980/filing-history?page=2.

520. Visor Consultants (2004), 'The team at Visor Consultants', https://web.archive.org/web/20040211022450/ http://visorconsultants.com:80/teamvisor.html.

521. MI5 (no date), 'Attack plots in the UK', https://www.mi5.gov.uk/attack-plots-in-the-uk.

522. *Independent* (2008), 'Terror plots and conspiracy theories: the hunt for Rashid Rauf', https://www.independent.co.uk/news/world/asia/terror-plots-and-conspiracy-theories-the-hunt-for-rashid-rauf-944064.html.

523. Nafeez Mosaddeq Ahmed (2013), 'Britain should prosecute terrorist suspects, not play shady games of geopolitics', *Independent*, www.independent.co.uk/voices/comment/britain-should-prosecute-terrorist-suspects-not-play-shady-games-of-geopolitics-8632402.html.

524. Raffaellio Pantucci (2012), 'A Biography of Rashid Rauf: Al-Qa'ida's British Operative', *Combating Terrorism Center Sentinel*, 5(7): https://ctc.usma.edu/a-biography-of-rashid-rauf-al-qaidas-british-operative/.

525. Lady Justice Hallett (2011), *Coroner's Inquests into the London Bombings of 7 July 2005*, London: The Stationary Office.

526. Sophie Hazan (2006), 'The CV of a bomber', *Yorkshire Evening Post*, www.yorkshireeveningpost.co.uk%2Fnews%2Fthe-cv-of-a-bomber-1-2149977%20.

527. Peter Power (2008), 'Visor drill on July 7th', http://powerbase.info/index.php/Peter_Power.

528. DRIVE (2005), BBC Radio 5, https://www.youtube.com/watch?v=aGE9FiuM06o.

529. Intelligence and Security Committee, op. cit.

530. Brian Castner (2013), 'The exclusive inside story of the Boston bomb squad's defining day', *Wired*, https://www.wired.com/2013/10/boston-police-bomb-squad/.

531. Mayor's Press Office (2012), 'Mayor Menino Announces Urban Shield: Boston Simulated 24-Hour Public Safety Exercise', City of Boston, https://web.archive.org/web/20130421060721/ http://www.cityofboston.gov/news/Default.aspx?id=5837.

532. FBI (2011), FD-302 (Rev. 10-695), 04/23/2011, https://vault.fbi.gov/

tamerlan-tsarnaev/Tamerlan%20Tsarnaev%20Part%2001%20of%2001/
view.

533. Michele McPhee (2017), 'Tamerlan Tsarnaev: Terrorist. Murderer. Federal
Informant?', *Boston Magazine*, https://www.bostonmagazine.com/news/
2017/04/09/tamerlan-tsarnaev-fbi-informant/.

534. Henry Grabar (2013), 'Boston Is One of the Best Prepared U.S. Cities to
Handle a Crisis', Strategic Operations, https://web.archive.org/web/
20130507200051/www.strategic-operations.com/news/article/2013/05/
03/strategic-operations-helps-boston-disaster-preparedness.

535. Dave Wedge (2013), '2012 drill braced for bombs at the finish line', *Boston
Herald*, www.bostonherald.com/news_opinion/local_coverage/2013/04/
2012_drill_braced_for_bombs_at_finish_line.

536. Local 15 (2013), 'UM Coach: Bomb Sniffing Dogs Were at Start, Finish Lines
for "Drill"', NBC, https://web.archive.org/web/20130415220245/
http://www.local15tv.com/mostpopular/story/UM-Coach-Bomb-Sniffing-
Dogs-Were-at-Start-Finish/BrirjAzFPUKKN8z6eSDJEA.cspx.

537. Guillaume Gendron (2013), 'Patrick Pelloux: "Violence is inseparable from
the practice of emergency medicine"', *Libération*, http://www.liberation.fr/
societe/2013/09/05/la-violence-est-indissociable-de-l-exercice-de-la-
medecine-d-urgence_929609 (Google Translate).

538. Alex Duval Smith (2003), 'French health chief quits, warning heat toll could
be 5,000', *Independent*, https://www.independent.co.uk/news/world/
europe/french-health-chief-quits-warning-heat-toll-could-be-5000-
100937.html.

539. Coralie Vincent (2015) 'Patrick Pelloux, "the friend of the president" has he
received favors after the attack on "Charlie Hebdo"?' *Closer* (French edition)
https://www.closermag.fr/vecu/faits-divers/patrick-pelloux-l-ami-du-
president-a-t-il-beneficie-de-passe-droits-apre-530489 (Google Translate).

540. Gendron, op. cit.

541. John Fleming (2015), 'Irishman Paddy Sherlock sings at "Charlie Hebdo"
editor's funeral', *Irish Times*, https://www.irishtimes.com/news/world/
europe/irishman-paddy-sherlock-sings-at-charlie-hebdo-editor-s-funeral-
1.2069114.

542. Gendron, op. cit.

543. Michelle Clifford (2015), 'Terror Threat: Docs Need War Injuries Training',
Sky News, https://news.sky.com/story/terror-threat-docs-need-war-injuries-
training-10338642.

544. Vincent, op. cit.

545. France Info (2015), 'Paris Attacks – "Multi-site Attack Exercise" Planned for
November 13', https://www.youtube.com/watch?v=QhyMzuWcVmU.

546. Eric Boodman (2015), 'Emergency response to Paris attacks worked, doctors

say', *Stat*,
https://www.statnews.com/2015/11/24/medical-response-paris-attacks/.

547. Sky News, op. cit.

548. *Saumur Kiosque* (2016), 'Saumur: Planque de Daesh découverte? Branle-bas de combat', http://www.saumur-kiosque.com/infos_article.php?id_actu= 32966 and *Le Courrier de l'ouest* (2016), 'Saumur Les terroristes de Daesh étaient en fait des militaires', http://www.courrierdelouest.fr/actualite/ saumur-les-terroristes-de-daesh-etaient-en-fait-des-militaires-22-09-2016-284131.

549. BBC News Online (2018), 'Westminster crash: Salih Khater named as suspect', https://www.bbc.co.uk/news/uk-45193781.

550. The SIA (2018), Twitter,
https://twitter.com/SIAuk/status/1027607989954457600/photo/1.

Index

Books to challenge  *your perception of reality*

A message from Clairview

We are an independent publishing company with a focus on cutting-edge, non-fiction books. Our innovative list covers current affairs and politics, health, the arts, history, science and spirituality. But regardless of subject, our books have a common link: they all question conventional thinking, dogmas and received wisdom.

Despite being a small company, our list features some big names, such as Booker Prize winner Ben Okri, literary giant Gore Vidal, world leader Mikhail Gorbachev, modern artist Joseph Beuys and natural childbirth pioneer Michel Odent.

So, check out our full catalogue online at
www.clairviewbooks.com
and join our emailing list for news on new titles.

office@clairviewbooks.com

CLAIRVIEW